Bombproof

Bombproof

A True Story of Second Chances

Leana Beasley
Stephen Sawicki

iUniverse, Inc.
New York Lincoln Shanghai

Bombproof
A True Story of Second Chances

Copyright © 2007 by Stephen Sawicki

iUniverse books may be ordered through booksellers or by contacting:

iUniverse
2021 Pine Lake Road, Suite 100
Lincoln, NE 68512
www.iuniverse.com
1-800-Authors (1-800-288-4677)

Because of the dynamic nature of the Internet, any Web addresses or links contained in this book may have changed since publication and may no longer be valid.

The views expressed in this work are solely those of the authors and do not necessarily reflect the views of the publisher, and the publisher hereby disclaims any responsibility for them.

ISBN: 978-0-595-47488-2 (pbk)
ISBN: 978-0-595-91760-0 (ebk)

Printed in the United States of America

Contents

Part II BRONSON

Part III TEAM

AUTHORS' NOTE

Pseudonyms have been used for a number of individuals mentioned in this book. Dennis Stockton; Dr. David Russo; Jen Simons; Dr. Laura Field; Deb Steiner; Martha, a psychiatric patient; and Harris, a prison guard; are fictitious names.

ACKNOWLEDGMENTS

It is with good reason that the powers that be put a time limit on acceptance speeches at the Academy Awards, the induction ceremonies for the various sports halls of fame, and other such proceedings. Life offers too few opportunities to publicly thank those who have been so kind to you. As the authors of these pages, we understand, because we too have many folks to whom we are indebted. If allowed, we could easily go on saying thank you deep into the evening.

Many people were interviewed, some numerous times, to share the experiences they had with Leana and Bronson as well to provide details about their own lives. Some individuals spoke off the record, confirming or disputing various aspects of this story. Others helped us find documents or track down people who seemingly had vanished from the face of the earth. Some people went beyond the call of duty: One government worker dug through stacks of Army records in a warehouse to help us find misfiled medical documents that would otherwise have been lost forever. Another person took it upon himself to knock on doors in rural Washington to help us locate Bronson's previous owners. Some provided background information, about post-traumatic stress disorder, for example, or the psychology of women inmates, service dogs or any number of topics. Some helped to interpret the unique language and symbols of medical records. Our benefactors are many, and our appreciation runs deep.

Thank you to: Dr. Silvia Amato, Dr. Jose Amato, Harry Beasley, Michael Beasley, Mark Bell, Mary Bell, Annie Bringloe, Margarethe Cammermeyer, Mimi Clifford, Tami Croft, Barbara Davenport, Rose Marie Davidson, Susan Duncan, Donna Durnford, Kim Farr, Michael Goehring, Dr. Richard Graham, Jeanne Hampl, Peter Hampl, Ray Hasting, Leslie Hays; Karl Iggers, Mona Jaber, China Jester, Tabatha Johnson, Richard Levandowski, Rachelle Lunde, Rolf Lunde, Cindy Mack, Glenn Martyn, Brendan Maye, Grace McCardle, Robert Newell, Sue Ortega, Alice Payne, Pam Reader, Lockheed Reader, Robert Reis, Beth Rivard, Marguerite Richmond, Dave Rodriguez, Dan Small, Jerry Strauss, Barbara Thompson, Patricia Toomey, Kyle Wilson, Bob Walter, and Yvonne Wood.

Various organizations, institutions and agencies lent a hand, in ways big and small. Whatever their contribution, our appreciation is sizable. Thanks to: Delta Society; Epilepsy Foundation; International Society for the Study of Dissociation; Prison Pet Partnership Program; Department of Corrections, State of Washington; People-Pet Partnership, College of Veterinary Medicine, Washington State University; and Sidran Foundation.

Leana gives special thanks to her family and friends, in particular her son Michael, Jeanne Hampl, Margarethe Cammermeyer, and everyone who supported this project.

Stephen offers his gratitude for encouragement, understanding, and favors granted to: Beth Albert, Michael Carroll, Verne Edwards, Jan Engle, Janet Fillmore, Leslie Graham, Keith LaBott, Mark Palmer, Christopher Sawicki, Rodger Stebbins, Genny Warren, Mary Alice Welsh, and Merri Yacenda. And of course his late great golden retriever, Abbey, who today surely carries her sticks amongst the angels, and his earthly Irish setter, Katie, who exemplifies the sentiments of a popular song–"don't worry, be happy."

INTRODUCTION

On the bulletin board in front of my desk, I keep a quotation from the thirteenth century mystic poet Rumi. It is a call to participate in life, basically, a summons to bring forth what is uniquely yours, to heed your inner voice when society's considerable influences tell you to do otherwise. "Start a huge, foolish project, like Noah," Rumi advises. "It makes absolutely no difference what people think of you."

Here is *Bombproof*, our huge, foolish project come to completion. It began one day in 1998, just as I was finishing the research for an article that would appear in *Animals* magazine about dogs who warn their owners of oncoming epileptic seizures. For a dog to detect a seizure before it strikes is a remarkable feat all by itself. Yet dogs who do this also provide great service. Among other things, they give people some time to seek help or to find a safe, private place to have their convulsions, which for someone who suffers from uncontrolled attacks is nothing less than a godsend. I had spoken to some interesting people for my article, from owners of such dogs to authorities who have investigated the phenomenon, and was about to start writing when my telephone rang.

On the line was one Leana Beasley, who been given my telephone number by the Prison Pet Partnership Program in Washington state, from which she obtained her seizure-alert dog, Bronson. A week or two earlier, I interviewed a woman from the organization and asked if she could put me in touch with any clients. Now, here was Leana, calling from Arizona, to share her experiences. Given my looming deadline, I figured I would let her talk and use maybe a quote or two. As it turned out, the story that Leana and later her husband, Harry, told me was so moving that it became central to my article. A wonderful photograph would eventually accompany the piece, showing a grinning Leana standing between Bronson and her neighbor's horse, the two animals touching noses in curiosity. (Looking at that picture today, I am struck less by the gentle behavior of the animals and more by the big smile on Leana's face. In the three or four years before Bronson came into her life, I doubt she ever wore that expression.)

Even when my article was done, I remained intrigued by Leana and Bronson's saga. So we began talking on the phone every week or so for an hour or two, my tape recorder running, with the thought that perhaps there was something more than a magazine article in all this.

Indeed, Leana's life–and that of her family–had been harrowing in recent years. Her medical and psychological ills were considerable, many of those problems growing out of her having been raped when she was in the military. Leana had spent a lot of time in medical and psychiatric hospitals, most of which did little to curb her problems. The stories she told were not pretty, and some were fairly unsettling.

The more we spoke, the more I realized that Leana could not tell this tale by herself. During much of what occurred, she was unaware of what was going on around her. Often, she was in the throes of convulsions. At one point, she was in a medically-induced coma. And at other times, she was in an altered state of mind, often stark terror, as a result of her post-traumatic stress. What's more, she knew little about Bronson's history.

As time passed, I interviewed dozens of people who knew or came in contact with Leana and Bronson, including family members, her doctors and therapists and dog trainers. I visited with Leana (and Bronson) and her family. I also spent time in the state of Washington for interviews and to gather records. There, I also traced Bronson's past, going to the farm where he was first found, the shelter where he was surrendered, the drug-dog training program from which he flunked out, and the women's prison where he was trained.

Leana and I also spent many hours tracking down her medical and psychiatric records from the various places in which she was hospitalized both in the Army and as a civilian, in the United States, Germany and Panama. There were also ambulance, police and military records to ferret out. In the end, I would pore over thousands of pages of documents. Taken together, they not only confirmed much of what Leana told me–her memory was remarkably good–but bolstered our research. Clearly, Leana's life underwent a marked change with the arrival of Bronson.

The dog, I found, touched a lot of people on the road to saving Leana. As I traced his pawprints along that road, I noticed a pattern. Although he had been given up on several occasions, it was not without human heartache. When Mary Bell, his owner from the farm, was driving to surrender him to a shelter, she was beside herself in grief. When Barbara Thompson, the prison inmate who trained him, gave him up and left the dog program, she was uncharacteristically weeping. When Rachelle Lunde, the volunteer who trained him for service-dog work in the community, finally delivered him to Leana, she turned back to her car in tears. Each of them told me that before they passed Bronson on to the next person that they were desperately searching their minds for some way to keep him for themselves.

There are special people who pass through our lives–and special dogs. Bronson is such a creature, though many folks I spoke with considered him more human than canine. When I met Sgt. Barbara Davenport, of the Washington Department of Corrections, who rescued him from the shelter and gave him a tryout as a drug-sniffing dog, she reported that he lacked what it took to make it in that particular field. He cared more about pleasing people, she said, than uncovering hidden narcotics. One point she emphasized, however, was that Bronson was unflappable, that he had a calm and gentle demeanor in the face of every challenge she and her fellow officers threw at him. "Bombproof" was the word she used, time and again.

When it came time to choose a title for this book, I suggested *Bombproof*, because it so aptly described Bronson's temperament, especially in regard to his experiences with Leana. My co-author said she liked it, then ran it by her then-teenage son, Michael. He gave it a nod of approval as well. "It sorta describes you, too, Mom," he told her.

Stephen Sawicki
Bridgeport, Connecticut

The people in flight from the terror behind—strange things happen to them, some bitterly cruel and some so beautiful that the faith is refired forever.

—*John Steinbeck,*
The Grapes of Wrath

PART I
LEANA

At the cycle's center,
They tremble, they walk
Under the tree,
They fall, they are torn,
They rise, they walk again.
                    —James Dickey
                        "The Heaven of Animals"

PROLOGUE

When my husband and I set out for the prison that first day, I asked God not to make this another time in which my hopes soared sky high only to later break apart and leave me more defeated than ever. "Don't let this one fall through, Lord," I prayed. "Let it happen. Watch over everything today. Let everything go well...."

Life had been difficult enough for the past ten years, starting with the rape and the flashbacks that haunted me. Then came my crash down a flight of stairs and the violent seizures. They struck often and unexpectedly, always at the worst times, and spat me out too frightened, too wary of further humiliation, to even leave my home.

The most crushing blow had come more recently, less than a year earlier, when I inhaled vomit during a seizure, ended up in a coma for more than a month, and nearly died. When I emerged, I had extensive damage to my lungs, among other woes, and a loss of memory that claimed even my ability to spell my name.

Harry and I had put our faith is science, in medicine, in well-respected health professionals with all kinds of degrees and specialties. Psychiatrists, psychologists, neurologists, cardiologists, and everything in between. They spoke of new drugs and new treatment regimens that promised to make a world of difference. They continually adjusted my medications, sometimes unwittingly increasing the frequency of my seizures, other times producing outrageous hallucinations that convinced me I'd lost my mind. They passed me along from one white coat to another, from one hospital to the next, always with assurances of better treatment right down the road. We chased after those dreams, hearts filled with hope, and more often than not came away dejected.

I don't know that I could have survived having my dreams crushed again. That's why I was praying that January morning as we left our home on the Fort Lewis military base for the Washington Corrections Center for Women near Gig Harbor, about forty-five minutes away.

This was going to be my first working session with a dog named Bronson. For the past several months, he was being prepared through a special program in which inmates trained service dogs for people with disabilities and in the process found a degree of redemption for their sins against society.

The animals, most rescued from shelters, mastered all kinds of skills, from the basics of obedience that every pet dog should have to towing wheelchairs or retrieving objects around the house. In my condition, especially in the post-seizure state when much of my body was paralyzed, the dog would be a tremendous help.

But Bronson was said to have another talent that no one taught him: He could detect and warn a person of epileptic seizures as much as an hour before they hit. The program, in fact, was renowned for placing several such canine partners each year.

A dog's ability to seizure alert is a phenomenon that man has yet to fully understand. Some people believe the animals perceive barely perceptible tics or patterns of behavior that individuals display prior to seizing. Others say they respond to electromagnetic discharges in the brain. But the prevailing theory–and the one I agree with–is that the canine's magnificent sense of smell is at work, detecting subtle changes in a person's odor brought on by the oncoming seizure. It's thought that all dogs are capable of picking up the scent, but that only certain ones–after witnessing one or two attacks and putting two and two together–choose to give warning.

That's why I so desperately wanted things to go well. For if it was true, if Bronson could do that for me, I could reclaim my life. Even just a few minutes warning would give me a chance to get to a safe place to have my seizures, preferably in private. It would spare me tremendous humiliation as well as countless injuries that came from flailing about in dangerous places or around furniture. The dog couldn't prevent the attacks, I knew, but to give warning was the next best thing.

Harry, who was a military police officer and a dog handler during the U.S. invasion of Panama, was less than sold on the whole idea. He had his fill of supposed solutions to my problems and he expected this one to go no better. My husband had become so jaded that he now considered pessimism a positive trait, his shield against the disappointments that battered us.

Harry figured I'd probably fail to qualify for a dog. Or maybe the animal wouldn't perform as expected. He regarded this entire expedition as a curious adventure. He was willing to come along because I wanted it so badly, but deep down he was convinced this too would end in heartbreak.

Rain is a way of life in the Pacific Northwest, but this day was gorgeous, sunny and crisp. Mount Rainier, unclouded and majestic, sat off in the distance. As our

Geo Metro rolled across the mile-long Tacoma Narrows Bridge, which spans Puget Sound and links Tacoma with the Olympic Peninsula, everything seemed fresh and new. The sky was a deeper blue than I'd ever seen it, the trees a richer green. I had crossed this suspension bridge before, but today its towers and stately rows of cables, even the fishing boats down below, seemed new to my eyes.

As we got off the highway and followed the wooded road to the prison, I tried to rein in my galloping anxiety. Years before my health conditions laid claim to my mind and body, I had been an MP like Harry. And though I was assured that the convicts today knew nothing about our personal lives, I was filled with dread. My post-traumatic stress only heightened the effect, causing even the least likely of threats to loom like thunderclouds.

The inmates, both in and out of the prison dog program, had been serious criminals. Some were murderers. Others were deadly in other ways. And though it was none of my business why they were incarcerated, I couldn't help but worry. My mind raced with outrageous scenarios, mixing the worst I'd heard about state prisons with the stuff of a made-for-TV movie. What if someone took a shank to one of us? What if a riot ripped loose, with Harry and me smack in the middle?

As unlikely as all that may have been, this wasn't a girls school. It was doubtful that any of the convicts felt kindly toward police officers of any kind, past or present, military or local. A cop was a cop, and somewhere along the line that was who had tracked down each of these women and took away their freedom.

Indeed, that was one of the ironies I found impossible to escape as we drove along: During the happiest, most self-confident time of my life I had been a law-enforcement officer, and now, in utter need, my last hope for anything resembling a normal life rested with convicts.

"Don't think of it as a prison," Harry said soothingly. "And don't think of them as inmates. Think of them as people who are helping you."

When we arrived, we were greeted by Jeanne Hampl, the director of the Prison Pet Partnership Program. Jeanne was in her fifties, a little shorter than average, and wore her graying hair in bangs. She had a professional friendliness, but a tone of voice and body language that left no doubt as to who was in charge.

Hampl guided us through the series of checkpoints and steel doors, each controlled by grim-faced guards, then led us outside and over to the aging gymnasium, where most of the inmate-trainers and their dogs had already assembled.

There I was introduced to convict Barbara Thompson. She was smallish and gaunt, with world-weary features that spoke of having endured some hardships herself. At her side was Bronson, a handsome black and tan dog, whom I'd met once before. Like most of the dogs, this Rottweiler-mix was clad in his working uniform, a red, double-sided backpack. Knee high, he was lean in the way of ado-lescent dogs, with but a stub of a tail. His hind end wiggled like mad as he whined an excited hello.

We barely exchanged greetings before Hampl put us to work. Joining seven or eight inmate handlers and their dogs, Bronson and I began with the basics. Everyone lined up along the sideline of the basketball court to have the dogs per-form what are known as "down-stays" and "sit-stays." As you might guess, my job was to tell Bronson to lie down or sit, followed by a command to "stay." Then, I was to summon him from across the floor.

I did, and Bronson exploded from his position like a sprinter. He weighed about seventy pounds, the larger side of medium, but in that moment and in the fear that ruled my life, he seemed massive and dangerous.

"Tell your dog, 'Front'!" Jeanne shouted.

"Front!" I yelled.

Then I cringed, folding myself up and throwing my hands before my face, expecting a body blow to send me reeling. When it failed to come, I cautiously peeked out to find Bronson seated before me, panting.

He met my gaze with a merry look, as if to say, "I did good, huh? Didn't I? Didn't I?"

Across the way, Jeanne and Barbara were smiling broadly and shaking their heads in wonder.

"What was *that*?" Jeanne yelled. "That was not proper obedience training. What were you *doing*?"

"He looked so big!" I stammered.

Jeanne came over and reassured me. We tried again. This time I called "Front!" and forced myself to watch as Bronson hit the brakes and again dropped into a flawless sit in front of me.

Jeanne said to finish with a heel, so I gave the command and Bronson leapt to my side, seamlessly pivoting on his hind legs before his front paws even touched the floor, and sat upright beside me.

The dog basked in the praise and good-boy pats I gave him. I got the feeling that he instinctively knew I was going to be his person. All through the class, his focus was entirely on me. He never even gazed over at Barbara or Jeanne.

The session flew by. When we were done, I walked from the gym with Harry, Jeanne, and Barbara, who now had Bronson on his lead. We followed the side-walk toward the gate; then Barbara said goodbye and she and Bronson turned in the direction of their cellblock.

My husband and Jeanne continued on, but I lingered for one last look at my partner-to-be. As Barbara and Bronson moved away along the fence line, the dog seemed reluctant to separate from me. Betraying his impeccable training, he fell out of step with Barbara and stared strangely at me for the longest moment, as if he didn't want me to leave.

"Well, what do you think?" I asked Harry when we got in the car.

"I don't know," he said, shaking his head. "That dog is trained awfully sharp. You're going to have to do a lot of work to keep up his training and not let him slide."

Jeanne had spoken to us about this very issue. A disabled person's problems don't magically end when a service dog enters the picture. Success and failure hinge on how well the person and animal come together as a team, and how dedicated the human half of that pair is to maintaining and supplementing the training as issues arise. Harry wasn't outwardly saying it, but both of us had to be thinking the same thing: With my considerable problems–and they were indeed considerable–and a young son to raise, was I really up to handling such an elite dog?

We started for home, each of us sorting through the day's events in our own minds. We got about two miles when I began feeling queasy. Harry noticed a change in me and asked how I was doing. I said I was exhausted. I had stayed awake the entire night before, worrying. Then the stress of the prison and wanting so badly to make a good impression took more out of me. Now that we were done, I felt like a boxer collapsing in his corner after the final bell.

"I don't feel too good," I finally admitted, though my timing could have been better. Harry had just pulled onto the bridge, and we had no place to pull over.

My husband, realizing that seizures were about to strike, went into emergency mode. First, he ordered me to lock the door, then told me to attach my seat belt. I got the first part done, but no more. In seconds, I was in full-blown convulsions.

There I was, thrashing about, while Harry tried to steer, shift gears, and prevent me from hurting myself, all while stomping the gas pedal in a blitz for the emergency room at Madigan Army Medical Center at Fort Lewis.

We arrived safely. The doctors looked me over and released me that day. But as usually happens when I have seizures, I was wiped out. The convulsions taxed every muscle, worse than the most rigorous workout. I spent the next couple days feeling like I'd been steamrolled.

When I was up to it, I called Hampl to fill her in. Rather than express much sympathy, though, she seemed to be chuckling.

"That's wonderful!" she said. "Very interesting."

What was this? Besides her work with dogs, Jeanne was a registered nurse. She knew that with all my problems the seizures could be lethal. What could possibly be so marvelous about my experiencing them in the middle of traffic on the Tacoma Narrows Bridge?

Jeanne explained that immediately after I left the prison on Friday, Bronson was acting up. It was completely unlike him, she said. He was pacing. He kept sniffing at the door of Barbara's cell. He refused to calm down. Barbara had come to her and said she didn't know what was the matter. No one knew what was going on with the dog.

I was bewildered, and concerned. Was Bronson all right? Was I still going to receive him? What was Hampl driving at anyway?

Jeanne surely sensed my confusion. She paused long enough to keep me dangling, allowing the possibilities to ricochet through my mind.

Finally, with the good-natured brusqueness that typified her, Jeanne spelled it out: "Leana, your damn dog was alerting."

1

The blackness of a summer evening wrapped around Harry and me as we slept. We were the picture of marital contentment, young parents stealing a few hours repose before another day of work and the demands of raising a two-year-old son. But in the recesses of my mind, unspeakable horror was breaking loose.

It was 1987. We were in Mannheim, Germany, where Harry was stationed as a military police officer. I was three years out of the Army. Now, in an explosion of memory, I was back in Virginia, in my barracks room at Fort Lee. And though it was Harry who drowsily slung his arm across me that night, in my mind it was that of my sergeant. Fueled by whiskey, he was upon me once again, invading me, taunting, and enjoying my pain.

Utter fear possessed me as I flailed wildly. In the darkness and tangle of sheets, I managed to wedge my feet beneath Harry and launched him from the mattress. He thudded to the floor between the bed and wall, scared and confused.

"What's going on!" he shouted. "What's going on!"

Harry scrambled for the lights. When he flicked them on, he saw me wrestling with the covers, my eyes crazed, my body quaking and drenched in sweat. The illumination flung me back to the present. And when my husband hurried over to ask what was wrong, all I could say was that I didn't know. It must have been a bad dream, I told him, and, God, I was sorry.

But this was more than a nightmare, as I had been calling these horrible intrusions. I was in crisis.

More and more over the past few years, similar episodes plagued my sleep. Unlike dreams, which have a certain ethereal quality, these visions seemed hard and true, as if I experienced them with all my senses, indeed my entire body. And though I didn't always remember the details, I'd always jolt awake, frightened beyond comprehension.

I did my best to dismiss the attacks and live my life. But their effects surfaced in ways I had no control over. My emotional reactions, even to something as harmless as a television program, were increasingly heightened. I'd grow furious, for example, or extremely wary without obvious reason. My stomach seemed constantly snarled.

Most disturbing, brief flashes of terrifying memory began to haunt me when I was awake. I might be doing housework and in an instant everything would fall away and my attacker would appear. Or I would be slicing a tomato and rather than see juice on the counter, there'd be blood. The episodes lasted just seconds, but with each instance I came away more deeply shaken.

My relationship with Harry suffered. Sometimes while making love I became so scared that I would tremble, freeze up, then dissolve in tears. At other times, reliving the rape, I would shriek and cry out. Some nights, I avoided my husband altogether and curled up beside our son in his bed.

Harry was never one for talking out problems, and I doubt I could have explained this anyway. Although he knew about the rape and tried to be understanding, it was obvious that he was wounded by my behavior.

It was also during this period that the blackouts, lost seconds of which I could give no account, also afflicted me. I had first experienced them when I was growing up, short stretches of staring blankly, my mind seemingly turned off. I even had a few such moments after I joined the Army, but attributed them to a lack of concentration.

They became more pronounced–and frightening–after our son was born, then followed me when Harry transferred to Germany. Once, I blacked out while I was standing in our living room, by the couch, with the baby in my arms. My body struck the floor, but to my lasting relief, I found Michael unhurt on the sofa.

At other times, I'd be watching television and the screen seemed to shrink, becoming distant in my perception, until it was a pinpoint in a sea of blackness. When I came to, half an hour would have passed.

The most unsettling incident occurred a few weeks before I ejected Harry from bed. I was watching a television talk show in which a guest recounted being sexually assaulted. Just then, as I was putting some water on the stove to boil, I fell unconscious. When I came to, I was writhing on the floor, desperately reaching overhead with my left hand to free my right from a non-existent restraint. I didn't know how much time had passed, but it was enough for the teapot to now be whistling like mad.

None of this made sense. Was I was losing my mind? Besides being too ashamed to tell anyone what I was going through, I worried that I was losing my ability to beat back these intrusions. If in this stricken state I could catapult Harry, a one-hundred-and-seventy-five-pound man, off the mattress, was I capable of unknowingly inflicting even worse harm to him or Michael?

I found myself in a crossfire of fear, bewilderment, and doubt over what was real and what was imagination. The distinction hardly mattered because the terror was devastating one way or the other.

CERTAINLY, this was a far cry from the fresh start I anticipated when the baby and I arrived in West Germany in the fall of 1985, a few months after Harry began his new assignment. I grew up in rural Washington state, and like most everyone in my family had never left the United States or traveled much. And though Harry and I had both been at Fort Lee for several years–I left the Army after becoming pregnant–we were looking forward to being out in the world and experiencing a different culture.

Our home in West Germany was Benjamin Franklin Village, a newly remodeled military housing community. Germany's a beautiful country, and I loved shopping and sightseeing around Mannheim and Heidelberg. On weekends, we would ride bicycles, with Michael strapped in a seat behind Harry, while I carried the diaper bag and other necessities. We splashed in a nearby lake, took in beerfests, toured historic sites, and trekked around the zoo.

While Harry was busy with his MP duties, patrolling U.S. installations around Mannheim, I tended to Michael. Having once been an MP myself, I also held a civilian job for awhile as a store detective at the PX.

These were uneasy days to be abroad. Cold War tensions ran high. Terrorism, too, was on the rise. In Germany, the notorious Red Army Faction was reaching its peak of activity, unleashing a series of bombings against U.S. interests. One of the scariest attacks came in 1985, as RAF members murdered an American soldier, then used his identification to enter an American airbase in Frankfurt. There, they detonated a bomb that killed two people.

Then in the spring of 1986, Libyan terrorists set off a blast at a disco in West Berlin that killed three more, including an American serviceman and wounded two hundred others. The U.S. retaliated with air strikes on Tripoli and Benghazi. All over Europe and the world, American forces went on high alert. Tanks appeared in our housing area to counter would-be car bombers. Even residents were subject to automobile searches and MPs passing mirrors under our cars. The precautions and potential for danger were like nothing I'd ever witnessed.

Then, three weeks after the Libyan attack, disaster struck at the Soviet Union's Chernobyl nuclear power plant. We were on standby for evacuation, in fact, out of concern that the radioactive cloud would shift toward Germany.

All this craziness intensified my already growing sense of fear and fierce protectiveness of our son. Michael's birth had been the culmination of a year of life-changing events: my rape, my marriage to Harry, the pregnancy, and my departure from the Army. My son arrived almost a month after my due date, by emergency Cesarean section, on February 17, 1985. That also happened to be my twenty-sixth birthday.

After the operation, infection set in–most likely from a pair of contaminated surgical scissors–and I was crippled with pain. By the time the doctors opened me up again, gangrene had spread through most of my reproductive system. In a shattering experience for me and Harry, a surgeon now removed everything but my ovaries.

I was a first-time mother who would never have another child, even though a large family had been our fondest wish. The result, fed by my emerging PTSD, was that I became consumed with keeping Michael safe.

Since birth, my son suffered from chronic ear infections. They were so severe that he was in large part deaf for his first three years, until he had corrective surgery. This, in turn, delayed his learning to speak. He could say a few words, but they were so garbled that for the most part I was the only one who understood him.

Michael's hearing difficulties also threw off his physical balance. As a result, he had more than the usual number of childhood accidents. Even walking down the hall was precarious for my son.

With my nightmares and flashes of memory coming on stronger, I became all the more fixated on Michael's well-being. Every new problem, no matter how slight, filled me with dread. Most first-time mothers are a little overcautious, but I took it to an extreme. Soon, I was bringing Michael to the clinic for bumps and bruises that most mothers would have kissed away. And when something truly dire occurred, like the time he was hospitalized for E. coli poisoning from a fast-food hamburger, I nearly fell apart.

My extreme reaction to events combined with my overprotectiveness of my son soon began to get the attention of clinic workers and others. It was increasingly obvious that I was in deep psychological distress. It was one of Harry's superiors, in fact, who finally urged me to seek psychiatric counseling.

I followed his advice, but in the end it only intensified matters. I had a severe reaction to my first Army counselor, a sergeant whose light hair and mustache, even some of the phrases he used, summoned memories of my attacker. I left one of our sessions in a frightened, near-shock state. And though I got home okay, I had no idea how I actually got there.

Soon, I all but stopped functioning. I was extremely depressed, not sleeping, not eating. And I was timid as could be. If anyone around me moved too quickly, or a car backfired, I jolted. When I went out, to the PX or church, I was wary of everyone. My speech became a frightened stutter. Often I would scribble what I had to say, sparing myself the shame of attempting to talk.

I was scared, no longer in control, and full of self-loathing. It all finally became too much. Late one summer afternoon, while Harry was napping, I emptied the contents of several containers of muscle relaxants and pain relievers into my mouth and washed them down with a glass of milk. I scrawled a note to Harry, saying I loved him and Michael and apologizing for the trouble I'd caused. Then I went out.

I ended up at the Benjamin Franklin Village chapel, where some workers were closing up for the day. They agreed to let me inside for a few minutes, and I found my way to the balcony where I murmured some prayers. When told it was time to lock up, I staggered out, sat on the stairs, and waited to die.

Harry, in the meantime, discovered my note and the empty pill containers. There had been some tension between us recently and he questioned whether this was legitimate or if I was looking to get a rise out of him. Leaving Michael with a neighbor, he set out on foot to see if I was with a couple we knew. If I wasn't there, he told himself, then this was serious.

To this day Harry says an angel was on his shoulder, for when he came to an intersection on his way to our friends' place, an inner voice told him to head in the opposite direction, toward the chapel. We attended services elsewhere, so he had no obvious reason to expect to find me there. But there I was, perched by the side door, sobbing hysterically and praying out loud.

Harry got someone to call the MPs, my stomach was pumped, and I was held at an Army hospital for observation. Making matters worse, I suffered a flashback a couple days into my stay and charged out of the building. A guard managed to grab me and return me to the ward.

Soon afterward, I was transferred to Landstuhl Army Regional Medical Center, about eighty miles west. After eight uneventful days, I was discharged with a diagnosis of "mild depressive disorder" and given a prescription for anti-depressants.

In Mannheim, I began seeing Jen Simons, a civilian psychologist at the Army mental health center. With her patience and encouragement, I came out of myself a bit, telling her about the rape and the frightening events of recent months. She assured me that despite all that happened, I wasn't losing my mind and that with time I could win back my self-esteem, and all else that had fallen away.

"It seems like everything you've been holding in for these three years is all coming out now," she told me.

Simons spoke about veterans from Vietnam, how they often experienced flashbacks and other aftershocks of war, and how my situation was not all that different. She brought out a sheet with the psychiatric criteria for post-traumatic stress disorder and showed me. Down the list she went, point by point. Practically every item described me, from the traumatic life event, my rape, straight on through the flashbacks, fearfulness, persistent avoidance, and hypervigilence.

Simons had one overriding theme she wanted to get through to me. It was going to take time, she said repeatedly, but life would get better; there was hope. Neither of us could have guessed how far I still had to fall–or the peculiar form that salvation would take.

2

Harry was completely on edge during the days and weeks after my overdose. When the doctors at Landstuhl deemed me stable, they sent me home. But "stable" was small consolation to my husband, who doubted I should have been released so soon. My respite in the hospital, he knew, resolved nothing.

The suicide attempt had caught him off guard. He was baffled by it and pained. We had always struggled when it came to sharing our deepest feelings, and this was as heavy as it came. Harry turned inward, figuring he was to blame, that something he said or did set me off. Now he worked diligently to keep me from becoming agitated. At home, he was on his best behavior, watching what he said and helping more around the house and with Michael. That angel on his shoulder, he worried, might not be around if I tried to kill myself a second time.

Storms were gathering on other fronts as well. Because of his worries about me, Harry's work began to slip and his chain of command took notice. Though initially supportive, the military had limited tolerance for mental illness, whether it involved one of their own or a dependent like me. The machine that was the Army was too rigid, its personnel schooled to trust only hard and fast rules, for anything so unpredictable. Harry's superiors wanted this to end, posthaste.

Stirred into the mix, my psychiatrist, David Russo, who worked with Simons, was prodding Harry to put in for compassionate reassignment. He knew that the U.S. military in Germany lacked the expertise and facilities for an affliction as severe as mine. To get the proper care, he explained, I needed to return stateside. Perhaps Harry and I were in denial. Certainly we underestimated what was occurring. But we liked Germany and we stubbornly balked at any suggestion that we leave.

I had grown comfortable seeing Jen Simons, and thought our weekly sessions might be all the professional intervention I needed. I became more apprehensive, though, after I blanked out one day at the PX and left Michael in his stroller, forgetting he even existed until I'd walked halfway home. Rushing back, I found him safe; no one even noticed him there. But I came away deeply distressed.

Then, one autumn night, another nightmare struck and I woke up soaked in sweat and shivering. While Harry slept peacefully, I padded into the living room, sank into the overstuffed chair to clear my head, and nodded off.

When I awoke, the room was bathed in a dim glow from outdoors, and somebody forgot to turn off the kitchen light. My left hand ached. I looked, and was puzzled to see both my hand and lap covered in blood. A red puddle had formed on the tile floor beneath me. Then, I saw a slash running deep across my wrist, as if someone had been sawing on it.

I went to our room and cried for Harry. He could hardly believe what he was jolted out of a sound sleep to see. But he quickly shook off his confusion and pressed a towel to my wound to stave off the bleeding.

He also found the bloody butcher knife in the kitchen sink. A trail of crimson ran from there to the overstuffed chair.

That evening I was deeply withdrawn and quiet. Whatever Harry told me to do, I obeyed almost like a child.

He bundled up Michael, who dozed through the entire ordeal, and we made off for the Mannheim clinic. The doctor there stitched my wrist and once again I was dispatched to the medical center in Heidelberg for observation.

This time, Dr. Russo, who oversaw my care, refused to release me so quickly: My depression had become incapacitating. My stuttering was worse than ever. And he was skeptical when I couldn't explain my mutilated wrist.

I got through my first couple days there without incident. But the hospital itself was feeding my anxiety: With the nurses constantly hovering, checking to make certain I didn't try to take my life again, I had no privacy. And while I was allowed to go to the stairwell for an occasional cigarette, a staff escort was mandatory.

The musty smell of that old military structure, moreover, stirred memories of the barracks at Fort Lee. My senses made the connection before my mind; I found myself trembling without comprehension. The place was stifling. The walls seemed to be closing in.

A couple times, I tried to walk outside for some air but was intercepted by a nurse who directed me back to my bed. Finally I just ignored her and kept going. I was outside for only a minute or two when staff reenforcements appeared and urged me to return with them. "Please, just a few minutes," I sputtered.

"I don't have time for this nonsense," snapped a male nurse He snatched my arm and pulled.

The past roared back and I was awash in naked fear. But before I could flee, the staff jumped me and wrestled me down. I fainted during the tussle.

The next day, I was strapped in four-point restraints to a gurney and loaded into an ambulance to again be transported to Landstuhl.

When they draped a blanket over me to keep me warm that morning, I was void of feelings. I wasn't angry or melancholy or introspective. If anything, "numb" best describes my state of mind. And bewildered. Since no one explained to me about the transfer, I had no idea what was happening.

A male medic climbed in front to drive and his partner, a petite young woman, got in the rear with me, to keep watch. She wasn't very attentive, though. Beneath the cover I managed to manipulate my hands enough to slide them out of the restraints, then my feet. We were halfway to Landstuhl when I sat straight up and stared quizzically at her.

I don't know what she thought my particular problem was, but at that moment she looked like she was going to be sick. She scrambled for the window to the front cab, pounding furiously.

"She's free! She's free!" she yelled, as if a wild creature had broken its chains

As you might expect, the vehicle came to an abrupt stop. When the medics went to switch places, I made a play for freedom, but the man blocked me and pushed his way in. Rather than try to muscle me into the restraints, he nervously convinced me to ease back, holding out a cigarette to soothe the beast.

It was when we finally arrived that trouble hit. The medics carted me out with no problem. But they made the mistake of leaving me unattended, in a wheel-chair, in a hallway outside the emergency room while they went to contact the staff.

I waited awhile, then got up, strolled past the admissions desk, and stepped outside to take a breather. I was minding my own business, standing in the ambulance loading zone, when I heard someone shout, "There she is!"

I looked up to see a group of medics charging toward me as if I had just fielded a kickoff. All I saw was the rush of military uniforms. My adrenalin surged. I didn't think, I just ran. They tackled me hard, right on the blacktop, and sub-dued me. Then everyone latched onto an arm or leg and hauled me back inside.

In the ten days I was in the Landstuhl hospital, I gravitated between a near catatonic, depressed state to one of utter fright. Not only did the place remind me of the room where I was assaulted, but when I tried to escape, which was often, the staff had no qualms about forcibly strapping me down and leaving me in a tight little "quiet room," which stirred all the more memories of the night I was raped.

Like Jen Simons, doctors there said I appeared to be suffering from a post-traumatic reaction. Rather than help, my stay at Landstuhl only further trauma-tized me. The staff's idea of treatment seemed to be either to lock me up or other-wise keep me quiet and groggy on mood-altering drugs.

When I was finally proclaimed stable and Harry brought me home, it was obvious what was coming. It took less than a week before my husband stepped into the living room late one night–his angel must have nudged him awake–and found me asleep in the same overstuffed chair, with the same wrist sliced open, my arm slung over the side, and blood pooling on the floor. And once again, I was mystified as to how it happened.

They stitched me together at the Mannheim clinic. Then Harry went in to talk to the doctors, who insisted that I stay in the waiting room, where Michael was playing with his toy cars.

I waited a bit. Then imperceptibly, my mind shifted. I suddenly had no idea where I was or why I was there. I left my son, marched past the office where Harry was, and stepped out the emergency room exit and into the night.

I had just lit up a cigarette and was considering the best direction to head when my husband appeared with two medics and the MP who was guarding the clinic. "Lee, where are you going?" Harry asked.

"I've got to get to work," I said. "You know how to get back to the company?" Harry surely thought I was crazy. I had no job. But more than that, it sounded like I might be referring to my days in the Army.

"Why don't you come on back in here and wait," he said carefully. "We'll figure it out when you're inside."

One of the medics, seeing how strangely I was behaving, turned around and went inside. He came back carrying a straitjacket.

It was right around that time, as the medics and the MP began to grapple with me, that Michael tottered out to see where everyone had gone. When he saw a group of men ganging up on me, he came running, shrieking.

Harry snagged Michael and took him off to the side, telling him that Mommy needed help and assuring him that the jacket was only to keep me warm. I never blamed my husband for allowing them to take me that way; I was out of control. But for years afterward I held it against him, sometimes furiously, for thoughtlessly allowing our son to watch as I was taken down and forced kicking and screaming into a straitjacket.

3

When I arrived at the sprawling Walter Reed Army Medical Center in Washington, D.C., I was trembling, less from my psychological problems and more because I realized that I was no longer in control of my life. I was back in the United States, alone and in fragile mental health. My husband and son were an ocean away. I was heavily sedated. And I had no idea what was in store. For all I knew, I was being locked away for the rest of my life.

I was considered a full-scale flight risk and tried, soon after my arrival at the hospital, to casually blend in with everyone who was bustling through the admissions area and simply walk off. My attendants quickly intervened, sat me in a wheelchair, and brought me five floors up to the psychiatric unit, Ward 55, for in-processing.

Unlike the Army hospitals in Germany, Walter Reed was thoroughly modern, with nice rooms, courtyards, a daily schedule for the patients, and varied therapeutic activities like arts and crafts or use of the greenhouse for those who earned the privilege. Still, Army personnel ran the place. Practically everyone was in uniform, even most of the patients, which I would later discover was a stressor for my PTSD.

The shock of being in America again, and in such a sophisticated facility, was substantial. It was only two weeks since I was overpowered at the Mannheim clinic. Harry and the doctors decided to ship me back to the states, but my husband needed permission from the German courts before he could take guardianship. Arrangements also needed to be made for my medevac flight.

Warped by the PTSD, I had my own perception of my "best interests." In my final days in Germany, I attempted half a dozen escapes. In one incident, I wriggled out of an improperly bound straitjacket and almost made it over a ten-foot-high stone wall to freedom before a pursuer grabbed my ankle and yanked me down.

In another instance, when the MP assigned to watch me stepped away from my hospital room for a moment, I casually walked out. Barefoot and in pajamas, I dashed down the stairs and across a parking lot. My guard gave chase, shouting, while the MP at the gate and some medics who had just arrived also tried to stop me. I was wielding a pilfered butter knife when one of the MPs finally blindsided me and the others piled on.

Then, on the day before I was to be flown out, while in a hospital in Frankfurt, I filched a safety razor from a hygiene cart. I broke it open and set to work with the blade, this time slicing my right wrist. I hadn't realized I was being monitored by a security camera. The staff got to me fast, before I did much damage, and once again I was stitched together. Now they stationed someone in my room to watch me.

But I wasn't done yet. The day I was to leave, they carried me, bound to a stretcher in five-point restraints, onto a cargo plane at Ramstein Air Base, but made the mistake of briefly leaving me alone. This time I managed to undo the little locks on my restraints. As the workers were busy loading and otherwise preparing the plane, I marched out the door and down the tarmac.

The sight of a woman hurrying along the airstrip, dressed only in hospital pajamas, in early November no less, was bound to catch someone's eye, and I was gang-tackled yet again. They forced me into the plane and injected me with something that knocked me right out. Whenever I emerged from the fog on that long journey to the U.S. someone jabbed me with another needle and I was gone.

By the time I arrived at Walter Reed, I was still feeling the effects of that and the other drugs administered to keep me docile. I can't say that at that point I longed for Michael or Harry or, in fact, had much feeling about anything. Between the drugs and an incapacitating depression, coping with the here and now was hard enough.

Settling in, I found life on Ward 55 to be more structured than my previous hospitalizations. Patients were awakened early each morning, with a half hour to get dressed and ready, then on to medications, breakfast, and activities. We had daily meetings to attend, including community sessions with the other patients and staff, in which we discussed and voted on rules for the ward. Participation was a way to earn privileges, but I remained detached, oftentimes in my own world.

I was at Walter Reed three or four days when I was assigned to my psychiatrist, Captain Laura Field. She was a resident, about my age, with a certain fair-skinned beauty you wouldn't expect in a military officer. She struck me as a soldier's soldier, impeccably dressed in her Class B uniform–light green blouse, with dark green pants or a skirt–and possessing a similar sharply-creased, to-the-point bedside manner.

To me, Dr. Field always seemed harried, with too many patients and too little time. Her overriding concern was my medication, with only a question or two about my state of mind.

A few weeks into my stay, I was given an electroencephalogram, or EEG, a less-than-perfect tool for ruling out potential causes of my condition, such as a seizure disorder or brain tumor. The test came back normal. My official diagnosis would read: post-traumatic stress disorder, major depression, and panic attacks.

From the beginning of my stay I drifted in and out of flashbacks, especially when I was bumped or jostled by other patients. I was so startled and scared that on several occasions I ran face-first into walls and doors, without ever seeing them, bloodying myself. Any sudden and loud noises, or those I perceived that way, be it the PA system, a toppled trash-can, or a dinner tray clanging to the floor, had me petrified. I was too anxious to make eye contact and too wary to turn my back on anyone. I skulked through the hallways, staying as close to the walls as possible.

Initially, Dr. Field had me on the anti-manic drug Tegretol, which also happens to be used for seizures, and the anti-psychotic Melleril. But one of them, or the combination, only heightened my terror. In one wild scene, I roared through the double doors of the ward, which were usually closely monitored, and into the outer hall. With staff members giving chase, I bolted down one corridor, past the elevators, and was just beginning to charge down another when a male attendant lunged for me. He missed getting a handhold, but knocked me down, and I slid face-down, as if on ice, over several yards of polished tile floor.

Next thing I knew, someone was on my back, struggling to flip me over. When I turned, the male attendant was straddling my waist, trying desperately to get me under control. What I envisioned, however, was my rapist.

"Get off! Get off!" shouted a female nurse seeing the terror in my eyes. When he finally did climb off, I fell apart, curling into a ball and crying uncontrollably.

They returned me to the ward, and as seemed to be standard procedure, strapped my hands and feet to the bed, supposedly to protect myself and others. But the restraints only intensified my fear. I would writhe on my bed until I passed out from exhaustion. Sometimes they kept me that way for entire days at a time.

My nightmares also continued. In some, I was being raped again. Or I saw hands grabbing at me, among other visions. When the nurses shook my shoulder or arm to awaken me, I was so startled that on several occasions I swung at them. Once, I backed into a corner and cowered. After awhile, staff members learned to keep their distance when they came to wake me, venturing only a step or two past my doorway and calling my name or reaching out with a foot to jostle the bed.

More than once the nurses would be making their rounds late at night and hear the spray of the shower in the bathroom attached to my room. Investigating, they found me in my bedclothes on the floor of the stall, sobbing and shaking, hot water raining on me.

At other times, I may have looked to them as if I was stable, but actually I was drifting in and out of a dissociative state in which I thought myself still in the Army, four years earlier. I regarded myself as Leana Proctor, which was my maiden name, private first class. In my mind the hospital became the barracks at Fort Lee.

Now and then, I addressed people as if they were soldiers in my unit, using names of individuals long gone from my life, or I would incorrectly identify the year. Invariably, the staff's reaction was to insistently correct me. I was baffled by this, but their remarks never changed my perception. If anything, they convinced me that keeping to myself was the best strategy for surviving in this peculiar place.

All of this was interspersed with stretches of lucidity. But even then I was gazing through the lens of dark depression.

One fellow patient, an active-duty soldier in his thirties suffered what I was told was a bad reaction to a change in his medication and remained confined to his room. All any of us heard of him were screams and cries from behind his closed door. His experience left me deathly afraid that something similar could befall me, that one wrong drug would leave me a raving madwoman, a vegetable, or dead.

The wife of a military man, meanwhile, was receiving electroconvulsive shock therapy for her severe depression, the very thought of which paralyzed me with fright.

As it stood, I was frustrated with the constant changes and adjustments Dr. Field kept making to my medications. Just as I got used to one, she switched to another. And with each change came new discomforts: dizziness, headaches, lethargy, confusion, and racing thoughts, to name just a few. After awhile, the side-effects seemed worse than my original problems.

By December, Harry and Michael finally arrived in the U.S. My husband took an apartment in Arlington, Virginia and settled into his duties at Fort Myer and Arlington National Cemetery. His mother, meanwhile, came from Arizona to look after Michael.

Citing regulations, the Walter Reed staff denied me physical contact with my son. He was a few months short of three years old, too young to be allowed on the psych ward. And they refused to let me off the unit until I earned that privilege. I found it maddening and cruel that Michael and I could see each other only by peering through a glass wall of the courtyard. It was like I was on display at the zoo. And it broke my heart to not be able to hug him and dry his tears.

IN THE COURTYARD at Walter Reed, I sat on the concrete wall of a raised flower bed, lost in a swirl of painful memories and emotions from that night at Fort Lee. I had always been reluctant and in many ways unable to discuss the rape, so Dr. Field encouraged me to try putting my thoughts down on paper. I was apprehensive, but she kept dangling the promise of privileges, including the chance to spend time with my son, as a reward. So, I agreed to try.

Day after day, I took a pencil and yellow legal pad, found a quiet place, and wrote, arduously, about my ordeal. Sometimes I became so overwrought that I would vomit or suffer flashbacks, to the point that a nurse would check on me or help me back inside. I would be out of commission for hours, sometimes a couple days, but when I recovered I commenced writing again. I worked for nearly three weeks, usually sitting in the courtyard, though sometimes the dayroom or my own room.

I produced a small stack of pages, recounting not only the rape, but my hopes when I joined the service, my aspirations to become a military police investigator, and how it all fell apart so rapidly. I remember writing something along these lines:

> It is close to eight o'clock at night. I am in my room at the barracks, about to go for a jog, when the rapping comes at my door. I open it, expecting to see a fellow woman MP, but I'm wrong. It's him. Terrified, I go to slam the door, but his foot is wedged there. Still, I push. More powerful, he shoves. The door bursts open and I fall backwards, striking my skull against a heavy metal locker. We struggle. I kick at him. Raging now, he catches me with a blow to the stomach. I can't breathe. He's on me, lips against my face, hands pawing beneath my clothing. I smell his aftershave, his sweat, his boozy breath. I resist again, and a fist explodes to the side of my face. He seizes my hair and thumps my head over and over against the rock-hard floor.

My attacker, I explained, was my supervisor at Fort Lee. Sgt. Dennis Stockton, a career soldier, Vietnam veteran, and fixture on the base. He was well known for abusing low-ranking soldiers with slaps and punches and was often inebriated on the job. In his mid-thirties, he lived off-base with his wife and children.

I was twenty-five. I came out of high school in rural Washington state with dreams of becoming a police officer. I attended college briefly, went through the police academy, worked in security, then joined the Army in 1982. And though I was a dedicated, hard worker–I'd held all sorts of jobs since I was a kid–I was naive about men and anything having to do with sex. I never had a boyfriend or went on a date, nothing like that.

At first, being in the Army was all I imagined. I did well in basic training, getting in great physical condition and rating expert on the firing range with the M-16, the .38 Smith & Wesson handgun, and grenades. I liked the camaraderie, too. For once, I felt good about myself. I was self-confident and with a clear-cut purpose to my life.

After several months of training, I became a full-fledged MP, stationed at Fort Pickett in southern Virginia. I was the military's equivalent of a street cop, having a hand in everything from routine traffic stops, to breaking up drunken brawls, to responding to thefts.

As time passed, I also got experience as a military police investigator–detective work, basically–through on-the-job training. I was in on a number of good cases, helping track down some drug suspects who escaped custody and assisting in a probe of how money and supplies were being siphoned from a military warehouse.

What's more, I received an Army Commendation Medal for my stint as a guard at the U.S. Disciplinary Barracks at Fort Leavenworth, Kansas, the military's legendary maximum security prison.

In late February, 1984, I was transferred to Fort Lee, in Petersburg, Virginia, for additional on-the-job training. Shortly after my arrival, plans changed: I was sent to work in an unrelated office job. Although disappointed, I had only a month before I left for Military Police Investigations school in Alabama. I figured I would grin and bear it.

From Day One, however, Sgt. Stockton was far too flirtatious for a supervisor. When I showed no interest in him, his behavior got worse. He began making lewd remarks–vulgar suggestions about his physical desire for me–and leaving suggestive notes on my desk.

Soon, painful pinches, slaps, even punches–some of which was witnessed by others, who did nothing–became daily occurrences. I told him to stop, to no avail. But I took no formal action because I figured that my sex, rank, and newness to the base would only work against me. And the last thing I wanted was a reputation for filing complaints against my superiors.

Before long, it got worse. After hours, Stockton would bypass the guard in my barracks, saying he had to check on his "people" (of which I was the only one), and rap on my door, making crude overtures. I fended him off, but he grew increasingly insistent.

On the night of March 16, he bulled his way in, raped and sodomized me, then slashed my arm with a knife as I went to escape. And though the attack itself proved deeply traumatic, it was the aftermath that shattered my faith in the Army.

I was in utter shock after the incident and didn't know what to do. The cut on my arm, however, required emergency care and raised immediate questions. Frightened and confused, I signed a statement saying I was attacked by some area toughs in a parking lot.

When I came forward the next day with what Stockton had done, my company commander accused me of lying, fiercely supported the sergeant, and promised I would pay a price if I sullied his company by even uttering the word "rape."

As the investigation expanded and word got out, people in the company took sides. Some, like Harry Beasley, whom I had just started dating and who witnessed one episode of Stockton repeatedly slapping me in the head, supported me down the line. Others believed Stockton and I were having an affair, that I cut myself that night, and that I accused him only to protect myself from getting into trouble for having sex with a married non-commissioned officer.

As it turned out, Stockton never faced the court martial he deserved. Instead, the matter was handled by the battalion commander, who had the power to dole out non-judicial punishment for certain offenses. In this case, charges of fraternization, sexual harassment, actions unbecoming an NCO, and adultery earned Stockton a fine, a reduction in rank, and ninety days of extra duty. The groundwork was being laid for his expulsion from the Army.

After his initial punishment was handed down, it got uglier–and scarier for me. The evening his case was ruled upon, Stockton went berserk at his home in a nearby town, complaining how unfairly the Army was treating him. In a drunken rage, according to police records, he was waving a knife and threatening to kill himself. Then he smashed a window, ripping open his arm in the process, and went charging through the streets like a madman. He tangled with the local cops and later the MPs who were summoned to round him up, screaming at one point that he would kill me.

That summer, he was ordered to appear before an Army board to determine his fitness to continue in the military. I was among those who testified against him, describing the harassment and assault but, as I was told, never using the word rape. When the board issued its ruling, Stockton was out–effective immediately.

Yet my career was tarnished, too. I was reprimanded for signing a false statement. As further punishment, my company commander tried, without success, to take away my MP status and have me assigned to pumping fuel. My orders for investigations school were now canceled.

Late that year, newly married to Harry, pregnant with Michael, and disillusioned with the Army, I opted for a pregnancy discharge and walked away from it all.

That was the gist of what I wrote and presented to Dr. Field at Walter Reed.

A few days later, I returned to her office to ask if she had read my account. She said that she had, then gathered my pages from her desk, and tossed them in my direction, as if disgusted. Astonished, I watched as all of my efforts, the compilation of my deepest pain, fluttered to the floor like a bird blasted out of the air.

"Who are you trying to impress?" she said.

I never learned what Dr. Field's problem was that day, whether she doubted what I wrote or if she was angry at me for an unrelated reason. (When asked about the incident years later, in the research for this book, Dr. Field said she didn't remember that episode but conceded she might simply have been having a terrible day.) Still, it was a response I never would have imagined from someone who works with the mentally ill, let alone from the one person I entrusted with my story.

At the moment, I was enraged. But rather than risk spending even more time in the hospital, I simply collected my papers and retreated. Sitting on the floor of my room, my anger and frustration giving way to inconsolable grief, I shredded what I had written, then flushed it all down the toilet.

The only positive result of all that writing was that Dr. Field made good on her promise to allow me to see Michael. I remember Harry came onto the ward and signed me out of the hospital while my mother-in-law waited in the hall with my son. We stepped out and I saw Michael in his stroller, head down, examining a toy truck that Harry had just bought for him. Harry's mother tapped the boy on the shoulder. He looked up at her, then over at me.

"Mommy!" he shouted.

With a big smile, he jumped from his stroller and ran into my arms. All of us had grins on our faces and tears in our eyes.

We took the subway to the Mall and spent the day seeing all the sights of Washington, D.C. that we could squeeze in before I had to get back. Michael and I took some time to play with his Legos and his toy cars. Then we happily rolled ourselves down a grassy hill.

When we returned to Walter Reed, Michael cried incessantly, unable to understand why I couldn't go home with them. I was aching, too. As I started to go, Michael handed me his new truck—to keep me company, he said. For the rest of my stay, I carried that toy in my pocket everywhere I went. It was a reminder, a source of strength and determination, until, armed with mood-stabilizing medications, I was finally deemed stable enough to go home, two days before Christmas.

4

Our possessions had yet to arrive from overseas. Harry's mother was staying with us in a small two-bedroom apartment, a couple miles up the road from Fort Myer. My husband and I slept on our bedroom floor with blankets, while my mother-in-law and Michael had Army cots. We had requisitioned pots, pans, and dishes from the military. And our only clothing was whatever came packed in our suitcases.

Christmas arrived. We had no tree, no decorations, and just a few gifts for one another. We were as poor as we would ever be. I was forty-eight hours off the psychiatric ward, with telltale scars across my wrists. Yet we enjoyed a pleasant holiday. We strolled to a restaurant for a Christmas dinner and as we were coming home it began to snow, which is unusual enough for Washington, D.C. I remember playing with Michael, showing him how to make snow angels, and for one day at least feeling free of my problems.

With the arrival of the new year, I was determined to reclaim my life. Harry's take-home pay was only a thousand dollars a month and I wanted to help with the mounting bills. So I took a job in security at a Sheraton in Arlington; Dr. Field assured my boss I'd make a capable employee, though she said I couldn't drive or carry a weapon. Despite being apprehensive about having a male supervisor, I liked the job. Dressed in plainclothes, I'd patrol the halls, take reports, monitor the maids for theft, whatever came up. It felt good to be busy again, and contributing to our family.

Early in January, I suffered a setback and found myself hospitalized in Dominion Hospital in Falls Church, which doubled as a psychiatric facility and nursing home. I would be fine for awhile; I was rational enough. Yet sometimes I found myself–or the staff found me–speechless, staring off into space, as if in a daze. As it was at Walter Reed, one thing or another would startle me and my perception dramatically shifted. For much of my stay, I faded in an out of a muddled frame of mind, usually with no idea of where I was or why I was there. Jumbled in the mix, I revealed flashes of private Proctor, making comments that made sense only in context of my former life in the military.

It was much later that I learned this to be a form of what psychologists call dissociation–essentially a disconnection from how the mind typically handles events and information. It is not unusual for victims of trauma to shut down or parcel out memories too horrible to live with, but dissociation can touch everyone. It is seen in the absent state of mind that anyone who has driven long distances knows, traversing ten or twenty miles without realizing it. At the extreme end of the dissociative continuum are those individuals with multiple personalities.

For many, dissociation is a means of survival, a sanctuary from overwhelming emotional pain. What form it assumes depends on the person. Some people block out or compartmentalize certain feelings or events. Others latch on to separate personas. A number detachedly harm themselves or others.

At Dominion, I mostly kept to myself. There was no indication that the staff ever fully understood the changes occurring in my mind. My dissociation, after all, only became an issue when I decided, in my old persona, to leave the facility. That's when I found myself carted off to a quiet room. But being forcibly handled only summoned flashbacks from the rape.

I spent six days there. And though the doctors urged me to stay for further evaluation, I desperately wanted to return to my family and work. Hurting myself was no longer an issue. My mental condition was better. So, having started me on an anti-depressant, my doctor recommended I continue therapy at the Arlington County Mental Health Center, urged me to consider joining a rape self-help group, and sent me home.

Harry was taken aback by the hospitalization. He figured that all that time at Walter Reed had cured me. Talking to the doctors at Dominion, however, he finally came to understand there was no quick-and-easy answer. We both, it turned out, had a lot to learn.

For awhile all was calm. We eased into a comfortable rhythm of life at work and home. We completed unpacking and arranging the apartment. Michael had the first of several surgeries to resolve his hearing problems. We also got him into speech therapy and a good daycare program at a nearby church.

With the passage of days and then weeks, however, my symptoms resurfaced: The nightmares kicked up again. Once or twice I wandered off in confusion, finding myself in a neighborhood park clueless as to how I got there. And I was having outbursts of anger that made no real sense.

Harry's responded by withdrawing. When it came down to it, he wanted to ignore this problem, even though it had reached every corner of our existence. When I tried to tell him how I felt, about any of it, he would tense up, change the subject, or find something to busy himself with. His silence made me feel more worthless and isolated. He wanted everything to be fine again, like it was during the first two years of our marriage. But nothing was fine. It couldn't be. I needed to talk, to come to terms with all that had happened.

That March, the anniversary of the rape, the flashbacks thrashed me. Even at work I had intrusive visions of Sgt. Stockton and chose to stay home for a week, keeping to our bedroom to ride out the storm.

If Harry was working graveyard shift, I would sometimes take my old MP handcuffs and bind myself to the radiator next to our bed, tossing the key across the room for Michael to retrieve in the morning. (Later, when we bought a bed set, I attached myself to the frame.) The handcuffing guaranteed that I wouldn't unknowingly hurt myself or walk off. And though no one liked it–my outpatient therapist demanded that I stop–I saw no other way. It struck me as better than signing into a hospital, where they might keep me for days at substantial expense but with no real results.

Four years had passed since the rape, and I was a cauldron of emotions, raging one minute over something inconsequential, then inexplicably sobbing. My skin was crawling, as if ants were devouring me, and I spent countless hours scrubbing myself raw under scalding hot showers.

I survived those difficult anniversary days, but I couldn't soldier through forever. That spring, my therapist discontinued our sessions. She gave me one reason, about needing to care for a sick child at home. But when pressed by my husband, she admitted to feeling unqualified to deal with problems as severe as mine. I took it as a major rejection.

Soon, my symptoms had me in a tailspin again. Flashbacks, nightmares, and headaches pounded me every day. Depression blanketed me. I went sleepless, sometimes for days on end. My weight fell ten pounds in three weeks. Again, thoughts of killing myself became disturbingly frequent.

Once, I would have gone to any lengths to avoid another psychiatric hospital. Now I just felt defeated. I asked Harry to bring me to the Psychiatric Institute of Washington, a facility I first heard about from their television commercials.

Compared to Walter Reed or Dominion, this was a less sterile and more home-like place, with manicured lawns and flower beds outside and comfortable furnishings and other personal touches inside. It sat in a peaceful neighborhood, surrounded by attractive homes.

The forty-one days I spent there, however, were chaotic, laden with dissociative episodes, impulsive acts, and a battle of wills with my doctor. I again tried to kill myself, first with a razor I smuggled into the hospital, then with a shattered light bulb, which I also held against my throat to keep the staff at bay.

That hospitalization also stands out in memory because of an incident with another patient. I had been sitting at a table in the dayroom, busying myself with something, a game of solitaire or writing, when a woman about my age came over and sat across from me. Martha was being treated for manic-depression. In her buoyant phases, she tended to become highly promiscuous, to the point of disrobing, parading naked, and coming on to all the men, patients and staff alike. Anyone who had been there very long was aware of her outrageous behavior, which explained why the patients around the television were now stealing glances in our direction.

The conversation began normally enough. She asked my name, where I was from, the usual. And though I was reluctant to talk to anyone, I grew more uneasy when she pressed me about what brought me there. She overheard some nurses say I had been raped, she said. I conceded that, yes, I had been assaulted by my supervisor in the military.

Several patients by the TV called for her to leave me alone, and as a result she quieted down for a bit. But then she dove back in, rambling on in graphic detail about how thrilling rape must be.

"Tell the truth," she said. "You liked it, didn't you? Tell me what happened. Was he rough with you? Did it hurt? I like a lover who's forceful."

By now the others were yelling, telling her to shut up and leave me alone. Meanwhile, I was frozen in place, trembling, and trying to beat back the memories.

"You like it rough, don't you?" she said. "You know, it's not rape if you like it. Was there oral sex?"

I exploded from my seat, flipping the table that was between us. It did a perfect one-hundred-and-eighty-degree turn in the air and hit the floor, upside down, with a loud bam. Incredibly, it never even grazed her. It did scare her, though, and she let loose a scream.

As I sank down on the sofa, crying, one of the female patients who had been watching came over to console me. "Someone should have warned you about her," she said. "I'm sorry we didn't make her stop. She had no right."

I wound up in seclusion for that incident, locked once again in a room that brought to mind the barracks at Fort Lee. I struggled as the staff stripped off my clothes, then dressed me in a disposable, paper hospital gown. I was on suicide watch again, this time with nothing but a mat on the floor—no sheets, no pillow, nothing. I lay there five hours, beset by flashbacks, before I was allowed out.

My stay at the Psychiatric Institute raised more questions than it answered. A consulting psychologist gave me a battery of tests: questionnaires, inkblots, story-telling, drawings. "She comes across as extremely vulnerable and in enormous psychologic distress," he wrote.

Meanwhile, an EEG revealed a "brief burst of generalized sharp activity." It was a borderline reading, too unclear to say for certain whether I was experiencing seizures or if it was an anomaly.

Still, I had experienced brief blackouts from the time I was a kid. It is impossible to say if they were in fact seizures or, in turn, if any specific head trauma caused them. My mother, for what it is worth, tells of my father accidentally clunking me in the skull with an errant golf ball when I was three or four. My head had also been slammed about during the rape, not to mention during an automobile accident a few weeks prior to that. And as I told the neurologist at the time of the test, headaches commonly followed my flashbacks.

He concluded that the EEG probably indicated nothing. The neurologist considered my problems—especially the suicide attempts—psychological, having nothing to do with brain injury or seizures.

But I wonder about that EEG. Even with the mental health issues I was enduring, could this have been the first clue of an underlying physical cause to at least some of my problems? Seizures, as maddeningly difficult as they can be to detect, can have a marked effect on behavior, moods, memory, even psychic states. They're often mistaken for mental illness, in fact, or overlooked when the two come in concert. Epileptic seizures can be hard enough to pinpoint, but other types, ignited by intense emotional stress, are not even discernible by EEG.

The test was never followed up. To this day I believe more was at play than post-traumatic aftershocks of the rape and a personality disorder. Given the horrors that were waiting in the wings, I have good reason to be skeptical.

I was released from the Psychiatric Institute of Washington early in the summer of 1988. My diagnosis remained PTSD and borderline personality, and I was given a new regimen of potent medications.

Once more, I tried to pull together my life. We had some happy times in Washington, D.C. that summer. The Fourth of July fireworks, viewed from our perch on Colonel's Row at Fort Myer, were spectacular. It was even more special because it was the first such display Michael ever witnessed. We flew kites on the National Mall. And trips to local pools or the beach were always an adventure because Michael, accustomed to going *au naturel* in Europe, would often discard his swimsuit, sending us scurrying to cover his bare bottom.

My marriage, however, was hanging by a thread. Harry avoided me at home and put in more and more hours at work. He refused to see a marriage counselor or the base chaplain, either with me or alone. His job performance declined.

His mother living with us only made matters worse. During an angry altercation, I finally demanded that she leave. But in the end, the real problem was between Harry and me. Too much that went unspoken was now pulling us apart. My hysterectomy and the fact that we would never have more children. The rape and its after-effects. Guilt. Anger. And simple, raw emotional hurt.

My husband may not have been spoken the words, but it was clear he was unhappy with our life together. We finally agreed to separate–to get some distance between us and figure out what would happen next.

It was an informal arrangement at first. He went to live in the barracks and I stayed at the apartment with Michael. Before long, Harry stopped visiting or even calling. I felt as if he had washed his hands of us. That fall we signed papers for a legal separation, granting me custody of Michael and allowing me to take him out of state.

I returned to work at the hotel to pull together some money. Out in Washington, my mother found me a small one-bedroom apartment in Kennewick, not far from where I grew up.

That December, Harry saw Michael and me off at Dulles International Airport. I knew he still loved me. Both of us were crying as we said goodbye. All he had to do was ask and I would have changed my plans then and there. But Harry never did ask me to stay.

5

I had to get away. From my troubled marriage. From the crushing cost of living in suburban Washington, D.C. From the trappings of the military world, which I was finally understanding to be a trigger for my flashbacks and other symptoms.

I didn't know where to go. So I went where anyone might head when their world falls apart and the future is uncertain: I went home, to my roots.

My mother still lived there, in southeastern Washington; she was getting divorced from her third husband around the time I arrived. My natural father had long since withdrawn to Alaska, where he worked for the railroad. My younger sister Kathy and brother Wade were building their lives up there, too.

The area to which I returned was a mix of scrub land, farm country, and a collection of municipalities known as the Tri-Cities–Richland, Kennewick, and Pasco–at the junction of the Columbia and Snake rivers. On the surface, it seemed like safe haven–a peaceful corner of the state, with a lay-back pace, and people who were for the most part friendly.

But for me the area stirred painful memories that had laid dormant for nearly seven years. Now, those hurts welcomed me back.

I had been an isolated, lonely child. I grew up in large part on a farm just up the interstate from the Tri-Cities, three miles outside of tiny Benton City. But the rural solitude affected me less than the feelings of rejection by my family and ostracism by other kids.

Above all was the tumult and instability of life at home. By the time I reached tenth grade, my mother had married three times. Beneath the appearance of a nice, respectable home, my childhood was marked by upheaval, neglect, and abuse. I felt myself the black sheep, an afterthought to the family, almost an embarrassment.

I was blessed with a brief stretch of kindness and understanding from Mom's second husband. But my real father wanted little to do with me. And her third husband, a heavy drinker with a mean streak, was a terror.

The Army was my way out. I had big dreams and disdain for the world that my mother grew up in: the oppressiveness of small-town living, the marriages straight out of high school, a job for life at the Hanford Nuclear Reservation. I wanted more and I was determined to get it.

Now, all that seemed shattered. I had been raped. My aspirations for a career in the Military Police were dashed. My marriage was coming apart. I could have no more children. And the past couple years were spent in and out of psychiatric wards, with a frightening mental condition I didn't fully comprehend. What future could I possibly have? What was the point of living?

The answer, of course, was Michael.

The four hundred dollars Harry agreed to send each month barely got us by. And with the threat of a flashback or anxiety attack ever present, a full-time job was out of the question. To make ends meet, I baby-sat for several children in our apartment complex. I also enrolled Michael, then four, in a Montessori school at a local church, taking an after-hours job there as a janitor to cover the cost.

Unfortunately, problems with his hearing persisted. Michael's eardrums ruptured and he required another operation. Worried that he might be unable to start school on time, I spent a lot of time working with him to strengthen his hearing and better develop his speaking and concentration skills. For several hours a day we played speech and listening games. In one, I would stand behind him and create a noise of one kind or another; Michael's job was to identify the sound or the object that produced it. We also played a variation of that game on our daily walks, seeing how many outdoor sounds he could pick out.

I often read to him. Or, I had him write out the letters of the alphabet then pronounce them. Spelling objects around the house was an everyday activity.

Having so much time with my son was a salve, the silver lining to all that had gone wrong with my life. We would go to the park and play. I taught him to fish. At other times, we worked on his swimming, went on nature walks, and planted flowers.

It was in Washington, too, that we added a young cocker spaniel to the family. All black, and female, Puppy was the perfect foil to Kitty, the black cat we got in Germany. They were inseparable, partners in crime–playing, sleeping, even eating together.

Primarily, the pets were for my son. Because of his ear problems he was often unable to go out and play with the other kids; the animals became his playmates.

As any mother can relate, I did the bulk of caretaking and training of those creatures. I didn't mind. Both were funny and quick to learn. My son and I got a lot of pleasure out of playing with them or watching as they cavorted around the apartment. They lifted my spirits as well as anything my doctors prescribed.

As the weeks passed, the symptoms of my post-traumatic stress began to recede. Being away from contact with the Army, the uniforms in particular, helped. As did my overall reduction in stress.

But those pets deserve credit, too. They were a calming force. They made no significant demands, passed no judgment, and looked upon me and the world with a pureness of heart that humans lack. Here in Washington, they were a reminder as well. Of times long past. And how I got through.

I ENTERED Benton City only once during the months we were in Washington state. Harry had taken a bus out, to try to work through our problems, and I showed him and Michael our old house and farm. We slowed as we drove by, but never stopped. I couldn't. Too many memories haunted that place.

I did not get off so easily, however. For the ghosts that haunted that structure and the fields where I once galloped my horse and shouted for my dog, already knew I was back. They visited when I least expected them, touched off as memories are by a familiar sight, a long forgotten manner of speaking, even something in the air. Unlike the recollections summoned to life by my post-traumatic stress, these were imbedded in who I was, and produced not terror but abiding sorrow.

Remembering … being just seven or eight years old and my natural father, a brakeman for the railroad, thrashing my bottom with his belt for an offense I never committed, the breaking of a bottle out behind our garage. I took the punishment stoically. And when he was done, I coolly asked him: "Do you feel better now, Daddy?"

He pulled up, and a look of such despair came over his face. In that moment, I believe, he realized that he was passing on the violence of his own upbringing to me. After that day he never struck me again.

Remembering … rejection by my dad. Growing up, I desperately craved my father's attention, only to be repeatedly turned away. From time to time, if I made a mistake or did something foolish, he would make a remark along the lines of, "I knew you couldn't be my daughter." It was cruel to say to a child, and my mother reenforced it by often saying that Dad truly did question fathering me–though she assured me his doubts were absurd.

All the same, I carried a lot of hurt and uncertainty through my youth. (Years later, Dad denied having such doubts. I also learned, during high school, that I share a rare blood disorder with my father's side of the family, more or less putting the paternity issue to rest.)

Remembering … my mother's cutting remarks–about my appearance, intelligence, and shortcomings. We had been close when I as little, but as the years passed she seemed indifferent toward me, unless I was doing something that got her mad. In my mother's eyes, I felt, I was never good enough.

Remembering ... bouncing along in a green pickup truck belonging to Les Weaver, Mom's second husband, heading home after a cattle auction. Broad-shouldered and husky, Les owned a farm near ours, as well as a lumber mill. I initially knew him through my friend Theresa, his daughter, and I would help out on their farm. I couldn't have been happier when less than a year after Dad left, my mother and Les hit it off, got married, and moved into our place with his teenage daughter and son.

Les was a decent man who took the time to listen to me and who boosted my self-confidence, trusting me with chores and responsibilities around the house and farm. He also had an instinct for what made me happiest, bringing me a beautiful German shepherd puppy, Sergeant, not long after he married Mom.

I remember Les and I were going home at the end of a perfect day, everything I imagined a father-daughter relationship should be. The stock auction had gone well and I was enjoying just being with him and talking. As we drove that day, I even found the courage to ask if he would mind if I started calling him Dad.

When he heard that, Les smiled. Then to my astonishment, he began sobbing. He brought me on the trip alone, he explained, because he wanted to give me some news. Mom wanted a divorce, he said. He and his kids were moving out.

Remembering ... being outside the window as Mom and my father argued about whether I could live with Les and his kids instead of her. "Let her go," I heard my father say. "She's never going to amount to anything anyway."

Remembering ... my mother's piercing scream.

After about a year of living with the Weavers on their ranch in Prosser, Les brought me back to live with Mom. Soon thereafter, she married again and life turned upside down. Her new husband was often drunk and abusive. Loud, ugly arguments were common. To escape the turmoil, both my sister and brother left home to live with our father in Alaska. And though I would have gone in a minute, he never asked me to come.

On the day I heard Mom shriek, a dispute in our house had reached fever pitch. My mother and I were upset at the death of Maylee, a young Pekinese I had given her as a Christmas gift. That day, Mom was yelling at my stepdad, demanding to know if he had killed the dog.

Now, with my mother's scream, I bolted up the stairs from the basement. I grabbed a butcher knife as I hurried through the kitchen, then burst into the dining room to find my stepfather, drunk and squeezing my mother's neck in a headlock. His other hand wrenched her arm up behind her back as if to twist it off.

I was certain he was going to kill her. And though I was only in high school, I was determined to protect her.

"Let her go!" I yelled, waving the knife at him.

My stepfather looked, then taunted me, holding Mom before him and daring me to come stab him.

"Leana, no!" my mother shouted, weeping. "He's not worth it!"

Finally, Mom got me to set down the knife; he responded by heaving her across the room. When I went to call the cops, he fled.

More commotion followed. But when it all settled out, after a few days, my stepfather was back under our roof.

ASSESSMENT: *"L. feels more kinship w/animals than w/people."*

That sentence, written in shorthand scrawl by a psychologist, is buried in the records of my out-patient counseling sessions at the Mid-Columbia Mental Health Center during my junior year in high school.

That I felt that way raised concern among my teachers and the mental health counselor at Benton City High School. That I liked animals, I'm sure, was fine with everybody. It was my sense of removal from other humans that had them worried.

School officials took note of my depression and isolation, much of it spun from the growing tension at home. I had no close friends, and I responded so ferociously to teasing that most kids kept their distance, mistakenly regarding me as something of a bully. When I was a freshman, the school recommended outside counseling, but I only went to a few sessions.

A couple years later, as matters at home intensified and my depression became worse, school officials insisted that my mother bring me to Mid-Columbia, where perhaps the entire family could get involved. I saw the psychologist almost every week that spring–with my mother, stepfather, brother, and sister even attending one or two sessions. We covered many subjects over those weeks–my disdain for the use of sex and alcohol to be popular, my anxiety over what I would do after graduation, and my distaste for my mother's new husband, as well as the turbulence he brought to our home.

As the psychologist noted, I had carved out a special place in my life for animals. There, I found kinship, comfort, and refuge from that which was uncontrollable or caused too much pain. With animals, I found the sense of belonging I could never find with people.

Creatures had always been a big part of my life, and in many respects I have my mother to thank. She had a deep affection for horses and dogs, and long dreamed of raising her family on a farm.

We still lived in Kent, just north of Seattle, when she got a sheltie named Penny, who was practically one of the kids. Mom bred that dog and entered her in a few shows, and they did quite well. Another dog that was around awhile was Suzy, my father's black lab, which he used for hunting. Growing up, we also had hamsters and rabbits, which I adored.

When I was about to enter sixth grade, we moved to the fifteen acres near Benton City. It was a gentleman's farm more than a moneymaker. But we had horses and cattle, and grew alfalfa, enough to provide some added income.

On a farm you learn fast about animals–their differing personalities, their dependence on you for nourishment and medical attention, and how mistakes in judgment or attention can cause them great harm, even their death. If you pay heed, you also begin to understand something of their emotional capacities–their need for love and their willingness to share it.

We had only been living in the country a short time when an adorable lamb claimed my heart. He was born on a sheep farm up the road. His mother died two days after his birth and the other sheep refused to nurse him. I asked the owner if he would give me the lamb rather than put him down as he intended. My parents gave their okay, so the man allowed me to have him.

Having recently seen the movie *Oliver Twist,* I named my little orphan Oliver.

The young lamb was like a puppy and I was his surrogate mother. I remember how he wobbled on his new legs, his pink skin covered with the tiniest coils of wool. Initially, I bottle-fed him six times a day and watched with pride as he grew bigger and stronger.

Oliver had a box next to my bed and at night he would bellow if he wanted his bottle or to curl up next to me. He never had an accident in my bed or my room. When nature called, he would simply stand up and I knew to return him to his box.

As Oliver matured, my parents insisted he stay outdoors. To ease his transition to the barn, Mom and Dad allowed me to bring my sleeping bag out and sleep there with him for a couple nights.

For close to two years, Oliver was my special friend. To my parents, however, he was a farm animal who over time began to get in the way. You can imagine my heartbreak to come home one day to learn that they had called the slaughter wagon and simply gotten rid of him. I never even had a chance to say goodbye.

We also had a Shetland pony, Black Beauty, that my sister and I shared as we learned the basics of horseback riding. Within a few years, my parents bought my sister an older thoroughbred-quarterhorse named Chili. Not long after, I got Daisy, a bay quarterhorse, who was three or four years old.

I spent countless hours with Daisy. We developed a mutual trust and respect. I loved riding that horse and did so nearly every day–around our land, the adjacent property, and on into town. Sometimes we competed in local play-day competitions, which tested her agility and quickness. I worked on training and devotedly groomed her day in and day out.

My other favorite was my dog Sergeant. Not long after Les Weaver married Mom, he asked me in passing one day what breed I liked best and I replied that I'd always dreamed of having a male German shepherd. So when Les surprised me by bringing the twelve-week-old puppy home from the breeder, I was overjoyed. He was tan and black, with big brown eyes, the most precious thing I ever saw.

With my interest in police work and the military taking seed around that time, I named him Sergeant. He would fill out to be a handsome, sturdy dog of about ninety pounds. Intelligent and attentive, he possessed an innate awareness of when I was feeling down and comforted me, pulling close by my side and licking at me.

From eighth grade through high school, Sergeant was by my side. He came with me to high school football games, joined me if I had work around the farm, trotted beside me when I rode Daisy, or busied himself nearby as I groomed her.

He also adored my second sheep, Baby. I'll always remember those two pursuing one another around the farm like kids playing tag. One year, on the evening before a Future Farmers of America contest, the three of us even slept together in the fairgrounds barn–to protect my prize sheep against theft but also so she wouldn't have to be alone in a strange place.

Which is not to say Sergeant got along with every species. Once, he routed a family of skunks from our chicken house, but paid the price. You can imagine my mother's reaction when she came home that day to a house reeking of skunk, with me in the bathroom scrubbing the dog. There was little I could say in self-defense other than that it seemed like a good idea at the time.

On another occasion, we brought Sergeant to the veterinarian with porcupine quills in his muzzle. Apparently, the dog came across the intruder raiding the grain bin or going after the chickens. It had to be excruciating for him, but Sergeant sat still, completely trusting, as I reassured him and the veterinarian plucked those quills one by one.

Another time, my sister burst into the house shouting that Sergeant had been shot. I ran out to the front porch to find him curled there, bleeding profusely from one of his hind legs. I wrapped it and Mom rushed us to the veterinarian.

Someone—we never learned who—had blasted Sergeant with a high-powered hunting rifle. The vet told us Sergeant was fortunate: If the bullet had struck just a inch higher, there would have been no saving the leg. As it was, he recovered just fine.

That dog was a true friend. Yet my mother's third husband detested him, as he did all animals, and forbade him from coming in the house (though I did manage to sneak him in late at night now and then to sleep in my room.) Who could blame Sergeant for standing on the porch growling, refusing to let my stepfather pass when he came home drunk late in the evening?

By my senior year in high school, desperately needing to escape the turmoil of our house, I convinced an aunt to let me live with her in the western part of the state. My emotional health improved as did my grades, but I wasn't allowed to bring Sergeant. It was during this time, when my dog was about five, that my mother and stepfather gave him away and I never saw him again.

THE SEPARATION from Harry allowed me to regain my footing from the onslaught of my post-traumatic stress. In all the time I was back in Washington, I required hospitalization on just two occasions. Both stays were brief and came within a month of the anniversary of the rape.

Harry in the meantime was able to get back in the good graces of his superior officers. For once, he felt, he could do his job without worrying about me or having to break away for one emergency or another. It also allowed him to gain perspective. He loved me and Michael. And now that he had some distance from all that happened, he began to understand that none of it was my fault, or that I brought it upon myself.

Harry had built up a lot of anger over the past couple years. Much of it, he directed toward me, feeling I should have been able to cope with my problems, to buck up and press on like a good soldier. Now, he was starting to see that life was more complicated than that.

We spoke regularly on the telephone. Then, Harry came to visit and we talked more. Neither of us wanted a divorce, we decided, and we made up our minds to try to work things out.

Harry was up for re-enlistment and had a number of options for his next assignment, including Germany, Korea and Panama, where he had been stationed earlier in his military career. When he got back to Fort Myer, he found that the Army made the decision for him: He was ordered to Panama.

Because of the Panama Canal, of course, the U.S. had long retained a military presence there. But now General Manuel Noriega was on the first President Bush's radar. Besides his indictment in the U.S. for drug trafficking, the military strongman had annulled his country's spring elections, won handily by the opposition. Then, he beat back a coup attempt. As 1989 progressed, Panama was growing increasingly volatile.

That fall, Harry spent six weeks at Lackland Air Force Base in Texas, training to become a dog handler. Come December, he touched down in Panama.

To help Michael, who was then four years old, feel closer to his dad, I read to him about Panama, telling him where it was and what it was like.

In mid-December, we were distressed to hear that a U.S. Marine was killed by Noriega's thugs. Also, a U.S. Navy lieutenant was tortured and his wife terrorized. Harry had landed in the hottest of hot spots.

A few days later, we learned just how serious the situation had become. Michael and I just came home from grocery shopping. While I was putting food away, Michael went to the living room to watch TV. A few minutes later, I heard him screaming and crying. I rushed in and he ran into my arms, sobbing about someone trying "to kill Daddy."

When I looked at the television I understood: Operation Just Cause, the invasion of Panama, was underway.

Harry, I would later learn, was assigned to monitor a key intersection in Coco Solo, routing civilian traffic away from the invasion area.

It was afterward–when he and his German shepherd Claire were assigned to looter patrol–that he faced the greatest risk. Snipers continually took potshots at him and the other MPs. Thankfully, he came away unscathed.

Noriega ended up in a Florida prison. Democracy returned to Panama, and with it came a calming effect. Military families would soon be allowed into the country again. We began to make plans to reunite.

6

Our family could hardly have been happier than we were the first seven months after Michael and I arrived in Panama.

When we stepped off the plane and into the furnace that is Central America at the peak of summer, I was in my best physical condition ever. During the half year of waiting for the Army's red tape to clear so we could go down, I made up my mind to look my best for Harry. I worked out with weights, swam laps in the pool at our apartment complex, went for long walks, jogged, and put many a mile on the exercise bicycle my mother loaned me.

I dropped twenty pounds, down to about a hundred and forty-five. In the meantime, I let my hair grow out and bought some nice summer dresses. I never felt better.

Although the main U.S. military installations in Panama were on the Pacific Ocean side of the country, Harry was stationed near the Atlantic, at Fort Davis. Because most families had been evacuated in anticipation of Operation Just Cause, getting housing was easy. We lived in a townhouse on post, with a back-yard and just beyond that, a wall of jungle.

We loved Panama. Some tension toward Americans lingered because of the invasion, so we were advised to steer clear of certain areas. Otherwise, we enjoyed the beaches, fishing, and sight-seeing. With the cost of living so much below the U.S., we could afford to eat out and found plenty of bargains shopping, especially in the duty-free zone in Colon.

Problems with my post-traumatic stress were minimal. I did have one hospital stay for depression and PTSD symptoms, including flashbacks and visions of my assailant. ("States she is seeing blood on her arms several times per day, a man in her house, someone in the hallway with a knife," read my admission report.) But that was mainly because my medications had run out and were next to impossible to obtain in Panama.

Life was going so well, in fact, that we talked about adopting a child from Panama. And since this was expected to be Harry's last duty station before he left the military, I began to consider going back into law enforcement when we returned stateside, perhaps with a local police department.

Panama was ideal for someone like me who was fascinated by animals. We could look out our back window to see the most gorgeous tropical birds in the jungle tree line. More dangerous creatures, of course, also ventured out from the jungle. Harry once found a seven-and-a-half-foot boa constrictor on our back lawn, which is why Puppy never went out unsupervised. One day, as a matter of fact, our neighbor discovered that his little dog was gone from his backyard. In its place was a giant snake with the pet's chain coming from its mouth.

The variety of species in Panama was incredible. Iguanas the size of a man were common sights. We saw tarantulas, crocodiles, and all kinds of monkeys. Ocelots, jaguars, and pumas were just some of the wildlife found there.

Among those that most captured my fancy were parrots. In the wild, these colorful and intelligent birds fly thick in flocks that can number in the thousands. One generation after another, they add to their family's flock and remain in it their entire lives. We would look up and see them, a wave of yellow in the Panamanian sky. Then they'd swiftly change direction and the picture magnificently changed: The wave turned blue and green. It was like watching a rainbow unfurl.

In Panama, I saw firsthand the plight of these gorgeous birds. Poverty was such that people would chop down full-grown trees just to get their hands on a nest of baby parrots, so they could sell them in the streets. They usually ended up crammed in a shoe box with dozens of others, many of them soon crushed to death. Others suffered from inadequate care or nutrition and were discarded at the roadside, some still half-alive, as if they were trash.

One day we were sitting in our living room when we heard something bang into the window. I looked out to see a baby toucan on our patio wobbling back and forth. He had flown into the glass and knocked himself silly.

I hurried out and looked around for the parents. I couldn't find them, though I did hear their calls. I looked over this kitten-sized baby, who seemed top-heavy with his extra-sized beak. One of his wings appeared to be hurt; he was clearly unable to fly back up to the canopy of the tree line.

I took him in and over the next week or so fed him crushed mangos and bananas and other fruit that toucans commonly eat and tried nursing him back to health. When he wasn't getting better we contacted the zoo, which sent someone out to pick him up. They assured us they would take care of him and set him free when he was ready.

Little did I know that this was the beginning of what would later become a passion for me: the rehabilitation of sick and abused parrots, of which there is no shortage.

Another incident that seemed insignificant at the time but foreshadowed events to come was an airing of the television program *Unsolved Mysteries* that we happened to catch one night. Between Harry's work as a dog handler and my own interest in anything having to do with animals, we were intrigued by the segment about a woman who suffered from epileptic seizures and who had obtained a service dog through a program at a woman's prison.

The golden retriever, we learned, had an ability to detect oncoming seizures and warn her owner, a young woman. We had never heard of such a thing and stared at the TV spellbound. But that's as far as it went. When the show was over, we filed it among all the other curiosities gathered along the way and resumed our lives, which for once were coming along fairly well.

Until the night of April 8, 1991.

It was about ten o'clock. Harry was working swing shift at the kennel. Since I'd never been able to sleep without him next to me, I did what I always do: I busied myself with housework. I was in a T-shirt, shorts, and my stocking feet, which with the air-conditioning I always wore to keep my feet warm. Down in the kitchen, the washer and dryer were going.

Michael's ears were acting up again and the doctor had given us some antibiotics. My son had an infection and a fever and couldn't hold down any food. Getting him to sleep that night had taken forever.

So when the washing machine's off-balance alarm sounded, I jumped. I was in the bathroom upstairs when I heard the loud buzz. Worried the racket would wake Michael, I bolted for the stairs. Dizziness washed across me just as I hit the first of about twenty steps, and I felt my socks slipping on the highly polished wood. My desperate grab for the handrail only caused me to pitch me forward. Next thing I knew I was crashing head-first down the stairs.

When I came to, my head was in a pool of blood midst a stack of Harry's tools I had set on the landing earlier, to be put away.

How long I was unconscious is hard to say. I was dizzy and confused. All I understood was that my head hurt. Bringing my legs down, I sat up. My head was throbbing. I rubbed my eye and my hand came away covered with red. Blood was running down my face.

I pressed a hand against the wound at the top of my head to stanch the flow and fought desperately to get up. But everything was reeling. I crawled off the landing, across the entryway, and into the kitchen, then yanked the phone off the table by its cord and poked speed dial for Harry at work.

HARRY BEASLEY

I was working CQ (charge of quarters) at the kennel that night. That's basically the night watchman. We always had a dog handler out on the road, but the CQ is there in case they need another dog. He can grab one and respond. Otherwise, my responsibility was to take care of and look out for the dogs.

I was on the couch when the phone rang. It was Lee. She was crying. She said, "I fell down; I hurt myself; I hit my head and I'm bleeding." She wasn't really coherent. I couldn't understand what she was trying to tell me, other than she was hurt and she was bleeding.

I knew Michael would be upstairs in bed, so I said, "Okay, I'm going to get on the other phone and I'm going to call for the MPs and an ambulance." So on the other phone I dialed the MP station and said, "I need an ambulance sent to my quarters and I need a patrol sent to my quarters. My wife is on the other line and apparently she's bleeding real bad."

I kept trying to talk to Lee but there was no answer at all. I figured that with a head injury she was probably out cold.

I stayed on the phone. Finally, after about three or four minutes I heard some movement in the house. I heard knocking on the door. When the MPs let themselves in, they found her on the kitchen floor. She was down.

One of them picked up the phone and told me, "This is Sgt. Such and Such and we've got your wife here. She's got a big cut on her head. Apparently she's having some kind of seizure."

The ambulance brought me, unconscious, to the emergency room at the military clinic in Coco Solo. It was only a short while before the doctors realized that my situation was more precarious than they were equipped to handle. I faded in and out of consciousness and repeatedly erupted into full-body seizures.

The staff got me on medication to quell the convulsions, hooked me up to an IV, then loaded me into an ambulance for the sixty-mile drive to Gorgas Army Community Hospital in Balboa, on the Pacific side.

Much of what transpired over the next day or so was a confusing blur. They had infused me with so much medication for the seizures that I had no idea what was going on. Most of my memories from those first days at Gorgas consist of brief images–of Harry visiting, of doctors and nurses coming and going. It was only later that I was able to piece together what happened.

Over the next week, matters only got worse. While I was in intensive care, the doctors took me off my PTSD drugs. Afterward, when they put me on the wards,

I got up and left my bed on three occasions, though I had no memory of doing so. Once, the MPs even found me in my pajamas outside, where I promptly suffered another seizure.

The doctors were baffled. The wanderings may have been part of the aftermath of seizures; indeed some people with epilepsy do find themselves walking, seemingly in a trance, often into danger. Yet it is also likely that this was the start of what would become a chaotic and baffling interplay between my post-traumatic stress and the seizures. The stress of the convulsions, it appears, was feeding the symptoms of my PTSD, and vice versa. Whether I was in a postical state as I wandered or dissociating, imagining myself back in the military and heading for work, is anyone's guess.

The doctors at Gorgas felt unqualified to determine what exactly was going on. Were the seizures truly epileptic and emerging from an injury or defect within the brain? Or did they have psychological roots, an uncontrollable full-body reaction to the intense aftermath of being raped? And how best to treat me given these complexities?

Two out of three EEGs that I was given in Panama revealed suspicious activity centering around my left temporal lobe, increasing the likelihood that the seizures had physical origins. But the tests fell short of conclusive.

Eight days after my fall, I was air evacuated to the United States and brought once again to Walter Reed. And once again I was dismayed to find myself on Ward 55, the psychiatric unit. Even though seizures were obviously at the heart of my problem, the doctors checked me in for *psychiatric* evaluation, focusing instead on my confused and amnesiac states following the convulsions.

I was at Walter Reed for three weeks. Neither a magnetic resonance imaging scan nor two EEGs revealed any abnormalities. Which is not to say none existed. I had a some significant seizures while I was there. In one, while smoking a cigarette in the courtyard, I dropped off a wall I had been sitting on, scraping me up, and scaring the daylights out of the patient who witnessed it.

The doctors at Walter Reed seemed as mystified as those in Panama and finally, they decided to ship me back to Panama. The neurologist reported that he could not rule out the possibility of an epileptic seizure disorder. But for the immediate future his only solution was to boost my levels of Tegretol, which I had already been taking for PTSD and which is known to help with seizures, too. That, he said, should do the trick.

7

Any thought I had of taking control of the seizures–and my life–upon returning to Panama was short-lived. Within just a week or two, the convulsions were back full force. They went from what I at first considered a temporary medical disturbance to an overwhelming crisis for me and my family.

For Harry and Michael, neither of whom had ever witnessed anyone having a tonic-clonic seizure, they were terrifying at first. One minute I would be fine and the next I was on the floor flailing around, my body jerking uncontrollably. Besides the thrashing, I would grunt or make other sounds. Usually I'd be incontinent. Often I'd vomit. And if my family failed to pay strict attention, I could suffer any number of injuries, from scrapes and bruises to busted bones.

As I regained consciousness, I was lost in confusion. What happened, where I was, sometimes even who I was were baffling. To have no control of myself was frightening beyond words. If it happened in public, I was also humiliated. All that in addition to a terrific soreness, particularly in the joints, that left me feeling as if a freight train had run over me.

Harry learned that not every episode required hurrying me to the emergency room, that often he could look after me at home and I would recover. But early on, emergency medical care was the safest choice.

To the doctors at Gorgas hospital, I became a familiar face. For the first few months, the hospital did have a neurologist. But he soon had an accident, falling off the roof of his house, and couldn't work. At the same time, Gorgas and other American military facilities all over the country were downsizing, in preparation for the turnover of the Panama Canal and a diminished U.S. presence.

The offshoot was that no single doctor oversaw my care. On my frequent runs to the clinic at Fort Davis or to Gorgas, I was seen by whomever was available. Making matters worse, it seemed like every physician wanted to set up his own treatment plan, virtually ignoring the previous regimen, sometimes before the drugs even reached therapeutic levels.

And though the MDs continued to debate whether my convulsions were epileptic in nature or pseudoseizures, few hesitated to prescribe potent anti-seizure medications.

Over the next year in Panama, I was given most of the heavyweight drugs then available for seizures–Tegretol, Dilantin, Valium, Phenobarbital–not to mention varied mood stabilizers for my post-traumatic stress and borderline personality diagnoses.

None of these medications, by the way, came without side-effects, be it headaches, nausea, or diarrhea, to name just a few. Some of the drugs rendered others ineffective, or produced unwanted results.

Phenobarbital, which they tried for awhile, had me hallucinating. At the time I thought I was going crazy. Walls melted before my eyes. One of my socks on the floor became a squirrel. And it felt as if ants were marching across my flesh.

Now, as had occurred at Walter Reed, my post-traumatic stress reactions returned, hastened by the seizures, anxiety, and adjustments in my medications. Following an attack, I might be resting in my room at the hospital only to look up and see my assailant clear as day. Time after time, I whipped off the sheets and fled, once again crashing into unseen walls and furniture and hurting myself. Phenobarbital only heightened the effect.

Afterward, almost as a matter of routine, they transferred me from the medical wards to psychiatry. The only problem was that the seizures would thunder again and I'd have to be rushed to intensive care.

So it was that I bounced between the wards. None of the medical people seemed to have the right answer to the seizures. It didn't help that many looked at my psychiatric ills and wrote the matter off as a mental-health issue.

At first, I tried to live down the seizures, denying they were anything but an obstacle to be overcome. Yet they relentlessly hammered away. With each episode and each hospitalization, I felt my will to fight ebbing.

Early on, the doctors emphatically told me to stay on base and not to venture into Panama by myself. Some of the indigenous people, they said, considered seizures a form of evil possession and that they might try to stone me.

It little mattered, because the seizures soon had me too afraid to leave home at all. I didn't even want to go into the yard to garden; losing consciousness there left me vulnerable to any creature that decided to venture from the jungle and gnaw on me.

As it was, the convulsions hit like a missile strike. When the doctors first asked whether I experienced an aura, I had no idea what they were talking about. It took months before I was in touch enough with my condition to make much of a connection between the seizures and the peculiar chemical taste and smell that often preceded them. Or the nausea. Or the black spots before my eyes. Even when I could identify the warning signs, they usually appeared just seconds before I went into spasms.

Often the seizures came in succession, usually a few minutes apart. One nurse at Gorgas was holding my hand, comforting me after an attack, when another wave hit. Unknowingly, I crushed her fingers. Nothing was broken, but the next time I saw her, she had a splint on one finger and her hand was swollen and bruised.

Then, about a week before Christmas, I was watching television, with our Christmas tree decorated and lit with flashing lights behind me. In an instant I was on the floor, writhing and thrashing. We later pieced it all together, and that's when I realized that the reflection of the blinking lights off the TV screen had triggered the convulsions. Not long afterward, we discovered that I had a similar photosensitive reaction to video games like Nintendo.

It seemed like nothing was safe. Before doing anything or going anywhere, I constantly worried about the likelihood of seizures. "What if" was always on my mind. I could no longer take a bath because I might drown. I was afraid to attend my son's swimming classes for fear I would fall into the pool. I was scared to cook, to drive, to use the stairs.

What if I had a seizure when I was out with Michael? What would prevent someone from abducting him while I was compromised? What was to stop my son from wandering off? Or from being hit by a car?

My emotions fluctuated from frightened to angry to sad to frustrated in a single afternoon, sometimes all at once. One minute I'd be weeping; the next I would be enraged.

The doctors simply could not get a handle on what was going on. Sometimes I burst into tears and begged them to help. Other times, I prayed with the chaplain, appealing to God with all my heart.

I'd be so upset I couldn't sleep. But lack of rest only provoked my condition. The more upset I became, the more likely I'd induce the seizures and symptoms of PTSD.

I had always been active. I loved the outdoors: hiking, skiing, fishing, hunting, you name it. But once the seizures entered my life, caution took over. I would awaken in the morning, get Michael off to school and Harry off to work, then stay in my rocking chair all day, watching television or staring out the window, wondering when the next eruption would occur.

Now, I was in and out of the hospital so much that I'd become as familiar as one of the staff. A typical entry in my medical records would begin, "This 32 year old, white female is well known to the medical service," then go on to describe my latest crisis.

Once, I had seizures on a shuttle bus. Another time, after washing dishes, a seizure hit as I was putting away a stack of plates. The dishes shattered on the floor and I went into convulsions right atop the shards. By the time I stopped, there were cuts all over my torso. Had one gone much deeper, in fact, it would have punctured my liver.

Before the seizures, I began to make friends with some of the MPs' wives. I was invited to get-togethers, baby showers and the like. All that stopped once my condition became common knowledge. It was subtle, never anything you could really confront someone about or discuss. When I ran into one or another of the women, they would never look me in the eye. I'd get the usual greetings around the base, but now no one stopped to chat. Or, I'd catch wind of a social event and lightly ask why I had been left out. "You didn't get an invitation?" they would say. "I must have forgot." After two or three such lapses of memory, I got the message. I even overheard one woman telling her friend that I must be on illicit drugs, why else the seizures? Did she think that because I had a seizure disorder, I was deaf as well?

It was painful, too, when other mothers, who had no problem with Michael playing at their homes, refused to let their kids visit our place.

Epilepsy is frightening, confusing, and surrounded by much misinformation and stigma. Yet none of those women would say anything or ask any questions, which I gladly would have answered. They were afraid of the awkwardness, I guess, or of hurting my feelings. Yet their silence was even more hurtful. I became more isolated, the last thing I needed.

HARRY BEASLEY

Down in Panama the seizures were bad. I'm talking on the average twice a week. It wasn't a matter of if she was going to have seizures but when.

One time, when Michael was at school and I was at work, she had a seizure on the patio. It was a concrete patio that over time the weather had done its worst on. It was like sandpaper. Real intense, heavy sandpaper. The whole time her face was just going back and forth on that concrete. What it did to her face you wouldn't believe.

Another time, we went fishing. We rented a boat and were out on Lake Gatun. We had expected clouds and rain because it was the rainy season, but there wasn't any. So it got hot. Real hot. And we got bit by the sun a little bit.

We're on the way back in, and toward the middle of the day the waves on the lake start up. We had a flat-bottomed jonnyboat that was hitting those waves as we were coming in, and it's going, slap, slap, slap. It's a constant rhythmic sound. That just happens to be one of the triggers for her seizures.

We get about three-quarters of the way in and Lee starts feeling sick. She got bit by the sun. So she's hanging her head over the side of the boat. In the meantime the boat is still going slap, slap, slap.

Then all of a sudden, out of the blue, she stands up. She looks at me, and she's got this damned panicked look on her face because she starts feeling the aura.

"Harry," she says, "I think I'm going to have a seizure."

Just in that quick second I realized, "You're in a boat and you're going to have a seizure and you stand up to say that?"

"Get down!" I'm yelling. "Get in the boat!"

Well, she doesn't move.

Then all of a sudden, it's just bloop, right over the side, right into the water.

The boat in the meantime is cooking along. We're doing a good eight miles per hour. And she's got a life vest on, sure, but she's not a light woman. I don't know if that thing is going to keep her head above water.

Don't forget, too, that the lake does have quite a few caimans and crocodiles, including what they figured was a fourteen to sixteen footer who always hung around off the docks.

Well, just as the boat is going past her I reached out and grabbed her by the life jacket. I cut the engine and I pull her to the side of the boat.

Now it becomes a predicament: How the hell am I going to get her into the damn boat? If I try dragging her up, it's going to flip over.

So eventually Michael and I, we ended up distributing ourselves, spreading ourselves out wide and far apart. Here Michael was only six years old and he had to help me pull her into the boat.

I couldn't get her in fast enough because all I could think is that I'm going to pull her up and find a crocodile attached to her feet.

We finally got her in and I mean, I hit the gas. We hauled butt as fast as we could. And when we got to the Aquativity Center, they called an ambulance, and the paramedics came and picked her up.

The seizures were bad enough, but now they worked in concert with my post-traumatic stress, a double whammy. During one hospitalization at Gorgas, I lapsed into a dissociative state in which I again thought myself private Proctor, from my days in the military, left the medical ward, and wandered outside. Missing nearly two hours, I followed a road that looped around and returned to the hospital. The MPs detained me as I was coming back. When a soldier snatched my arm, I panicked and suffered a flashback, which in turn ignited the seizures. An ambulance came and got me.

During another episode, I walked out of Gorgas in a dissociative state and traveled nearly ten miles in the middle of the night, arriving at the front gate of Fort Clayton, where the MPs rounded me up. Had I gone much farther, I would have ended up in the jungle.

As you might expect, all this affected my husband. When he was at work, he would call the house repeatedly to check on me. If he couldn't reach me by phone, he summoned a couple from next door to go see if I was okay.

As a soldier, Harry didn't feel he could express much of what he was going through to his superiors or vent his dissatisfaction with my doctors. At home, he let down his guard a bit. He could be a comfort, hugging me. Or, he would grow sullen and withdrawn. Or he cried. Because he knew that his feeling badly only made me feel worse, Harry tried to keep his emotions in check. Often I found him quietly strumming his guitar, engaged in his own private therapy.

My greatest pangs of guilt were reserved for Michael. Constantly checking in and out of Gorgas or being shipped back to the United States for weeks on end, I felt like a failure as a mother. These were my son's formative years and I wanted to be there for him. I felt his childhood was being stripped away and that I was to blame. Someone had to look after me when Harry was at work or away on maneuvers, sometimes for several weeks. More often than not, that job fell to six-year-old Michael.

In some ways, our roles became reversed. At a time when Michael should have been care free, he was given grave responsibility. We taught him that if I was having seizures, the first thing to do was put a pillow or something soft beneath my head, to keep me from banging against the floor or furniture. When the spasms ceased, he was to roll me onto my side and wipe any saliva or vomit from my mouth. Then, we told him to call Harry at work or if he wasn't there, the MPs. Michael also knew how to find the pulse in my neck as well as to lift my shirt and look at my ribcage, to determine if I was breathing.

All in all, it had been one rough year. Frustrated, the doctors at Gorgas remarked that I would be better served by regular care in the U.S. But that meant Harry would have to request another transfer. As it was in Germany, we were reluctant to leave. I figured this should be a manageable problem; I didn't fully appreciate what I was facing. What's more, we liked Panama and simply weren't ready to say goodbye.

But my care was putting a strain on the under-manned staff at Gorgas. Repeatedly, I had to be air-evacuated from Fort Davis to the medical center on the Pacific side of the country, never a run-of-the-mill or inexpensive operation. It reached the point where the hospital commander finally exploded: "She ought to have her own fucking helicopter!"

Finally, Harry was called in and matters were made clear: We do not have the facilities your wife requires. We do not have the staff.

The paperwork for compassionate reassignment moved quickly. In June 1992, we were winging our way back to the United States and my return to Washington state.

8

Being back in my home state, this time in the shadow of Mount Rainier, filled me with optimism. My family was together again. The hospital at Fort Lewis, where Harry was stationed, was said to be among the Army's best. And this part of the state–with its summits, the ocean, and lush countryside–was my favorite place on earth. Not only was it gorgeous, but it was free of the bad associations I held when living in the Tri-Cities.

Despite my bright outlook, my health conditions refused to make the transition easy. We were only in the United States two or three days when the seizures hit. I was at the hotel on base that morning when a series of three tremors tore through me. In what was an all-too-familiar scene, the medics rushed out, loaded me into the ambulance, and set off to have me treated–only now at Madigan Army Medical Center.

The more things changed, it seemed, the more they stayed the same.

Harry, Michael, and I soon found an apartment in Tacoma, where we would live about a year, before something opened up on base. Harry settled into his assignment as a garrison MP, the Army's equivalent of a municipal patrolman. I resumed my role as stay-at-home mom, keeping Michael involved in activities and serving as a chaperon for field trips and the like when school started that fall. I also had plenty of sewing projects to keep me busy, making shirts for Michael or drapes for our bedroom.

Both Puppy and Kitty contracted heartworm disease while we were in Panama. Puppy was on medication, but the cat died. Now, we added a long-haired tabby, Sam, to our household.

It was also shortly after our arrival that Harry told me he ran into an old military friend of ours from Germany. Lyle Shaffer, who had been in Harry's unit, was now at Fort Lewis, too. When I called to say hi to Lyle and his wife, however, I found he had remarried.

His new wife, Mona, was a sweetheart. We got talking and went on for two straight hours. I felt I'd known her forever. She told me she was in cosmetology school. Lyle had two kids from his previous marriage; she had two from hers; and they were all living out in Olympia, waiting like us for quarters to become available on base.

The following weekend we joined them for a cookout.

Petite, with long brown hair flowing down her back, Mona was a bundle of energy. She was outgoing, friendly, and caring. I found it easy to tell her about my life, even the worst of it.

Our friendship grew. We got together now and then—on Halloween, for example, so the kids could go trick-or-treating together. After so many months alone, it felt good to finally find a real friend.

Not everything was going so well. My relationship with Harry was again strained. We were without a car and money was tight. And though I did my best to keep my anguish from him, making love remained traumatic. Sometimes I emotionally shut down during the act itself, then afterward rolled over and cried myself to sleep. Other times, I had flashbacks and on occasion blacked out.

Even though I had seizures for more than a year by this point, new triggers continued to make themselves known. My upstairs neighbor, for example, was crazy about rap music. He played it frequently, at full volume. The racket would have irritated anyone, I'm sure, but I took particular notice since the endless, repetitive beat sent me to the floor in seizures.

The doctors at Madigan, in the meantime, picked up where my previous caregivers left off, assuming I suffered from a combination of epileptic seizures and pseudoseizures. Yet treatment never really progressed. I still had no primary physician. With every visit, it seemed, it was a new face, in many cases an intern or a resident, looking me over. My drug regimen was altered. The doctors settled on Dilantin by itself, but convulsions still struck every week or two.

New tests were conducted. As an EEG in Panama had found, the doctors at Madigan picked up possible epileptic activity in my brain's left temporal lobe. It made sense that the seizures might originate there, for that's the region of the brain responsible for emotions and memory, which played an integral part in setting off my attacks.

What's more, damage to one side of the brain often affects the opposite side of a person's body. Injury to the left temporal lobe, therefore, might explain why after a seizure my right side was ravaged by a condition known as Todd's paralysis. It was temporary, lasting as long as a month, but my limbs became so weak that I sometimes needed a walker, and later a wheelchair, to get around.

In five days of continuous EEG monitoring at Madigan, I failed to have a seizure, thwarting any hopes of better pinpointing the epicenter. But when the device was removed, they struck. My doctor concluded that the seizures were not epileptic. He cut off my medication and ordered me to throw away my medical-alert bracelet for epilepsy. It was like unleashing attack dogs. As the Dilantin wore off, the seizures rolled in fast and furious, joined by their partner in my destruction, the PTSD.

Living off base complicated matters. Being out of the Army's jurisdiction, we had to pay several hundred dollars every time I needed an ambulance. If the paramedics brought me to a private hospital instead of Madigan, all costs were out of pocket. And by now the bills were stacking up.

In the meantime, Madigan's psychiatric unit was often understaffed and filled to capacity and couldn't take me as an in-patient.

Life became one incident after another, a tornado steadily plowing through my existence and that of my family.

One day that September, flashbacks had me hiding from my attacker–imagined, of course–in a wooded ravine a block or two from our apartment. A police K-9 unit, sent to flush me out, discovered me hiding behind a log, covered with leaves and other debris, making no sense whatsoever. I resisted the cop and he sprayed me with Mace, then handcuffed me. I ended up at Western State Hospital, a state-run mental institution, where I was held for a day, evaluated, and released.

Come mid-November, I was back. All that day I had been having momentary visions of my rape. That evening, for whatever reason, I drifted into a dissociative state and marched out into the freezing rain, wearing only a T-shirt, sweatpants, and tennis shoes. Michael was asleep and Harry, although home, was unaware I left.

Much of that night remains a blur, but I walked for several hours, covering ten miles, apparently believing I was private Proctor again and that I had to get to my MP post.

I ended up in a seedy, unfamiliar part of Tacoma, drenched, shivering, and frightened out of my mind. I had no idea of my location. And though I had some grasp of my first name, my surname was a blank.

All the stores were closed; I couldn't comprehend the signs; the writing looked like gibberish. No one was around. I didn't have a cent.

I did manage to find a pay phone, however, and poked 911.

"Hello," I told the dispatcher. "My name is Leana and I'm lost."

She kept me on the phone until a patrol car showed up. As it turned out, the reason I couldn't read the signs on the storefronts was because they were written in a foreign language; I was in the Korean section of town.

The police transported me to nearby St. Claire Hospital, where the ER staff treated me for hypothermia. The mental health professional, concerned about why I was walking outdoors so underdressed, saw that I was transferred again to

Western State. This time they detained me for a mandatory seventy-two hours of observation.

Western State, located in Lakewood, was a tough place. The largest of the state's mental hospitals, it housed not only those individuals unable to afford care but the criminally insane and those under court-ordered evaluation.

Built in the 1930s, Western State's exterior design called to mind a medieval castle. And though modern inside, it was crowded and understaffed.

Over the years, my care had predominantly been at military hospitals, which for the most part handled acute, more manageable forms of psychiatric problems. After all, people with long-term conditions are not allowed in the Army, or are mustered out when their symptoms become evident.

Western State was another story altogether. Patients there spanned the range of psychological woes, from the ravages of depression to schizophrenia. As you might expect, most were deeply troubled.

When I arrived, I was strip searched for contraband, no small event given my mindset, and I was put on the general ward. Fearful of everything and everybody, I pressed my back to the wall of the dayroom and surveyed the scene.

Some patients sat quietly and read or watched television. Others murmured to themselves or imaginary companions. A few remained solitary, emerging from their rooms only for meals or medications.

One patient, an eighteen or nineteen year old man, was notorious for smearing feces on the walls of his room, the nauseating odor wafting onto the ward. One woman was caught several times attempting to have sex with the male patients. And before I left, a female patient stole an expensive sweatsuit of mine, among other items, then traipsed around the ward in it, insisting it was hers.

"Oh, my God," I told myself. "What am I *doing* here?"

We had just moved to a new place. A new life was before us. As I saw it, I was ruining everything. I berated myself. "Never again!" I said. "This is never happening again! I don't care what I have to do! I'm stopping this!" But I wasn't stopping a thing. Not by force of will at least. And not by myself.

The doctors put me back on the Dilantin that Madigan originally prescribed. And though they proposed holding me longer, I refused and left when my three-day hold was up.

A week later, trouble hit again. This time I had a seizure while walking through a vacant commuter parking lot at night, again after an argument with Harry. God knows how long I was unconscious.

When I came to, I had a gash on my forehead. I was trying to work my way through the post-seizure fog, sitting on the curb outside a 7-Eleven, sipping a cup of coffee, when a police cruiser pulled up.

They looked me over and said they were calling for medical assistance. The last thing I needed, however, was a huge bill for an ambulance and hospital visit, especially when all they would do is examine me and hold me for observation.

I tried to get away–walking, then running down a dark side street. Elements of the PTSD may have been at play–certainly I was in a panic mode–but more than anything, I was lost in the thickets of post-seizure confusion.

Voices in the night shouted for me to stop. It was the officers, I know now, but in the moment I had lost all sense of who was behind me. Up against a wire fence, I withdrew my pocket knife from my pants and opened the blade, as if to protect myself. I dropped it without a major incident, but the cops didn't know if I was suicidal, a maniac, or what. Once again, I ended up at Western State.

By the time I got to the hospital, my anxiety level was through the roof, and my stuttering was so bad that I could hardly say a word. To compensate, I answered my assigned doctor's questions with nods, shakes of the head, and by writing notes.

More chagrined than compassionate, he wanted nothing to do with communicating that way. Thinking I was being obstinate, he constantly demanded that I speak. Before long, no doubt following the doctor's orders, the staff refused to acknowledge my notes, denying me even the chance to take a shower or brush my teeth unless the request was made verbally.

It became a Catch-22 of nightmare proportions, especially considering my already fragile mental health: They wanted me to cooperate, but I couldn't speak. And until I spoke, they refused to acknowledge me.

This being my third trip to the hospital that autumn, the doctor also sought a court order to force me to stay two additional weeks, to better understand my problems and to get me on an adequate treatment plan.

I assume his heart was in the right place; he probably did want to stop the revolving door and help me. But he went about it all wrong. No one was going to force me to do anything. It was force, after all, that eight years earlier had started all this.

I wrote a letter, six pages in length, to the judge, explaining my resistance to being legally committed. Despite my outrage, it was a neat, well-organized letter, hardly the rantings of a crazy woman:

The hospital environment has always bothered me and is very stressful to me. I was tied up during the rape and could not get away. I can't get away here either. I am locked up. It's the same to me.

The staff complains about me writing everything down. But then they can't understand my stuttering. So how am I to talk to people? The more pressure they put on me to speak, the worse it gets. I am not suicidal. I am not homicidal. I don't want to hurt anyone or anything. And I am not depressed.

The staff has upset me so much that I have cried, but that doesn't mean I'm depressed.

If that were the case we better lock up all the people that cry or stutter or can't talk. Just because I stutter does not mean I'm depressed or crazy. And epileptic type seizures is no reason to commit someone.

I must have done well. The judge came down in my favor, saying he saw no evidence that I was incompetent. Whether I stayed at Western State or went home, he said, was up to me.

As it turned out, I returned to the apartment for a few days, then checked myself back into the hospital, this time under the care of a different psychiatrist, Dr. Robert T. Sargent. During that week-long stay, I had a couple flare-ups, including one late-night flashback in which my roommate awoke to find me trembling behind the door of our room, wiping non-existent blood from my hands. "Wash, wash," I told the nurses who guided me to the seclusion room.

Otherwise, Dr. Sargent and his treatment team reassessed my situation and adjusted my medications. By the end of my stay, my mood was better–at least for awhile. But despite extensive workups, Dr. Sargent settled on the same diagnoses as my previous doctors.

One piece of advice he offered, however, made the entire stay worthwhile: He asked if I'd ever considered seeking treatment at the Veterans Administration hospital in Tacoma. It had an excellent neurology department, he said, and it was probably the best place around for treatment of post-traumatic stress.

I had always thought the VA was for elderly veterans, like my grandfather who lived out his years at the Seattle VA's nursing home, not someone like me who'd served three years in the Army and was out. In all my hospital stays, over all these years, not a single person mentioned the VA as a possibility.

It was like a light flicked on; my life seemed on the verge of change. I told Dr. Sargent, I'd certainly look into it.

9

At first glance, the American Lake VA Medical Center looked like a college campus, spread out as it was on a few hundred acres of gorgeous property, surrounded by woods, the lake, and a breathtaking view of Mount Rainier. The yellow Spanish-style buildings, with their red-tiled roofs, dated back to the hospital's origins in the 1920s.

I was cautious when I first met with Grace McCardle, the clinical nurse specialist assigned to me when I called. I had a variety of therapists over the years, but none for very long. Most were men and because so much of my care was through the Army, they were usually in uniform. Both factors contributed to my simmering anxiety and undermined any attempt to help me confront the past.

But from the very start I had a good feeling about Grace. She was in her sixties and called to mind a kindly grandmother. She was soft-spoken, non-threatening, and non-judgmental.

We spent our first couple meetings getting acquainted and finding common ground. Grace herself had been a military wife; her husband was in the Navy during the early years of their marriage, before he became a Congregational minister.

Grace's husband, I would come to learn, succumbed to cancer years before, leaving her to care for four young children. Back then, living in Chicago, she was consumed with anger at God and the world at the unfairness of his death at age forty-one. Yet as time passed, she found that same pain served her well as a counselor because she too knew something about hopelessness and despair.

Her mother urged her to come home to Tacoma, convinced that she and the kids could never survive on their own, but Grace, who could be stubborn when provoked, set out to prove otherwise.

She had been working as a nurse at the Chicago VA's alcohol and drug treatment program, but wanted to be there for her children during the difficult months after their father's death. Grace loved animals, so she took a class, and for awhile groomed dogs at home. For a time she also bred poodles.

Eventually, she received her degree in counseling and finally did transfer to American Lake and moved back to her native Washington.

Grace appeared innocent and mild-mannered, yet quietly knew about life's dark places. Post-traumatic stress disorder was common in her patients. Over the years she walked many a veteran through waking nightmares of Vietnam and other killing fields. Grace had been punched by a couple patients, too, the blows of men frightened or not in their right minds. But she always forgave and forgot.

As accommodating as Grace was, I still had to tell her my story, and that in itself was a road fraught with landmines. I was so anxious during those first appointments that I could hardly sit still and often broke down crying. It didn't help that the anniversary of the rape, my toughest time of year, was rapidly approaching.

I told Grace about myself, including my tribulations of recent years. I also gave her an eight-page account of the rape, which I wrote at home, simply because it was too agonizing to discuss for very long.

Coming in for our third session, I was overwrought. Flashbacks kept me awake the night before, and I'd gotten little sleep all that week. The rape was bubbling near the surface of my consciousness, but I was also afraid of Grace's reaction now that she knew what happened. I'd already been through one rejection by a person I trusted: Walter Reed's Dr. Field. I didn't think I could survive another.

We got started that day, Grace would later report, and I soon drifted into a daze. One of my legs began shaking; a hand twitched uncontrollably; and my eyes were locked in a blank stare. When I failed to answer her questions, she reached for my arm to see if I was all right. But her touch alone sent a current of fear charging through me. I scrambled for a corner of the room, cowering.

Grace got on the phone to the psychiatrist she worked under and asked him to hurry over. When he opened the door, I saw Sgt. Stockton, my attacker, coming at me. I rushed out of Grace's office. Only after I caromed off a wall did the staff catch up with me. They assured me I was in a safe place and among people who wanted to help.

What followed was a voluntary hospital stay that stretched to thirty-eight days, from late February into April. The staff could now see firsthand the terror and confusion that had taken over my life.

Flashbacks bombarded me. Being around men, which nearly all the VA's patients were, was a particular problem. My second day on the psych unit, Ward 61B, I seemed to be doing better. I ate well, played cards with a member of the staff, then a nurse took me out to the fenced-in patio for a cigarette and some fresh air. I was sipping a soft drink when a male patient happened to walk in my direction, setting off such naked terror that I dropped the can and bolted for a distant corner, murmuring, "Go, go, go." They brought me to what's known as a quiet room, where I curled up on a mattress on the floor, trembling.

Such incidents came and went. I'd recover, then something else would trigger a reaction. When a technician was drawing blood for a routine test, the needle became in my mind a knife. I swung at him and fled. They found me just outside the building, "completely frenzied, legs shaking, teeth chattering," according to the records. I was "wild-eyed" and "hypervigilant to the max."

February turned to March, the anniversary of the rape. Nightmares tormented me. Crowded or busy rooms had me on red alert. And when a fellow patient prodded by his own demons suddenly slugged a staff member, I was once again off for the races, doctors and nurses frantically chasing behind.

Then there were my seizures. When I zoned out in Grace's office, no one was quite certain whether I was having a dissociative episode or a less obvious form of seizure. That same day they sent me to the seizure clinic for a consultation.

When the woman who ran the unit entered the room, I remember thinking that this was the tallest woman I'd ever seen. Margarethe Cammermeyer would later tell me she was six-foot, but she seemed tall as a building to me. Hers was such a welcoming smile that even in my troubled state I couldn't help but grin back. She was fifty years old, with a Nordic, wholesome appearance, and short blonde hair. What impressed me more than anything, was her air of complete authority and self-confidence.

Cammermeyer, I learned over time, was a nurse in Vietnam, married, and had four children. By the time we met, she was divorced and worked in neuroscience for the VA in California and Washington for more than fifteen years. In 1985, she was honored as the VA's top nurse in the country. These days she oversaw American Lake's seizure clinic, treating hundreds of patients a year.

At this time, she was also engaged in a legal battle with the U.S. Army that was beginning to attract attention. Having reached the rank of colonel and chief nurse of the Washington National Guard, Cammermeyer had been dismissed in 1992 because she admitted to being a lesbian. She turned to the courts seeking reinstatement, and before long became a focal point in the national debate over the military's policy toward homosexuals.

On the Friday afternoon we met, I knew nothing of all that. I simply answered Cammermeyer's questions and filled her in on the basics of my problems.

I was given an EEG, using photic-stimulation, which is basically strobe lights designed to induce electric activity in the brain. Over the years, I had a number of such tests, some using the flashing lights and some without. The difference this time was that it showed marked signs of epileptic activity.

For the first time, I had proof positive that my seizures–in the very least, some of them–were originating in the circuitry of my brain, that they weren't purely psychological, and that I did indeed need to be treated with anti-convulsants.

MARGARETHE CAMMERMEYER, RN, Ph.D., CERTIFIED NURSE SPECIALIST IN NEUROSCIENCE, RETIRED, AMERICAN LAKE VA MEDICAL CENTER

Seizures are really just abnormal electrical activity in the brain. One type of seizure stems from something that occurred during fetal development. In other words, people are born with it. In those individuals, the epileptic activity spreads over the entire brain at the same time. They don't have any warning beforehand. They just have a seizure, which may be the typical shaking and jerking with loss of consciousness or brief lapses of attention.

In our population at the VA, however, seizures were usually a result of some sort of head trauma or underlying brain tumor or stroke or something like that.

With somebody who has what we call a post-traumatic seizure disorder, meaning after a head injury, there is a scar on the brain that for some reason becomes more electrically charged. When that charge begins to become active, that's when they have a seizure. The seizure activity can spread to involve the entire brain or it can stay very circumscribed in a very small area.

If it stays circumscribed, if the scar is in the area of the brain that controls the hand, for example, then a hand may begin to jerk and nothing else. That's a focal motor seizure. It doesn't spread. You just deal with it.

Then you have the kind that spread. Those are called secondarily generalized seizures. That's what Leana has. There's a scar–perhaps as small as the tip of a pin—where the brain was injured. In Leana's case that's in the left hemisphere towards the vertex, which is near the top of the brain.

We know that something happened to this part of the brain—probably during her fall down the stairs–because even when she is not having seizures there is some unusual electrical activity there.

For Leana, when there was photic-stimulation or when she became particularly stressed, then this electrical activity would become more apparent and she would begin to have a seizure. It would start in that area, then spread to involve her whole brain, so that she would end up losing consciousness.

With seizures, we know there is a scar and a focus. We don't know what triggers the focus for everybody. That's very individualized.

Some people develop seizures in response to a sequence of musical tones. Others respond to photic-stimulation, such as the flicker of a television screen or a computer monitor.

If Leana had a repetitive number of seizures or she had a particularly long and hard seizure, she would awaken from it with what is known as Todd's paralysis, which is a motor weakness or physical weakness that is a direct result of having had the seizure. For her it was a weakness in her arm and her leg on her right side, which supported our diagnosis that the seizures originated on the left side of the brain.

Some people have said that after a seizure they feel like they have just run a marathon. That's because of the tremendous motor movements that take place, the flexing and relaxing of the muscles. It's a tremendous physical workout and many people have injured themselves as a result or feel really sore and stiff and end up needing to sleep for twenty-four to forty-eight hours afterward. It depends on the type of seizure and how long it lasts, but in many cases it is both a physical and an electrical storm.

Over the next few weeks, Cammermeyer tinkered with my medications. By the end of my hospitalization, we would settle on Depakote, which improved my seizure control a bit, though it did cause stomach distress.

Still, convulsions rocked me for much of my stay, igniting my PTSD. At one point, as I was being escorted across the parking lot after an appointment with Cammermeyer, I went down in spasms. The staff got me to the emergency room. But just as I was coming around I saw someone drawing blood from my arm, then noticed a smear of blood from where they inserted a catheter. Panicked, I ripped out the IV, scrambled off the table, and to the amazement of everyone, charged straight out the door.

Heading toward the ER, meanwhile, was Dr. Richard M. Koerker, the neurologist who worked with Cammermeyer. He had been summoned to look me over, but now stood stunned as I tore past him in the hall. "Stop her!" someone cried, and now Koerker joined the chase.

With my right leg weak from the Todd's, I fell several times, smashing my knee on the tile floor. Still I kept charging, right out the exit. I bound down the steps to the sidewalk, then galloped across the grounds—over lawns, blacktop, shrubs, even a hedge.

Koerker—as cerebral and non-aggressive an individual as you could imagine—managed to angle across the property and cut me off. He grabbed for me, fearing I was heading for the lake to drown myself. But I broke around him like a halfback in open field and rumbled down an embankment. He kept pursuing, and just as I hit the rocky shore, Koerker slammed into me. My knee twisted painfully as I crashed against the rocks. Everyone else piled on, but still I surged forward, dragging myself across some brambles, and slashing up my arms, until I felt the water.

All I knew was that I had to wash away the blood–the actual blood from where the IV had been as well as the imagined blood that covered my arms. Frantically, I splashed lake water on myself, as my neurologist and the others desperately hung on.

Someone wisely summoned Dr. Muriel Taylor, the psychiatrist overseeing my case while I was in the hospital, who hurried out and ordered the men to get back.

Gray-haired and in her fifties, Taylor sat down with me on the shore, spoke in hushed tones, and gently massaged my shoulders and back.

"Everything's going to be okay," she said, brushing the hair from my face and soothing me. "You're safe now."

I curled up, set my head on her legs, and sobbed uncontrollably.

So it went for the rest of that hospital stay. Back and forth I bounced between seizures, flashbacks, and dissociative episodes in which I relived a segment of my stint in the military. I was a time traveler, of sorts, destination 1984.

To those around me, I was the subject of much bewilderment and chagrin.

When the psych nurses brought my medications, for instance, I declined. "I never take drugs," I told them, because nine years earlier I did not.

Harry and Michael came by one day to cheer me up, but I saw my husband only as my boyfriend, which he was back in the days where I lingered. At one point I teasingly asked if he wanted a rematch in putt-putt golf, a reference to the drubbing he endured on one of our first dates.

I also broke little Michael's heart. He had been so looking forward to seeing me, but I didn't recognize him. "Who's the kid?" I asked Harry. "You baby-sitting for someone?"

Most persistent while I was dissociating, however, was my compulsion to either return to my company or report to duty as an MP. Time and again, I set off walking, refusing to be stopped, determined to get wherever I imagined myself going.

Once I managed to get off the unit. When the staff intercepted me across from the VA police station all I would say was that I had to return to Fort Lee. Told I needed to go back to the psych unit, I struck a nurse and tried to escape. Backup help was called and I was carted back to the psychiatric unit in four-point restraints.

On the ward that evening, a series of powerful seizures rattled me and I was transferred to the medical ward for treatment and observation.

It was there, a couple days later, that the nurses found me up and about, GI'ing my room–wiping surfaces, polishing fixtures, and stripping linens from my bed.

Private Proctor was preparing for inspection.

They tried to reason with me, explaining that I was in the hospital, not on a military installation. The year was 1993, they insisted, not 1984.

I figured these were lunatics, or pranksters, and went about my business. It frightened the nurses, who'd never seen such behavior. Within a couple hours, everyone was uneasy. When was this going to stop? What would I do next? How best to manage me before I further damaged my leg or matters spun out of control? Forcible restraint was becoming a distinct possibility.

Pretty soon I was asking if anyone had some Brasso, so I could clean the pipes under the sink.

Cammermeyer, who'd tried talking sense to me without luck, figured she better try *something.*

"Who are you?" she asked.

"Private First Class Proctor."

"And what are you doing here?"

"Inspection is at 1000 hours. I want my room in shape so I can get a seventy-two-hour pass."

At this, a light bulb flashed over her head. I was in another time and place, she understood. So wouldn't it be easier to enter my world than force me to return to hers?

Grethe drew herself up to her full military persona, summoned her most authoritative voice, and informed me in no uncertain terms that she was my commanding officer.

In my hospital pajamas, I snapped my heels together and stood at perfect attention.

"Private, you are *not* part of this inspection," she said. "You have been sick. And no passes will be granted at this time. You are confined to quarters for the next seventy-two hours. Have I made myself clear?"

"Yes, sir!"

I went over and sat in a chair. Someone gave me a sedative. Then they led me to bed, and I dropped soundly to sleep.

MARGARETHE CAMMERMEYER

When the incident in Leana's room occurred, I wasn't sure what was going on. It was so eerie because it was though she had moved back in time in a time machine. She had been brought up to the ward and I was asked to go see her. When I did, she began to refer to me as ma'am. Then she spoke of herself just like she would if she was in the barracks.

I remember she was totally obsessed with cleaning the sink. I encouraged her to get back to bed and she said "Well, you know, there's going to be inspection at 1000 hours and I want to make sure my room is in tip-top shape so I can get a seventy-two-hour pass."

I thought, "What is this?" Then it sort of dawned on me that she had moved back in time. I remember wondering, "Is she lost in this time and space? Are we going to be able to bring her back?" I still remember thinking that: How do we bring her back?

Finally, I said, "Okay, if she wants to play Army, I can do that." I just assumed my colonel role and in my best military voice I ordered her back to bed.

It was very clear that what she was responding to was this military milieu. At the time we were able to give her a sedative and she went to sleep. Over the next couple days she began to come back. But it took awhile for her to reorient to real life.

10

I felt safe in the controlled environment of the hospital. It was tedious, but life also had a certain rhythm. Somebody else decided when I would get up, go to bed, and eat. I wore the same clothes, hospital pajamas, every day. Should anything go wrong, doctors and nurses were ready to come running.

It was in the outside world where life got tricky. The anniversary of the rape receded and I became more stable. Come April, they released me. After being in the hospital so long, even the act of selecting what to wear each day was a struggle. Independence brought too many choices. What should I have for breakfast? What to do all day?

Every aspect of day-to-day living was a challenge. Establishing normal relations with people seemed impossible. I didn't need to be struck by a seizure or terrified during a flashback to feel off kilter. Simply worrying about them–and people's response–was more than enough.

Little by little, however, change came into my life.

We were finally assigned housing on Fort Lewis, which allowed us a little extra money each month and lowered our stress all the way around.

I regularly saw Mona, who was now living on base with her family.

I also ran into the younger sister of a girl I sometimes rode horses with when I was a kid back in Eastern Washington. Theresa Buchanan, now in her twenties, had also married a soldier. She and her husband had a little boy and a girl and lived right by us on base.

Now, I had at least a small circle of friends to visit or go out with now and then. Ever so slowly I emerged from my shell.

One night, Mona and her family came by and I had a seizure in the middle of a card game, flopping from my chair like a fish on the dock. I had always been cautious, never wanting her to see that. But she astounded me by calling the next day to check on me. It was absurd, she said, for me to worry that she might abandon our friendship just because of a seizure.

MONA JABER

I didn't feel sorry for Leana, but I felt she needed a friend, somebody to be there for her, because a lot of people would shy away from her. They would see one seizure and would be like, "Oh, my God," and that would be it. A lot of people, even in this day and age, think she's possessed by the devil, that people who are epileptic are possessed by Satan.

When we were living on Fort Lewis, she was always afraid to go outside of her house. She hated to have a seizure in public. It was embarrassing for her. A lot of times she would wet her pants, too. It was hard.

I remember one night I was over her house. Harry was working late and she wasn't tired. She couldn't sleep. So I stayed up with her until a little after eleven o'clock. Harry was going to be home soon, so I left.

A little after midnight I got a phone call from Harry:

"Is Lee with you?"

"No," I said, "what do you mean? I was at your house a little while ago and she was fine."

"Well, there's a puddle of blood here in front of the TV and she's not here."

So I came down to get Michael and took him to our house. Harry got in his car and went looking for her. He ended up going to the front gate, and that's where he found her.

She had fallen and hit her head. She said she remembered slipping and falling, and then she had a seizure. She said that when she got up nothing looked familiar. I remember Harry had to take her to the hospital for stitches.

The very next day, she and Harry were having a spat of some kind. She and Michael had come over to my house and she was looking through a newspaper, reading the classified ads. She told me she was going to find a job.

So she sat there for a long time and just kind of stared at the paper, just very spaced out. I got up to go to the bathroom and came back.

I said to the kids, "Where did Lee go?" They said they didn't know, that they thought she walked out the front door. I went out and didn't see her anywhere. I called Harry. Then we both got in our cars and started looking for her. Once again Harry found her at the front gate, completely spaced out.

Around this time, after the move to Fort Lewis, I began taking in parrots. The seeds of my affection for them that were planted in Panama had started to bloom.

I fell in love with my first one while on a shopping trip. Michael and I were going to browse around a pet shop while Harry picked up some items from a nearby computer store.

When we walked in, I was pained to see the most gorgeous orange and yellow parrot, a sun conure, in a cage that was obviously too small for it. I peered in and spoke softly to the bird, but every time I tried to walk away, she'd squawk wildly, as if crying out for me. The clerk told me the parrot had belonged to a family on Fort Lewis that was being transferred to Germany and had to leave her behind.

I asked if I could get a closer look. The saleswoman agreed to bring her out, but cautioned me that this one was a biter, and in fact had taken a piece out of her finger just the day before. The parrot climbed on my finger and cooed. Then I put her on my shoulder where she preened my hair.

Harry came in and I showed him. He agreed she was beautiful but reminded me of our rickety finances.

So we left that parrot and went on with our lives. That is, until a couple days later when my husband came home with a suspicious expression on his face.

"Remember that bird from the pet store?" he asked.

"Sure I do."

"Well, I dropped by again to look at her and it turns out that somebody made an offer on her."

My heart dropped a little, even though I knew we couldn't have afforded her anyway.

"But they didn't put any money down," Harry continued. "So before they came back, I went ahead and bought her."

He reached just outside our door, lifted the cage, and held her up. We named her Tangy, which seemed to match not only her tangerine coloring but her sassy disposition as well.

Tangy, as with all parrots, was intelligent and had a distinct personality. Playful and affectionate, she loved having her tummy stroked and being pet under the wings.

Tangy was a quick study and I taught her some impressive tricks. I would point my finger at her as if my hand was a gun. "Stick 'em up!" I'd say, and Tangy would lift her wings. I'd say "Bang," and she'd drop on her back in the palm of my hand and flutter her eyes shut.

Our flock became larger. Michael got a couple parakeets from a pet store. A neighbor on Fort Lewis, meanwhile, had a beautiful cockatiel named Picks that she'd been mistreating, screaming at and whacking his cage when he got noisy. I offered to take him off her hands and she happily obliged, handing the parrot over in a cage she actually dented while trying to silence him.

I loved having the birds around. Winning their trust required patience, but that was no problem. If anything, working with them relaxed me and helped pass the lonely hours.

As much as they provided me, it was also satisfying to be giving them a second chance. These birds–and the many parrots that followed–could never survive in the wild. But at least they'd have proper care. They could come out of their cages and play when they wanted. No one would be banging on the bars or shrieking at them to shut up. No one was going to harm them. It was the least that they, or any of us, deserved.

11

I managed to avoid another long hospitalization for the rest of our first year back in Washington. Yet that was more a determination to stay out of the hospital than an improvement in my condition. The seizures and PTSD, in fact, struck with such regularity that they seemed like one ongoing crisis. Most incidents stood out only when other people were affected or the hazards were particularly dire.

One such instance came in the spring of 1993, when I'd gone to the VA for outpatient physical therapy. The knee I had wrenched down by the lake was still on the mend. For the most part, my regimen involved stretching exercises and a good soaking in the whirlpool. But heat could be hard to take. Not long after I settled into the tank, a seizure hit and I slipped beneath the swirling waters. If someone hadn't looked over just as I was went under, I'm sure I would have drowned.

Other pressures were also chipping away at me.

Any time Harry was off on field maneuvers was difficult. When we lived in the apartments in Tacoma, I was uncomfortable being home alone with Michael. With so much crime in our neighborhood, I'd stay awake dusk to dawn with one of Harry's loaded handguns at my side. But even living on base I found it impossible to sleep without Harry alongside me. Instead, I'd stay up all night cleaning or otherwise keeping myself occupied.

Getting used to Depakote, in the meantime, was tough. Like a number of anti-convulsants, the drug had a mood-stabilizing effect, which for me was good. Yet it left me fatigued—to the point that I could hardly stay awake–and easily irritated. With five active kids in the mix, I often felt like I'd reached the end of my rope.

I also gained thirty pounds on the drug, which only made me feel worse, both physically and emotionally.

The months passed. I settled into a routine of weekly visits with Grace and regular appointments with Cammermeyer.

I found over time that I had developed a loyalty to the American Lake VA. It seemed a world apart from all the hospitals I'd been to before. Most reassuring, the staff knew a lot about PTSD, which they often encountered in their war veterans. For once, I was among people familiar with the forces that had been tearing me apart and how they changed me as a person, a parent, and a wife.

Grethe Cammermeyer, in particular, became one of my favorite people. Her field of expertise may have been neuroscience, but she helped me in ways that went far beyond my seizures.

Cammermeyer won my everlasting trust and affection the day she played into my flashbacks instead of resorting to restraints or other forceful methods to get me under control. Maybe it was her own experience with PTSD, a consequence of all she witnessed in Vietnam, that gave her such insight, or her work with thousands of veterans. All I knew was that she was the one person to pay close attention to what was going on in my mind and to try to solve the problem from my perspective.

As Grethe's legal battle with the military began to bubble over, I found her name was well-recognized at Madigan Army Hospital, where I continued to be brought when seizures hit as well as for orthopedic treatment of my knee. Because of her sexuality and stand against the Army, not everyone had kind words for her.

As I learned more about her dispute, I became increasingly defensive on her behalf. Over at the VA, everyone knew Grethe was excellent at her job. She had the utmost respect of her patients and people who worked with her.

When she applied for a higher security clearance with the Washington National Guard, so she could be considered for a promotion, Cammermeyer chose to tell the truth about her sexual orientation. A lot of people felt the Army had no business asking about such matters in the first place. A lie would have been quick and easy, but Grethe chose to tell the truth–and paid a heavy price.

Yet she refused to sit back and accept the military's banishment. By pressing her case, she not only took on a juggernaut; she exposed to public scrutiny the most private aspects of her life. Rather than shy away, she became an outspoken advocate of gays in the military, testifying before Congress and even questioning presidential hopeful Bill Clinton about his position on the issue during a town meeting in Seattle.

That Clinton made overturning the ban one of the first battles of his administration in 1993, resulting in the infamous "Don't ask, don't tell" policy, only put the spotlight all the more on Grethe and her case.

Here I was, living every day in fear. I didn't want to go out in the yard because someone might see me have a seizure. Yet Grethe was taking on the U.S. government. I had never known a woman–or anyone–so courageous.

Grace McCardle, for her part, was by far the best counselor to come my way. Although I still had anxious moments, she seemed to take them in stride. When my stuttering got so bad that I had to write out my side of the conversation, she never revealed any frustration or insisted that I speak.

Almost from Day One, Grace taught me relaxation techniques to cope with my anxiety, which if unchecked could evolve into worse problems. It was important, she said, to become aware of my own feelings and the circumstances that caused me stress. She taught me to breathe deeply, filling my entire chest with air, holding it for a moment, then slowly releasing it. Another method that was useful, she said, was to shake out my arms, clench my fists, then relax them. She also encouraged me to take long, hot showers to soothe tense muscles and, in turn, my mind. (Baths, of course, were out of the question, as my experience with the whirlpool made clear.)

Certainly the VA doctors prescribed their share of powerful drugs. Besides my seizure medication, Depakote, I was also on mood stabilizers. Cammermeyer and McCardle, however, provided me with more than medication. In both, I had caregivers who understood that true healing meant more than reining in my symptoms. They wanted me to regain control of my life and to understand that I did have power over myself, not to mention the responsibility that came with it.

Over the years I had been to countless doctors and hospitals. So much of the care, especially at the military facilities, was about doing what I was told. And usually what they told me was to take my drugs and be quiet. As someone who had been raped, it was distressing to find myself powerless all over again. As someone desperate to become whole once more, I was being taught dependence. The message was that everyone else knew what was best for me, and that I knew nothing.

That first year at the VA, my condition was as rocky as it had ever been. But somehow a seed was planted. I had faith in these people. And for the first time in ages, I was discovering faith in myself.

GRACE McCARDLE, CLINICAL NURSE SPECIALIST, RETIRED, AMERICAN LAKE VA MEDICAL CENTER

Leana was probably the most interesting of all the patients I've worked with. I felt a very strong bond with Leana, and empathy. I felt that she didn't want to be the way she was but she couldn't help the way she was.

When I first met her she was very wary. Even her physical appearance. She would pull back in the chair, like a little child that's scared. She was very cautious about what she would tell me. I can remember this kind of cowardice appearance. Very quiet. And it took a long time for her to come out with an answer. I felt she was sorting it out, what she wanted to say.

I felt Leana was a person very much in need of help. I felt like she was honest. I didn't feel like she was playing games. Besides her seizures, Leana was diagnosed as having post-traumatic stress disorder, dissociative episodes, and borderline personality disorder. Often these are not pure diagnoses. They're interwoven. It's hard, for example, to separate the borderline personality traits from the PTSD.

From the very beginning I had to accept that progress would be very slow. She would go forward, then fall back. My goal was to help her deal with the trauma and set it behind her–though it will always come up every so often–so she could deal more with the here and now. And learn how to function so she could feel comfortable in society and strengthen her own self worth. I also wanted to make sure her son was all right, because I felt like the child had to parent her too much.

Leana needed someone that would be a friend and would listen to her. I didn't expect miracles, but I encouraged her to find out what her strengths were and to follow those. My first concern was to try to gain her trust. I felt that was the number one priority, because otherwise you can't go anywhere. And she was not an easy one.

Some therapists insist on being in control and are very rigid, but with someone with Leana's problems that will probably only bring out their rebellious side. With PTSD, people often have explosive anger. Most of them don't want to be controlled. You give them a command to do something and they're ready to fight you.

I don't think rigid rules work with people with Leana's problems. It either will throw them back into memories or cause them to create more problems. I'm talking about the veterans I knew with PTSD. You become rigid with them and they'll just go into a rage.

The theory I followed is that the best way to help somebody through trauma is to try to make them walk back through it, which I wasn't sure how far I could go with her. She did a pretty good job writing it, as I recall, although she said she vomited all the time she was trying to write it because it was so disturbing.

I felt like we made some progress in at least getting it out, and I had to let her know that I accepted it as she wrote it and as she told me, because it seemed like in the past many people didn't believe her.

There's still many that don't believe the rape story, but I do believe her. I believe her because I've heard similar stories from female veterans.

And the exact facts of the matter were not what was important to me anyway. It was her reaction to that event that was most important.

Much of Leana's behavior was a result of the PTSD. A lot of people with PTSD, for example, will hear a car backfire and jump under something as though it were a bomb. Well, Leana reacts in much the same way. She overreacts.

A lot of times, those with PTSD don't fit in. It's often because they're quick to anger and get angry over some things that the other person doesn't understand. Something they've said or done or the way they looked. They're often argumentative and carry a chip of their shoulder.

It's a simple explanation, but they've been through a whole lot that nobody understands.

One thing I liked about working with Leana is that she would take the initiative to follow through on suggestions I would make. Very often people just sit back. You suggest things and they say, "Oh, yeah, that's a good idea." But then they do nothing. Leana followed through.

I used to enjoy talking with Leana–when she was in her right mood. She has a good heart and she was excellent with animals. She would share some very interesting things with me, like bringing in her parrots. Did she tell you that she trained them? That she trained one to act dead? I was so impressed with that parrot. He would sit on her shoulder. And then he would start pecking at her ear when he wanted something. So she would give him a bottle of liquid.

I never knew what Leana was going to come in with.

12

On New Year's Eve–with Harry working graveyard shift and Michael sleeping soundly–I had a seizure in the enclosed patio off of our kitchen. I suffered a deep gash along my hairline, most likely from striking my head on a table. I also scraped the right side of my face raw while thrashing around on the rough cement floor.

Somewhere during this episode, most likely as I lay unconscious, 1994 arrived. When I came to, I once again took to walking in a postical stupor, though I only got so far. The MPs saw me, confused and bloodied, detained me, and got a hold of Harry.

So it was that I spent the first few hours of the new year in the ER at Madigan Army Hospital. In retrospect, it seems only appropriate that that's how I would usher in the most trying year of my life.

I was groggy and disoriented for most of that January. After a run of seizures early that month, another head wound, and several weeks of feeling even more out of sorts than usual, I went to see Cammermeyer, who felt I'd probably suffered a concussion when I struck the table, and that much of my unsteadiness was the after-effects of that. Concerned about the continuing seizures and weight gain, she adjusted my medications, reducing the Depakote and starting me on Felbamate, which had just come on the market, and told me to see her again in two weeks.

Eleven or twelve days passed and I was getting along okay. The seizures had diminished quite a bit. But then I was hit with excruciating migraine headaches, which got worse with each passing day. Just the slightest bit of sunlight, artificial light, or noise was like a dagger in my brain. They got so severe that I grew nauseous, to the point that I couldn't hold down food.

Finally, I could stand no more. It was a Tuesday afternoon when we called Dr. Koerker, who urged me to come right to the VA. He was on-call for the emergencies that day and said to meet him at the ER. But as we were waiting in the lobby, I was toppled off my chair by a seizure that lasted a full minute, and I was rushed in for treatment.

I recovered soon enough, but Dr. Koerker thought it best for me to stay for observation and once again to make changes in my medications.

Initially, it looked like it would be a brief hospitalization and that I would be home in time for Michael and I to celebrate our mutual birthday that Thursday. But the seizures dogged me, with four of them pounding me in the first day-and-a-half I was in the hospital. The Todd's paralysis also set in, requiring that I be in a wheelchair if I got out of bed.

The night of my birthday, February 17, Harry and Michael came by with gifts and a white-frosted sheet cake. As was our tradition, half was decorated for Michael, with plastic dinosaurs, palm trees, and a candle shaped like the number nine, and half for me, with flowers and candles in the shape of a three and a five. Some of the nurses came by to join us. Considering where I was and the troubles that brought me there, we still managed to have a nice time.

That night, I couldn't sleep. The overnight shift came on and surprised me by remembering my birthday and bringing out another cake. I had a bite and stayed in my wheelchair by the nurses station deep into the morning, reading and occasionally chatting with the staff.

Just before five o'clock, I dozed off. A nurse would later recount that I suddenly opened my eyes wide and stared at her uncomprehendingly. She said she asked if I was okay, but that I never answered her. Instead, I fell into convulsions.

Over the next ninety minutes, I was hit with five more seizures, ranging in duration from forty to fifty-five seconds, many of them with vomiting. Medically speaking, this is known as *status epilepticus*, and it's deadly serious business. If cascading seizures aren't brought under control fairly quickly a lack of oxygen can cause severe and permanent brain damage and could even be fatal.

That morning, the doctor on duty was able to quell them with Valium. But as I lay in bed over the next twenty-four hours, I was tormented with visions of Sgt. Stockton and once again the rape was happening all over again. I desperately struggled to beat those images back, like one might slap his coat at a spreading grass fire.

That Saturday night, more seizures hit and the medical officer on duty decided it was time to put me in intensive care, where I could be monitored more closely. And when further convulsions rocked me the next day, they took the next step to control them, rendering me unconscious, intubating me, and putting me on a respirator.

Soon afterward, the staff's concern grew deeper. My breathing was becoming labored and tests showed the oxygen levels in my blood had dropped precipitously. A chest X-ray was ordered and, sure enough, fluid was building in both lungs.

During the seizures, I had aspirated vomit, and a bad situation suddenly became worse. I was to develop Adult Respiratory Distress Syndrome, which is basically the ravaging of the microscopic systems within the lungs that process oxygen and carbon dioxide. Although aspiration can trigger ARDS, the process remains somewhat a mystery. For me, the bottom line was that if something wasn't done quickly, I would die.

I had slipped into a battle for my life. They injected me with antibiotics. Through the ventilator, oxygen was pumped into me at levels as high as one hundred percent, which can be deadly in itself if continued too long. At the same time, the machine was producing pressure enough to keep my lungs expanded and functioning at least minimally. Yet my condition only worsened.

Any medical person glancing at my X-rays could tell that something terrible was happening. Because the lungs are usually filled only with air, they generally come through on a radiograph as black. But in my case, a buildup of inflammatory cells, fluid, and infection caused the image of both lungs to become completely opaque.

At one point, I woke up from the fog of sedation to find my hands loosely bound with gauze to the rails of the bed. It was the tube running down my throat, however, that really caught my attention. Understanding nothing other than that I felt I was choking to death, I reached up, straining against my restraints, and began yanking on the tube that was giving me much needed oxygen.

A nurse looked over from across the unit. "No!" she cried. "Don't pull that out!"

Too late.

For awhile, they allowed me to stay awake and use an oxygen mask instead of intubating me again, but when breathing became too difficult, they anesthetized me and ran another tube down my throat. Now designated "seriously ill," I remained for the most part paralyzed in a medically induced coma.

With my condition still tenuous, the doctors finally decided to transfer me to Madigan, which was better equipped for long-term monitoring of respiratory crises. The Army hospital was also better manned to go in surgically on a moment's notice if the staff could not get a needle in my thread-thin veins. At various points, IV lines would be running to veins in my neck, groin, even my forehead, where doctors had to cut down the skin to reach the vein, then hold it in place with stitches.

Once there, I was put on a rotating bed, which shifted about forty degrees, paused thirty seconds, then shifted again, to help clear my lungs as well as prevent bed sores.

My entire body was hideously bloated, making me virtually unrecognizable. Fearful that the swelling would make it difficult to pass tubes down my throat, the Madigan doctors performed a tracheotomy, slicing an opening at the base of my throat and running a tube straight to my windpipe.

Harry contacted my family and everyone–my mother, father, brother and sister, aunt, grandmother, adopted grandmother, and cousin–came to see me for what could well have been the last time.

I couldn't move. I had no understanding of what happened to me. Yet I did have a few moments of comprehension through the fog of sedation in which I could hear people around me.

I also recall the sound of Harry's voice and what a comfort it was and how it lifted my spirits. Once, I felt him hold my hand. Yet I couldn't speak a word, move a muscle, or even lift an eyelid. His face pressed against my hand. He was praying but crying, too.

I wanted to scream, "Harry, I'm alive! I'm here! I hear you!" But nothing came out.

For as long as I live, I'll never forget that feeling of my husband's tears against my skin and being utterly helpless.

HARRY BEASLEY

I would go to the hospital every day and see Lee laid out on the bed, out cold. Her entire body had swollen up hideously. It was just horrifying. And she had no response to anything. Not touch, sound, smell. Nothing.

She was on a bed that gently rocked, so the fluid in her lungs would shift, to help it dry up and clear. When a person aspirates, when they inhale vomit, the acid and all that material goes into the lungs. The acid damages the lung tissues, causing them to weep, so that the lungs just fill with liquid. Then the debris causes infection and the lungs fill with infection and pus.

The real telltale factor through the whole thing was her oxygen levels. The meter was reading how much oxygen was getting from her lungs into her blood, and throughout the whole time those levels were real low.

Day after day, I would go to the hospital and sit with her. And I would watch the meter.

Lee's oxygen had been going down slowly, surely, and steadily until she reached the point where she had no more room to go down. That's when the doctor told me, "If she goes down any more, she will die. So you best contact your family, contact her family, and if you know anything about making funeral arrangements, you should consider it."

Boy, I tell you, that hurt. I went home and I was sitting there crying and I realized that never in my life did I have to deal with anyone close to me dying. I didn't know a damn thing about making funeral arrangements.

When it first happened, I told Michael that his mother had seizures and she was in real bad shape, that she was in the ICU. Then, after I realized that this was going to be a very long-term affair, I explained to him as best as I could what happened, that she had vomited and taken it into the lungs, that she was out cold and couldn't respond, and that they were keeping her like that.

I didn't want him to see her that way. I told him it wouldn't really serve much purpose to see her. Basically, I told him she wouldn't really know he was there and she wouldn't respond to anything he had to say or do.

Over time, that built up into hostility on his part. In his mind what it came down to was he wanted to see his mother and Daddy wouldn't let him.

Each day I would go and see her. I would come home and he would say, "How is Mommy doing?" I'd say, "Things are just the same." And the hostility built up even more.

It was after about three and a half weeks that I pretty much had to let him see her, because he was really getting hostile. He had made a scene in front of one of the doctors, who was also an officer, at the hospital. He was just really angry. And it was getting to the point where he might never have another chance to see his mother alive.

Finally, I said, "Okay, I'm going to let you go in. I'm going to let you see your mother this time."

Well, when he saw her he was so shocked. And he hurt. And he cried.

I remember him saying his prayers that night. He was praying to God to make his mommy better, to make her all better so she could come home.

I know that he had prayed plenty of times before. But in those instances it was more like a little kid talking to a God he doesn't really understand. That night, though, he was really praying to God.

Not that I wasn't praying, too. I was praying through the whole thing. But my prayers were different. With my prayers it was, "Lord, this whole thing is in your hands. Make her better, take the pain away, whatever you choose, it's your will." But with Michael it was emphatic: "Make my mommy better. Bring her home."

It was just a couple days later that her oxygen levels actually started going up.

You should have seen the nurses at Madigan. They were almost rejoicing they were so happy. Just by their reaction, I don't think they had expected her to pull through.

But she did. She was getting better.

And to this day I believe it was the prayer of a little boy that made the difference. A little boy's prayer.

13

The drugs that paralyzed me were discontinued and I emerged from the coma in a haze. I assumed I was alive, yet I lacked the ability to so much as open my eyes or raise a finger. I was a mind inside a petrified body, and a confused and frightened mind at that.

My circumstances–where I was, what happened to me–were a mystery. My first impression, given both Harry's and my backgrounds in the military and in law enforcement, was that an unknown assailant shot me, perhaps in the head. Then I figured I somehow broke my neck. Given the uncertainty and darkness that engulfed me, my imagination ran wild.

When I finally could open my eyes, I didn't recognize Harry. His voice was familiar, but I couldn't place him. Eventually, it registered that this was my husband, but little else made sense: I came into the hospital for one set of problems only to wake up and find myself shipwrecked. I could barely breathe. I couldn't talk. Someone said it was spring, though in my mind it was still February. What was going on?

Harry brought Michael to visit, but the best I could do was wink at him.

Eventually I could grasp a pencil and produced some scribbles on a notepad. It irritated me when Harry and Michael said they couldn't decipher a single word. My writing, I later learned, looked like a two-year-old's scrawl. This wasn't just poor penmanship either; somewhere in the depths of my coma, a large part of my most basic education had been obliterated.

By my family's next visit, I could write the letter "Y," then next to it, a shaky question mark.

Harry considered this for a moment before it dawned on him.

"You want to know *why*?" he said.

I blinked twice, my version of yes, and he set about trying to complete the question for me.

"Why are you in the hospital?" he proposed. "Why did it happen?"

I blinked twice again.

My husband did the best he could, explaining about the seizures, my being in ICU, and that I aspirated vomit. He also filled me in on the tracheotomy and why I was unable to talk.

I was devastated to learn the extent of my injuries. Among other problems that would soon reveal themselves, my lungs would never be the same. And my assumption—wrong, as it turned out—was that I'd never be able to utter another word.

When the nurses sat me up in bed, my first time upright in more than a month, I was so weak and I'd lost so much muscle tone and coordination that I kept expecting to topple over the side.

I felt, and looked, horrendous. My eyes were sunken. I was swollen, pale, and feeble, with a plastic trach tube lodged in my throat. Along the back and sides of my head, clumps of hair had fallen out from weeks of resting on the pillow.

Harry and Michael got permission to push me a bit in a wheelchair. I couldn't go outdoors, but my doctor said it would be okay to wheel me around the immediate area. A telemeter kept me connected to the heart monitor in case something went wrong.

They strapped me in and Harry rolled me over to the nurses station. Michael, so excited you would think it was Christmas morning, had convinced himself my problems were over. He was so thrilled, in fact, that when his father stepped away to ask someone a question, he commandeered the wheelchair, pushed me out of ICU, and charged full tilt down the corridor.

I was helpless. My eyes wide open, tile floor streaking beneath me, I felt the air rushing across my face like a dog with his head out the car window.

Back in ICU, my heart monitor was flatlining, jolting the nurses into red alert. The problem was that I was beyond the range of my telemeter, but for all they knew I was in cardiac arrest.

When Michael reached the elevators some nurses intercepted us.

"Michael, honey, where are you going?" said one. "You can't take your mother anywhere."

"You've had my mommy long enough!" he snapped. "I'm taking her home!"

Everyone had a good chuckle over that; for as determined as my son might have been, home was still a long ways away.

As March came to a close, I was transferred back to American Lake VA to finish recuperating. And though the staff tried to reassure me, I was in constant anxiety over my condition, often to the point of hyperventilating. Sleep, meanwhile, brought frightening dreams of drowning.

I was alive. That was a blessing. So was the fact that the convulsions and worst symptoms of my PTSD for the most part stayed at bay.

Being incapacitated and medicated for so long, however, left me helpless as an infant—and about as strong. Once, I tried to make the shift from my wheelchair to the bed unassisted and dropped face down on the floor, unable to move or call for help. I lay there several humiliating minutes before someone discovered me.

The trach tube, in the meantime, was a burden. Although I was soon permitted to take soup and other liquids, I constantly needed to disable the device, thereby clearing passage down my throat.

Only my inability to speak was more disheartening. Writing was my sole means of communication, and with my memory loss I could produce only the simplest of words or phrases.

Then one day, Grethe Cammermeyer came by accompanied by a stocky, middle aged man with dark hair.

"Hello, Leana," she said matter of factly. "How would you like to learn to talk?"

Grethe could not have missed my quizzical expression.

"We're going to teach you how, using your tube."

She introduced me to her guest, a good-natured fellow veteran, who had a permanent trach tube in place. He moved his finger over the opening and greeted me. His gravelly voice sounded odd at first, but I could understand him perfectly.

For the next half hour, Grethe and the veteran taught me how to place my finger while simultaneously forcing air up my throat to bring forth sound.

At first I could only produce grunts and squeaks, but pretty soon I was pronouncing simple words like "yes" and "no." Eventually I could string together short sentences, though given my ravaged lungs I could only get out a word or two with each breath.

I continued practicing much of that day, and when Grethe returned she seemed pleased at my progress. She asked if I had anything in particular I might like to tell Harry. When I wrote it out she smiled, then sat and helped me practice, having me repeat my chosen phrase until I got it down pat.

Then she took the telephone and poked in my home number....

HARRY BEASLEY

When Lee first came out of the coma she couldn't talk at all. She had to write everything down. We would go and visit her. We'd put her in a wheelchair and we'd push her around the hospital. She couldn't say anything, though. She just wrote.

Then one day I was at home and the phone rang. It was Grethe Cammermeyer. She says, "Hi, Harry, I've got somebody here who wants to say something to you."

Then Lee got on the phone and the first words out of her mouth were, "I love you."

That hit me hard. And that's pretty much the point that I knew everything was going to be all right.

I was at American Lake about a week when the staff helped me take my first wobbly steps. Around the same time, the tube was removed from my throat and before long I was talking normally again.

For all my physical gains, the coma had wiped out much of my memory, most likely the result of oxygen deprivation to the brain. Long-term skills like writing and math were substantially diminished. More frustrating, I found myself groping to recall information I'd been given just five or ten minutes earlier.

Emotionally, I was fragile. When my doctors scheduled my first physical therapy session, I was excited but couldn't recall the time of my appointment. In my wheelchair, I'd wheel over to the nurses station and someone would tell me. Then I would return to my room and forget again.

On my third or fourth trip back, I got into a dispute with a male nurse over my medical records, which I needed to bring to my appointment. It ended with him blowing up at me. I retreated to my room trembling. Then I got out of the wheelchair, made my way to the elevator, and simply left. I staggered across the grounds to Grace's office, the one safe place I knew. I fell half a dozen times, bruising and bloodying myself, only to learn once I got there that Grace had departed for the day.

By then, the nurses on the medical ward realized I was gone and contacted the VA police. They found me not long afterward and I agreed to return. But the incident left me scared and infuriated. Despite the objections of my doctors, I insisted on signing out of the hospital.

Harry brought me home, but it took only a day or two to realize I'd made a big mistake by leaving. I couldn't get out of bed or rise from a sitting position without assistance. Climbing stairs alone was impossible. Sometimes, if no one was there to help, I crawled to the bathroom or kitchen. On several occasions, I lost my balance and fell off the toilet.

Harry did his best. He was so attentive that he became more like a parent than a spouse. But he also had to report to work. And though Mona or one of my neighbors would look in on me during the day, I still had long stretches of being alone.

My face was swollen and puffy. The edema was so bad in my legs and feet that I could hardly walk. My hands swelled so much that I had to stop wearing my wedding band because it would cut my skin. My watch band no longer reached around my wrist.

Eating was its own form of hell. The tracheotomy site was healing improperly and soon required corrective surgery. I had no control over the workings of my own throat. Often I'd choke on my food–sending Harry and Michael scurrying to slap my back. That led to uncontrollable coughing, then vomiting. Every episode renewed fears I would aspirate again.

Holding a normal conversation with anyone outside my family was all but impossible. My neck was swollen, with a puckering, baggy scar from the tracheotomy. If I was talking to someone, their eyes would always be drawn to my throat. That, and my appearance, made me so self conscious that I failed to pay attention to swallowing between words. Inevitably, I'd start coughing, which again led to choking, gagging, and throwing up. The humiliation was so great that I just avoided seeing anyone.

Nor did I find much peace at night. I often awoke in agony with cramps in my calves and shoulders, the result of my muscles going unused for so long. Bleary-eyed, Harry would massage them. Then I'd fall back to sleep only to be struck a half hour later by another attack.

What beat me down most, however, was my loss of memory, which in many ways left me like a child in navigating the world:

I could see colors perfectly well, but lacked any sense of how to coordinate them, making getting dressed every day an adventure.

I could no longer tell time, nor did I have much sense of its passage. Ten minutes and two hours were equally bewildering concepts.

Everyday tasks became a source of continual confusion. The washer and dryer were baffling, the stove a puzzle.

Harry came home from work one day to find me in the living room sobbing. I'd been crying all day because I couldn't figure out how to work the coffee maker, an appliance I'd used hundreds of times. Another day he discovered our place filling with smoke and a kettle melting on the burner. I had begun boiling water for tea, forgot about it, and took a nap.

When I started getting around better on my feet, I would step outside now and then for fresh air. I'd walk around a bit then forget which of the brick townhouse apartments was ours. Confounded, I once set off to find help, then got lost. Two hours later, the MPs located me and ferried me home.

Depression engulfed me. When my problems were only the PTSD and the seizures, I always had hope that one day I'd resume a normal life, maybe even go back to work. All I saw now was despair. I felt I'd lost the last vestiges of control in my life. I could do almost nothing without someone helping me. My self-confidence was shattered. Attempting even the most simple activities became a source of dread. Disaster seemed to be waiting at every turn.

Then, in early May, the seizures and symptoms from my PTSD were back full force and I returned to the psych ward. During my stay, on Mother's Day, Michael presented me with a card he had made, which depicted me as an angel. He wrote that if I died, he wanted to die as well, so he could join me in heaven. Reading that left me inconsolable.

14

It now became clear that I was ruining the lives of the people I loved most. Harry was wearing himself out on my behalf and it was clearly taking an emotional toll. Michael, meanwhile, had already been denied much of his childhood worrying about me.

Since the coma, my son had grown even more vigilant. Each day he returned from school and refused to leave my side. Some days I practically had to order him to go out and play. Even then, he'd linger around the window and peer in every few minutes.

When he presented me with the Mother's Day card, the repercussions of my problems hit home. I considered it damning evidence of the harm I was causing.

At the same time, I was stockpiling my anger over all that happened–the rape, the PTSD, the fall down the stairs, the seizures, and now the events surrounding the coma. I began self-medicating with tequila and wine coolers, not the wisest decision given the wide range of drugs I was on. One night, after about six drinks, I ended up in the hospital again for seizures. In the meantime I stopped taking my medications, telling Grace McCardle that I hoped a seizure would strike and finally kill me off.

Grace, in fact, witnessed a lot of my fury during our weekly sessions. To my lasting regret, I also drew her into the vortex.

One day in late May she decided to hold our session outside, at a picnic table not far from the VA's canteen. "I just wish I'd die," I told her. Then, in a cry for help as desperate as they come, I emptied my newly-filled prescription of Clonazepam, a potent anti-anxiety drug, into my mouth and began furiously chewing and swallowing. With Grace stunned and calling behind me, I strode off.

Authorities found me in time; my stomach was pumped; and I was sent to Western State Hospital for several days of court-ordered psychiatric observation.

I tried to resume my life after I was released. I wrote a heartfelt letter of apology to Grace, because I knew I'd done a terrible thing, not only to myself but to her.

Around the same time, I appeared as scheduled for an appointment with Cammermeyer, who by now had also gotten wind of the suicide attempt. Grethe did little to disguise her displeasure with me. "How dare you do such a thing," she said. "This hospital has spent more than one million dollars in resources to save your life. But because you're feeling sorry for yourself, you go and do something so foolish. It's time you stopped your self pity and started to fight back. The only way you'll ever get better is if you get serious and get to work on your problems."

Cammermeyer has a gift for bringing a person into line without crossing into humiliation. She's straightforward, honest, and to the point. What shamed me that day wasn't so much what she said but that I had so clearly disappointed her.

I went home certain that Grethe was right, that I needed to stop running from my difficulties and confront them.

But how? I had no idea how to get better or how to even take the steps to begin.

The best I could do was start small and deal with one problem at a time. My friends Mona and Theresa helped to show me how to cook and do the laundry once again. Michael, meanwhile, helped devise a series of color codes, symbols, and illustrated instructions for the appliances around the house.

Cammermeyer said it would be a year before I'd know the full extent of my memory loss, but I was impatient. I contacted the Literacy Foundation, which sent someone out to test me and determined my reading level was about that of second or third grade.

Michael and his fourth-grade teacher, in the meantime, hit upon the idea of sending home extra copies of his homework handouts—one for him and one for me. His teacher figured this would be a good way to help me reclaim some of my losses. And by teaching me, Michael would deepen his understanding of his lessons.

For hours on end, I sat at the dining room table with my son, revisiting the very basics of reading, writing, and math. We used flash cards; Michael read to me; we even used the face of a clock, so he could show me how to tell time. And every day when he turned in his homework, he also presented mine.

Those were humbling days. But they brought me closer to my son. And I'll always treasure the memory of Michael jumping off the school bus and running across the lawn, waving my latest assignment. "Mommy, Mommy!" he yelled. "You got an A!"

Still, many hurdles remained.

The anticonvulsant drugs kept my seizures in check for awhile, but not without breakthroughs. I might go weeks without incident, sometimes as long as a month, then a seizure would hit like a wrecking ball. Once, I slashed open my head against a coffee table. Another time, I cut up my face on toy parts that

Michael had left on the floor. At the hospital, my CT scan–to check for head injury–had to be stopped because I had a series of convulsions right in the machine. Given my new health problems, particularly the possibility of aspirating again, those convulsions loomed more menacing than ever.

As did the Todd's paralysis. Before the coma, it weakened the right side of my body following a seizure, an inconvenience but something I could work around. Now I was unable to move my right arm and leg for weeks, leading the VA to issue me a wheelchair.

Making matters worse, someone from the VA contacted the Department of Motor Vehicles about my condition and caused the cancellation of my driver's license, thereby killing off my last vestige of independence. (Although I didn't know it at the time, Grace McCardle was behind that, fearing that I would have a seizure on the road and run someone over.)

Given their regularity, the seizures were distressingly expensive. If I suffered an attack off base, Harry and I ended up with big bills for the ambulance and a private hospital stay, which his military medical plan only covered in part, if at all. What's more, to gain quick access to my body, the paramedics and emergency room workers were constantly shearing off my clothes–even when it would have been simple to unbutton or pull them off–destroying every nice blouse or T-shirt I owned.

Life only got tougher when Harry and his unit were assigned to Panama to process some 8,500 Cuban refugees who has taken to the sea that summer. The mission was expected to run four months–exceedingly trying, given my condition and Michael's needs. In the days after Harry left, I had more flashbacks and visions of my rapist. I'd lock myself in the bathroom and tell myself, "He isn't real, he isn't real." Once I even took our handgun out of its strongbox to protect myself against this all-but-authentic vision.

On occasion, I went back to manacling myself to the bed at night to prevent my walking off after a seizure or during a PTSD attack. When Grace heard about this she was aghast, dreading what could happen if there was a fire or other emergency, and made me vow never to do it again.

Through everything, Grace provided the ideal sounding board. I worried, for example, that Michael would have to go to foster care if I was hospitalized while Harry was away, which I felt would reveal that I was a failure as a mother. And I was distraught when one of the chaplains on base intimated that Satan was behind my many problems, trying to shake my faith.

Beyond being a good listener, Grace had suggestions for my more practical problems, such as how best to get around or ways to work through my memory loss. Almost every other psychologist or psychiatrist I ever had dictated to me, as if I was a helpless child. Grace never spoke that way. She posed her ideas as questions, involving me, and helping to rebuild my self-confidence. "What do you think of this?" she would say, or "Have you ever thought of this?"

Since McCardle was an animal lover, it was not completely out of the ordinary one day when she commented that she had recently seen the cutest picture in the newspaper. It was at a community college graduation and a woman was receiving her diploma with a service dog at her side. What made the picture so great, Grace said, was that like everyone else the dog was wearing a mortar board.

"It's amazing what these dogs are doing for people," she said. Service dogs could be found pulling wheelchairs, opening doors, retrieving telephones, even summoning emergency assistance.

"Given how you feel about animals, I was just wondering if this was something you might want to look into."

Acquiring a helper dog had never before entered my mind. But once it did, it stuck. Grace's remarks also touched off the haziest of memories, from my days in Panama. It was that television program Harry and I had seen, *Unsolved Mysteries*, and a woman whose service dog had the ability to warn her of oncoming epileptic seizures. No one really knew how it worked—most likely the animal was picking up a distinct change in his owner's body odor—but work it did. Having advance notice of her seizures, the woman in large part had turned her life around.

During my next appointment with Cammermeyer, I asked what she knew about such dogs and whether that was something I could dare to hope for. Grethe, who owned dogs herself, had a passing knowledge of the phenomenon and of a training program at the Washington Corrections Center for Women, but not much more.

A lot of medical people, enamored with their own expertise and locked into traditional approaches toward treatment, would have dismissed the idea. But Grethe remained as open minded and encouraging as ever. She suggested I contact the Epilepsy Foundation's branch in Seattle, saying people there surely knew more. They did, and sent me a package of information, articles, and contacts, including the Prison Pet Partnership Program at the prison.

As it turned out, this was the very place that the woman on *Unsolved Mysteries* had obtained her seizure dog. In its thirteen years of existence, the program had earned a certain renown for giving prisoners a second chance, teaching them to train dogs for the disabled, among other skills. It was also among the first programs anywhere to identify and turn out a steady number of dogs that alerted to seizures.

I called, and late that August, Grace and Grethe each filled out the program's medical history questionnaire, recommending me.

I also set about completing my application form, which was no small assignment. The memory loss from the coma had severely affected my spelling and ability to form proper characters. But day after day, I sat at the kitchen table with an electronic spell checker and a child's plastic ruler with the alphabet and numbers cut out and traced one individual letter after another, until I'd completed four pages of questions and six more pages that I attached.

As awkward and embarrassing as it was to reveal to strangers the most intimate details of my life, I was willing if it meant finding some relief. There were questions about income, my daily routine, and whether we had any animals. I explained that our cocker spaniel Puppy died recently, and though we did have our cat Sam and the birds, we could probably find good homes for them if that became necessary.

I wrote about the seizures and how they beat me down to the point that I was afraid to leave the house. I told of the dissociative episodes and the postical wanderings, of handcuffing myself to the bed, of my husband being away for months at a time, and how my nine-year-old son had lost much of his childhood worrying about me and watching out for my safety. I wrote of my dependence on friends to shop for me when Harry was gone, of ordering through catalogs instead of going to the mall, of eating off paper or plastic plates because of my experience of having seizures on shards of shattered flatware.

Above all, I stressed that an assistance dog could make a tremendous difference in my life. Even if it wouldn't alert to seizures, I had plenty of needs that it could help with, not the least of them being a calming effect and anchor to reality.

"I live in fear all the time," I wrote. "I can't go anywhere or do anything without my husband with me. I don't even go upstairs in our house because of fear of having a seizure and falling down the stairs or falling out a window. I never leave my house alone because I may have a seizure and walk into traffic or away from my home.… I used to be very independent and on the go all the time. Now I live in constant fear and my home has become a prison and my illness is my warden.…

"A service dog could hopefully learn to seizure alert for me. If it could not learn to alert, the dog would still be of great value to me with my severe post traumatic stress and dissociation episodes.… A service dog would be a godsend in my life and my family's.

"Please help us have some freedom and peace in our lives."

For weeks after I sent in my application, nothing happened. I called, but the response was less than encouraging. Jeanne Hampl, the program's director, was cordial, but she informed me that seizure dogs were hard to come by and they didn't just go to anyone who had epilepsy. The individual client's circumstances had to be taken into account, as well as how comfortable they were around animals, and even how they meshed with their would-be partner.

By October, I was desperate. Harry's command had announced to the spouses on Fort Lewis that his unit's assignment in Panama was being extended two months, through the holidays, bringing me to the verge of a breakdown.

My attacker, Sgt. Stockton, meanwhile, was appearing in flashbacks with disturbing frequency. Once, real as could be, I felt him seize my wrist, terrifying me and causing me to drop the frying pan I'd been holding, sending it and whatever I was cooking across the floor.

Twice that month, I would be hospitalized for PTSD-related problems, including one incident in which I had a seizure during a counseling session with Grace and when I came out of it again thought myself back in 1984.

It was late October when I contacted Hampl again, hoping against hope for good news about a service dog. Jeanne remained non-committal, saying the program couldn't help me at the moment. We spoke about a former inmate-trainer, out of prison at this point, who might work with me if I acquired a dog elsewhere. We also discussed another training organization that might be a possibility.

I swallowed hard. Jeanne was trying to help, but none of this seemed very likely to happen. Then, almost as an afterthought, she mentioned a dog that had come into the program five days earlier and that had been sent off to be neutered just the day before.

It was too early to say if this dog would even make it through the program, she said. For what it was worth, he was a black and tan mixed breed, maybe part Doberman, or Rottweiler. A nice dog, though. His name was Bronson.

"Let's talk in a couple months," Jeanne told me, "and see where we stand."

PART II

BRONSON

Don't try to tell me what's on your mind,
The sorrow of having been left behind,
Or the sorrow of having run away.
All that can wait for the light of day.
                        —Robert Frost
                                "One More Brevity"

15

The surrender card, dated August 19, 1994, was a death warrant.

"Bruce," as the dog was identified, was listed as an eight-month-old Rottweiler mix, though his age and heritage were at best a guess. (He was probably older, in fact, maybe a year to fifteen months.) His attributes, according to what little information was listed, were that he was good with children, a good watch dog, housebroken, and fetched anything. He was given up because he "kills chickens."

Like animal shelters across America, the Tacoma-Pierce County Humane Society was inundated each year with thousands of unwanted dogs and cats. Located in a gritty, industrial section of Tacoma, the shelter was where people came to surrender animals that they either couldn't or wouldn't care for anymore. Too often this was a place where perfectly healthy, potentially wonderful pets went to die.

Fifty-two kennels, each with three or four dogs, were usually at full capacity. The clamor was tremendous as the barking and whining of confused, scared, and simply vocal dogs of all shapes and sizes echoed off the cement-block walls. Would-be owners shuffled by, gave a cursory glance through the wire gate, then moved on.

The minutes of the creatures' lives, meanwhile, ticked down. The shelter staff tried to save as many as possible, but space limitations and the rising tide of the incoming often turned their work into an exercise in probability and numbers. It was difficult for the staff to get to know any of the animals, let alone give them a brushing or provide minimum training to increase their chances of adoption.

Each animal had about five days to win a stranger's heart. Failing that, they were ushered into a back room, administered a lethal dose of sodium pentobarbital, and heaped in a barrel for disposal. The best they could hope for was that a kindly attendant would comfort them when the end came and if not shell-shocked herself from the sheer volume of animals being killed perhaps shed some tears on their behalf.

The cute and cuddly, especially puppies or kittens, were most likely to find homes, while the older or more vicious detainees faced all but certain extermination.

Being of Rottweiler stock with a sketchy history and an indictment for crimes against poultry, Bruce was unlikely to be recommended as a good candidate for adoption. Some shelters, in fact, refuse to allow Rottweilers, pitbulls, or other breeds with reputations for aggression to walk out their doors.

Even if Bruce was of good temperament, as his owners claimed, the numbers were not in his favor. Almost half of the 5,295 dogs surrendered to the Tacoma-Pierce County shelter that year would be euthanized. Being a feisty adolescent who needed consistent obedience work did nothing to help Bruce's chances.

As it was, his past was a mystery. It would only be years later, in researching this book, that anyone would piece together some of the facts of his life, though even that left questions unsatisfied:

Sometime around the late winter or early spring of 1994, the dog materialized on a forty-acre farm just outside of Orting, a small town thirty miles southeast of Tacoma. It was assumed he was part Rottweiler because of his black and tan coloring and somewhat stocky build, though some considered his more narrow nose and figured there was Doberman pinscher in him.

Clearly the dog had been someone's pet. He wore a choke chain, but no identification tags. Also, his tail was docked and the rapid-fire waggling of the stub that remained had an endearing quality. He adored people and seemed to have at least some training basics.

How he arrived at the farm is anyone's guess. Certainly it is not unusual for the ignorant or irresponsible to drive their unwanted pets out to the country and let them fend for themselves. On the other hand, maybe this dog simply strayed too far from home. Or he might have been separated from his owner during an excursion. In the shadow of Mount Rainier, this was gorgeous country, especially along the Little Puyallup River. Hikers and canoeists commonly passed through.

It was the children–seven-year-old Annie and her brother Johnny who was ten–who spied him first. They lived with their parents in the larger of two houses that the farm's owner rented out.

Initially, the kids were wary. The dog's stare was such that it was difficult to know his intentions. Yet it quickly became obvious that he was friendly and liked nothing more than to be patted and to romp about with them.

He seemed to need a name and Annie settled on Bruce. The dog came and went, stopping to play then following his nose and curiosity to other attractions.

Well known to the children were Mary and Mark Bell, who lived nearby in the smaller farm house. Mary was in her late twenties, going to school to be a dentist's assistant, and working in a tavern on weekends. Mark was in his mid-thirties, making decent money operating backhoes and laying pipes for a construction company.

The couple, who had no children of their own, enjoyed chatting and playing with the neighbor kids. That's how they learned about the latest dog to appear on the farm. But they never saw the celebrated canine until they arrived home one day and found him at their door.

Four years later, the Bells would divorce and go their separate ways. But both have fond memories of life on the farm and of the friendly mixed breed who padded into their lives.

MARK BELL

We definitely liked it out there. It was quiet and kind of secluded. We had the one house and then there was the landlord's sister and her family living on the corner of the property. That was all of us. At night, all we'd hear was crickets and frogs chirping in the pond. It was fantastic.

We were only paying two hundred and fifty dollars a month for rent. Our place was really small—a two-bedroom, single-story farmhouse. It had a covered porch that went three quarters of the way around the house. That's where we found the dog. We came home from work and he was sitting up by the door, waiting for us. He was just hanging out and saying, "Hey, I'm going to live here now."

He wasn't a neighbor's. We asked the neighbors. And there really were not that many houses near us. I went uptown and checked the post office, the food center, the restaurants, the tavern and asked around if anybody had lost a dog and looked for signs posted. But nothing ever came up and we never saw anything in the paper.

I don't know if he was a drop-off or if he was lost. A lot of people would drop off their dogs and cats around where we lived and they would always find their way to our farm. But this one was in such good shape and you could tell he already had some training. I find it hard to believe somebody would have just gotten rid of him.

I really think someone lost him. We were less than a quarter-mile from the Little Puyallup River. Someone could have had him down along the river and he ran off chasing something. Something like that probably happened and he just found his way to the farm.

He was very loving. He just wanted affection. He was the friendliest dog you could imagine. All he wanted was to lay by your feet and be petted.

The problem was that we just couldn't keep him in or confine him. He just didn't want to have anything to do with being confined. At first we tried to put him on a dog run. I ran some cable off the one shed and up to the house and attached a line. First I connected it to his collar and then a harness, but he wouldn't stay tied up. He'd find a way to pull out of it.

So I started buying and collecting up fencing and tried to fence him in. Well, he'd either find a weak spot somewhere or he would jump over or go under. He would just work it until he finally got through. He liked being out, but once he was out he really wouldn't go very far. He liked to be on his own. He wanted to be free.

MARY BELL

There were two barns on the property. One was a two-story barn and it was an actual animal barn. It housed cows. And the landlord kept all his hay in there for his cattle and stuff. Every year he would fill it with hay from the field. The other barn was for hopps.

We always had a lot of strays coming in and out. We had a German shepherd for awhile. There were a couple of other dogs that came and went. We'd find homes for them or they would just leave. We didn't really pen them up or anything. But with all that open space, we couldn't not have a dog.

We didn't decide to keep Bruce at first. We had a black lab at the time named Biscuit. She was in the backyard all the time and Bruce started hanging around. So I gave him bones and he sort of moved right in.

Most of the dogs we had were Mark's, but Bruce was more mine. We just got along very well, which is funny, because I'm not a real dog person.

I don't know why the kids picked the name Bruce but it just seemed to fit him right off. I thought it was perfect for him.

We lived right near the river. I used to walk every evening after dinner and Bruce would go with me. I usually didn't take the lab because she would immediately take off. But Bruce was so good. He would just walk right with me. You know, sniff around like a dog does, but he never left my side basically.

He was really protective. Not aggressive, but if I met anybody on the path he would sit next to me and just kind of look at them while we talked.

Everybody was a little intimidated at first because he was a real stocky dog and he had a definite stare. He would just look at you. He wasn't sizing anybody up or anything. He was just alert.

He was really attached to us. I mean, he was content to lay by your feet while you were watching TV or he would follow me around the house. If I took a shower he would go in the bathroom with me and lay on the floor.

One thing he would do is just sit there and look at you. He did that and you could not help but pet him. He was a sweetheart.

He liked tug of war, playing with the rope, tugging on the rope.

We'd bring him with us if we were going somewhere, like the grocery store. My husband had a little Ford Ranger and I'd tie Bruce down in back so he wouldn't jump out. He loved it.

I also remember that the field they grew the hay in, they would spray it with liquid manure and Bruce would go out there and roll in that stuff, and so he had at least two baths a week because he would come home stinking so bad.

The lab usually stayed outside at night, because she was so hyper. She wouldn't settle down. Bruce would just lay down, though, so he was in the house way more than she was. He slept in the living room most of the time, because our bedroom was too small. We had a wood-burning stove, so he pretty much slept on the rug in front of that.

The problem was that we just could not keep him in the yard when we were away. He was really good at jumping over the fence. We had nice sized fencing, but he could jump over anything. If you would hold a stick up, he could jump as high as you could hold that stick.

One night I was out for a walk. I think I had both dogs with me. I was just about to turn down the river road when a car pulled up. It was the neighbors who lived down by the river. "Is that your dog?" she said to me. I said, "Well, kind of, yeah." And she said, "Well, it's been getting in and killing our chickens." I apologized to her and told her that I'd replace the chickens. She said, "No, no, don't worry about it." I said, "We're really trying to keep him in the yard, but we just can't do it."

I never saw him go after the chickens, but I think he thought it was fun. He was far from violent. That's why I was so surprised when she told me that.

So that was one reason we had to get rid of him. The other one was that the landlord, who owned a number of properties, had already been sued once by a tenant who was bit by a dog. We already had the lab and she started getting aggressive and biting at the kids and nipping at people. She bit one of my friends right in the rear end one day going out the front door. So I had to take her to the pound. That's when the landlord said we had to get rid of Bruce, too.

I took both dogs in at the same time. I brought my nephew, who was about seven, with me. Oh, it was just terrible. We both cried all the way there.

My nephew was real confused because I was so upset and I didn't want to tell him what could happen to the dogs. I didn't want him to be hurt. But he knew something was going on, that we were taking the dogs to the pound, and he was full of questions. I was trying to answer him as best as I could, all the while trying not to cry. Every time he'd ask me a question it made it so hard.

It took about forty-five minutes to get there. I took the back roads because the dogs were tied in back of the truck and I didn't want to be on the freeway going that fast with them in back.

They came and took Biscuit. I knew they were going to put her down right away because she was biting. And I knew there was the possibility Bruce could be put to sleep, too. But he was such a good dog that I was hoping they would find a family for him.

I remember telling the people at the shelter, "He's a good family dog." In the waiting room that day there were kids all over the place and they were all petting him. He was so good. He just sat there and let everybody pet him and fawn over him.

I was really upset. As for Bruce, he just seemed like he wasn't quite sure what was going on. Like I said, he was just so mellow. He just sat there. They took him in another room, and we left.

16

I've often wondered what it was like for Bronson–or Bruce, as his name was then–in the days after he was given up to the shelter. This dog lived for people. It must have been a shock to go so rapidly from life on a farm to being crowded in with three or four other dogs in an austere and narrow pen, with a concrete floor and cinder-block walls, the biting smell of antiseptic, and barking and howling from dozens of other scared dogs echoing day and night.

No doubt he was fed and got water, but he must have been baffled about his circumstances. My guess is that he waited for Mary Bell to return. And waited, and waited.

I'm sure, too, that the smell of death pervaded the place. With all of the animals that are regularly euthanized at the shelter, a sensitive dog like Bruce had to know danger was in the offing. How could it not be frightening?

If all that wasn't strange enough, I could only imagine Bruce's reaction a few days after his arrival, when he heard the repeated thump of a tennis ball somewhere in the distance, coming ever closer. Playing ball was one of his favorite activities back on the farm and the sound surely perked up his ears.

Bouncing the ball against the floor that day was Barbara Davenport, a former MP and Army dog trainer who now worked for the Washington Department of Corrections. Sturdily built and possessing a strong military bearing, Davenport trained narcotics dogs for the prison system as well as law enforcement agencies across the Pacific Northwest and into Canada. (Her husband, meanwhile, trained patrol dogs for the Pierce County Sheriff's Office.)

Barbara drew her drug dog candidates from a variety of sources, the primary one being the Pierce County Humane Society. After all, it was the largest shelter anywhere near her facility on McNeil Island in Puget Sound; it always had an ample supply of dogs; and the cost was negligible.

Periodically, Davenport showed up and strode the shelter's aisles, patiently bouncing her tennis ball, and waiting for reaction. Plenty of dogs raised their heads, but the sergeant was after more.

Davenport was looking for young dogs, preferably medium-sized. She cared little about their pedigree or lack thereof. She wanted dogs who at the mere sound or sight of a tennis ball took off like heat-seeking missiles, flinging themselves against the kennel gates with the passion of one possessed.

Any dog that displayed such mania for a tennis ball, Davenport knew, might show equal zeal for finding marijuana, cocaine, heroin, or methamphetamine–if at the end of their quest they were rewarded with the object of their affection.

Illegal narcotics were of major concern in the Pacific Northwest. Interstate 5, which ran from Mexico to Canada, was a renowned trafficking corridor. A shared border with Canada, hundreds of miles of coastline, and a large military population made the region a busy place for the drug trade. At the end of the day, there were more than enough airports, seaports, and individuals with dark intentions to keep drug dogs–and Barb Davenport–gainfully employed for years to come.

When she found dogs she liked, Davenport adopted them and brought them back to McNeil Island. A twenty-minute ferry ride out of Steilacoom, this was also home to the medium-security McNeil Island Corrections Center, the last of America's remote island prisons. Once it housed inmates Charles Manson, for an auto theft conviction long before the California homicides that brought him infamy, and Robert Stroud, before he became the Birdman of Alcatraz.

Each year Davenport ran several classes of law enforcement personnel and their canine counterparts through a rigorous, well-regarded training program. (Despite the location, none of the prison's one thousand-plus convicts had anything to do with Davenport's work.)

Not all of her dog-recruits had the right stuff. Some were too aggressive. Others had physical problems, such as bad hips. And a handful were simply too nice. These animals may have liked a good tennis ball as much as the next dog, but lacked the fire–some say neuroses–to put it at the center of their existence.

Most of the animals who flunked out were returned to the humane society to face a dark fate. With scores of other dogs waiting in the wings, none of the shelter's staff was going to spend much time on those that Davenport deemed unworthy.

Now and then, however, the sergeant spared a particularly nice dog, to be passed along to a different type of organization.

At another prison, the Washington Corrections Center for Women, the Prison Pet Partnership Program had won acclaim for giving convicted criminals a chance to give back to society by preparing dogs for the disabled. (Located in unincorporated Pierce County, just outside the prosperous community of Gig Harbor, the penitentiary was formerly named the Purdy Treatment Center, and to many is still known as Purdy.)

Many of these dogs, too, had been secured from shelters. But unlike Davenport's hellions, these were people pleasers of the highest order. Their job would ultimately be to help level the playing field for individuals in wheelchairs or who otherwise struggled to navigate a world designed for the able-bodied.

These dogs were destined for serious work. It was mandatory that they be even-keeled, dependable, and unflappable. A human life depended on it.

SGT. BARBARA DAVENPORT, MASTER CANINE TRAINER, McNEIL ISLAND CORRECTIONS CENTER

When I'm going down the rows and rows of kennels, I'm bouncing a tennis ball and I'm looking for that dog that disregards the other dogs in the kennel with him. That is, I watch for his eye contact on the ball. He's not looking at me. He's watching the ball as it bounces to the floor and back up. You'll see the ears come forward. The body language of the dog is just totally inclined forward. He is totally focused on that ball.

I'm looking for that dog that will hit the fence or whose head is bopping up and down in time with the ball. He might be in a kennel with three or four other dogs and he totally ignores those dogs and goes for the ball.

I'll stop in front of that kennel and then sort of stick the ball in the fencing and see if the dog jumps up to try to pull the ball through. If I stick my fingers through the fence, does the dog leave the ball and go to my hand? Or does it stay focused on the ball?

For the average dog, going into the humane society is a stressful situation. From the dog's point of view, he's wondering who are all these strange dogs and these strangers handling him. He might not have ever been kenneled before.

If the dog can disregard all that stress and that new environment and still show me he has drive and interest in the ball, then I'm going to pull that dog out.

Before it was renovated, the humane society had a back room, a feed room, where I would bring the dogs I picked. When you store that much dog food, you have spillage, so there's that distraction to the dog. Sometimes there would be a goat or a pig being held in an area just outside the feed room, which would also compete for his attention.

Basically I would toss the ball around and watch how the dog behaved. Does he stop to eat dog food that's spilled or is he just totally focused on getting that ball back? Does the dog line-of-sight go to get it? I don't really care if he brings it back. We're looking for the dog to retain possession of the ball—not for whether he's a good retriever.

Then I'll hold the dog back and throw the ball in among some boxes. Will the dog use his nose to look for the ball? Will he sustain his interest long enough for him to discover where it is?

If the dog passes all these tests, I'll bail him out and bring him back here.

Bruce, as I recall, was in the mediocre category. Maybe he would make it as a narcotics dog, maybe he wouldn't, but we'd give him a chance.

He looked okay in the kennels. He looked okay in the feed room. But he did need a little bit more handler interaction. If I threw the ball in a pile of boxes, for example, he would search for it, but only as long as nothing distracted him. If somebody walked in the room, he would go say hi to that person instead of continuing with his mission. And once he had the ball, I had to be right there to interact with him and play with him because he needed that.

Now some dogs do need that handler interaction in the rewarding process and still make okay narcotics dogs. But the dogs that make the best narc dogs are the ones that don't really care if it's you that throws the ball or if I throw the ball or if the stranger down the street throws the ball.

There are dogs that use the ball to get the handler's attention and then there are dogs that use the person to throw the ball. Do you see the difference?

So, Bruce passed the initial testing at the humane society. Once they're selected, I'll usually crate the dogs and bring them back with me on the ferry.

Once here, I always give them a couple days to get used to being at this site because, remember, these dogs come from private homes or they were running in the streets and they are not used to all of this.

Then we will bring each dog into the compound yard where there's a whole kennel of barking dogs to distract them. We throw the ball for the dog. Does he stop to mark territory? Does he retain an interest in the ball after he goes and gets it? If he drops it and walks away, he fails.

Another thing we'll do is hold the dog back, throw the ball out, then cover his eyes so he doesn't see it land. Then we look to see if he retains the drive to go look for the ball though he doesn't know where it's at, despite the sights and smells out there.

Inside, we'll throw the ball underneath a desk. Will he crawl under the chair and the desk in the dark to get the ball? Will he jump onto a desk or use a chair to get on a desk? Can I coax him onto a desk? Will he accept the ball as a reward that makes him more willing?

Then, to teach the dog to find marijuana, we bring in what's known as a scent box. It's a tall, rectangular wooden box with compartments. You put the dope in the first hole and nothing in the rest of the box. You put his nose on the first hole, where he can smell the marijuana, then immediately throw the ball. After a few repetitions, we give the dog a break, then move around the marijuana. What we're doing is making an association in the dog's mind that when he smells an odor, the ball shows up.

The next step is to ask the dog to search along the box on his own. By this time, he recognizes the box as fun because the ball shows up in the vicinity. What we're looking for now is if the dog has odor recognition. As he moves along the box does he stop at the right hole? Do you see his tail start to wag faster when he smells the odor? Do his ears come forward in attention?

Bruce would have passed all of this. We went ahead and X-rayed him and he had clear hips.

Usually all of the dogs have an equivalent of one week training before they are assigned to the handlers from the different law enforcement agencies. That way, half the team—the dog—knows what's going on in the first week of training.

When the handlers come, we teach them how to reward the dog. We work on timing, how to hold the leash, how to present for the dog, so the dog knows where to look. We go back through the scent box drill, with them working with the dog. Then we move on to simple finds on furniture.

Class started on October 10th. From our records, it does not look like Bruce had a particular handler during that class. That was an oddball class because each handler had his own dog with him already. We had a returning narcotics dog who was getting a new handler; I had a patrol dog from Idaho that came over to be cross-trained; and I had an officer from Spokane, who had been sent with a dog to be trained. The fourth student was technically an observer. So, Bruce would have been one of the dogs that were available that the students collectively all worked with together.

As I remember things, he actually went into the second week of training, which is when it becomes more like work.

At first, the dogs might have to search an entire room. They probably get anywhere from five to eight finds. But they had to do a lot of searching to get those finds. By week two, we're using classrooms for them to search, complete with desks and bookcases, simple furniture. It gets more complicated as time goes by.

Sometimes we'll get dogs that are just really nice tempered and sweet, that love everybody, and it may be that that dog will be too handler-conscious to work independently. He could be afraid of getting into trouble. All he really wants is his own person. If he can have his person, then he's happy. And if his person wants to play ball, well, that's okay, as long as the person wants to.

Well, that's not an obsessive dog. And what we go for here are the dogs that are obsessive.

Bruce was more people oriented. He had such a good-natured attitude. He just had all of the temperament qualities that I would look for to place at Purdy. And, believe me, any dog I would send over to Purdy is almost bombproof.

JEANNE HAMPL, FORMER DIRECTOR, PRISON PET PARTNERSHIP

Barb Davenport and I go way back. I knew her when she was in 4-H. The 4-H leader in Gig Harbor, where both of us lived, also happened to be the local dog obedience trainer. I was in my twenties and Barb was about sixteen. When we met I was taking an obedience class with my first golden retriever and she was training her malamute. I used to drive her to the American Kennel Club obedience shows in Seattle.

After high school, Barb went into the Army and we fell out of touch. But then one day I ran into her at an obedience class. We became reacquainted and found out we were both still involved with dogs.

Over time, we would help one another out. I donated one of my golden retrievers to her drug-dog program. And when I became director of the prison program, she would call to offer me dogs that didn't cut it as narcotics dogs but that she thought had the temperament to be good service dogs. And if I had a dog that I thought would make a good drug dog, I'd call her.

In many ways, we were looking for similar qualities. We were both looking for dogs that were very trainable. We wanted dogs that were not aggressive. Drug dogs can't be any more aggressive than service dogs. You can't worry that they're going to be biting someone. They also have to be friendly. They have to be physically sound. And for different reasons, we both wanted dogs that would retrieve.

The difference is that for Barb's type of dog, a narcotics dog, the ball is the ultimate goal. For a service dog, the ball is a task; finding the ball is not the end-all. Pleasing the person is the end-all.

In July, 1994, I started as director of the Prison Pet Partnership. Every now and then the phone would ring and it would be Barb.

"I think I have a dog for you," she would say.

"Tell me about it," I'd reply.

When she called that October and said this latest one was a rotty-mix, I'm sure I said, "What?" Because at that point in my development as a service-dog trainer, I normally wouldn't even consider a dog that was part Rottweiler. The public perception is that Rottweilers tend to be aggressive. With all the access issues, paramedic issues, and so on, I preferred dogs that the public considered more user friendly, like a golden or a Labrador retriever.

But Barb herself has rotts. She said, "No, no, no, Jeanne, it's really a very nice dog." I trusted Barb. She had working-breed dogs of her own. Plus she handled so many of them in the military. If she told me this dog was trainable, willing to please, and non-aggressive, I believed her. If she said this was a good dog, this was a good dog.

17

By the time Bruce reached the Washington Corrections Center for Women, he was a two-time reject. He had bounced from one institutional setting to another, each with severe restrictions on his activity and worse yet, limited interaction with people.

It is difficult to imagine this animal growing mean or belligerent, like a junk-yard dog. But the dog is a social creature—being among the pack means everything to them—and Bruce was more personable than most. It is safe to say his stress levels were climbing and frustration, if not outright depression, was surely setting in.

Purdy was spacious for a prison. Inside, it was flat and campus-like, with blocks of parched grass and stretches of sidewalk connecting the various one-story structures that either housed or serviced the convicts. There was even a crumbling tennis court, a vestige of a bygone approach to rehabilitation. Never mind that years had passed since anyone stroked a backhand here; when a tour group of politicians or law enforcement officers shuffled through, someone always noticed the tennis court and clucked about how easy the inmates had it. "Where do they keep the horses?" was a typical jab.

Yet prison fencing and coil upon coil of razor wire seemed to mock the open space and dilapidated tennis court. Hanging in the air at Purdy was a sobering awareness of freedom lost and a stark realization that others, with an agenda all their own, held the keys to freedom.

As for Bruce, I'm sure he was initially excited by the new sights and smells. Plenty of people were around, not to mention other dogs, either boarded in the kennels or going through the paces of their daily training and playtime.

The first person he would have met was Jeanne Hampl. As director of the Prison Pet Partnership Program, she oversaw what was then just a handful of inmates who not only trained dogs but ran the non-profit's grooming and boarding operations.

The program was but a small part of the prison's world, but it generated a lot of media attention. For reporters, it was impossible to resist a story about convicted criminals, dogs, and the disabled, all down on their luck, coming together to forge something good for society.

For some inmates, this marked the first time in their lives that they worked to benefit someone besides themselves.

Created in 1981, the Prison Pet Partnership's mission was to use dogs to show inmates a better way. Its impetus came from Kathy Quinn, a remarkable woman who for many years lived on the fringes, caught between an abusive upbringing and mental illness. She was lost and troubled, homeless and traveling around the country, but found comfort–indeed, salvation–in her dogs.

Quinn knew firsthand that animals could heal a broken person and sought not only to spread the good word but to put it into practice for others. She enlisted the help of Leo Bustad, who headed the veterinary school at Washington State University and shared her outlook. In turn, they recruited trainers and pulled together a program with Tacoma Community College to teach the prisoners how to train service dogs. Intrigued, the Department of Corrections signed on.

Quinn, once dismissed as a "mental case," went on to become a Dominican nun. Known today as Sister Pauline Quinn, she has since launched similar programs at other prisons in addition to her extensive efforts on behalf of refugees.

The Purdy dog program blossomed. It won particular fame for placing canines that warned individuals of oncoming epileptic seizures, starting in 1984 with Sheba, a German shepherd that won a degree of fame for helping turn around the life of Angie Barnam, a Gig Harbor teenager with chronic seizures. Others seizure dogs followed and before long, the Prison Pet Partnership was turning out two or three a year.

Only a handful of organizations that trained service dogs had been able to consistently identify the behavior, reenforce it, and help direct it toward something clients could use, getting themselves to safety before a seizure struck. For a dog to display such a skill–one most likely attributed to changes in a person's smell as a seizure draws near–seemed to border on the supernatural. Thus the arrival at Purdy of a film crew from PBS, the syndicated *Unsolved Mysteries,* among many others.

By the early 1990s. however, the Prison Pet Partnership was on the shoals. Prison officials wanted to drop the program, and with good reason. Despite a convict population that had burgeoned to well over five hundred women, the program employed but three inmates. Placement of dogs had dwindled to just a few a year. So little seemed to be getting accomplished that at least one member of the board of directors felt guilty about accepting the state's dollars for the program. And that summer, the pet partnership's director suddenly resigned.

Hampl, a former board member, took command in July. Trained as a nurse, she had stayed at home until her children were grown, then for nine years managed her husband's oral surgeon's office.

But training dogs was Jeanne's passion, and she had years of experience in obedience work, tracking and hunting competitions, and the demanding world of field trialing. She'd been teaching obedience to local dog owners, in fact, since the early eighties. An admirer of golden retrievers, she and her husband had several of the breed at home.

Jeanne was good-hearted. She also had a certain sarcasm and unvarnished honesty that could throw a person off stride. Yet Hampl had another side of her personality that was more difficult to ignore. Her force of will and determination to get things done—her way—was awe-inspiring to some and infuriating to others.

There was no mistaking who was in charge of the Prison Pet Partnership Program. Jeanne made that clear shortly after she took over, when she met with her inmate employees and pronounced a new way of doing business. Their "life of Riley," as Hampl called it, was over.

If an inmate failed so much as one of the state's random urinalysis tests, Hampl decreed, she was fired and permanently out of the dog unit. No more coddling the criminals with an extra Alcoholics Anonymous session or enrollment in prison rehab. This, Jeanne told them, was for the safety of the dogs, who stayed with the prisoners twenty-four hours a day and depended on them like children depend on their mothers.

Hampl also wanted the dogs trained faster. They should be placed with recipients within six months, she said. If they couldn't learn what they needed to know by then, they were never going to learn. Adopt the less than perfect dogs out to outside families as "paroled pets," if possible, but move on.

Some inmates, closely bonded to their dogs and reluctant to say goodbye, had become experts at slowing the training down, sometimes keeping a dog under their care for a year or more. Jeanne acknowledged the emotional needs of these women, but this had gone too far. Certain dogs, she pointed out, had done longer stretches than some of the inmates.

Hampl was also determined to expand the program—to bring in more trainers, rescue more dogs, and help more disabled people. Among Jeanne's early recruits was a tall, attractive prisoner in her early thirties named Yvonne Wood. Six years earlier, the woman was convicted in the murder-for-hire of her husband, an Army first lieutenant out at Fort Lewis. Wood liked dogs and worked well with them, but she had extra value in Hampl's eyes:

Yvonne suffered from uncontrolled, severe epileptic seizures. Her addition meant that after a year or two of going without, the program again had what amounted to a test subject for those dogs who showed a willingness to give warning about oncoming seizures. If one of the animals alerted to Yvonne, Jeanne knew, trainers could encourage and reenforce that behavior. In the end, someone with epilepsy was going to receive not just an assistance dog but a second chance at life.

At five-foot-four, Jeanne was less than physically imposing. As anyone who has witnessed a Scottie or similar breed take command of bigger dogs can attest, dominance and submission had more to do with attitude than size.

Now, even the dogs seemed to know who was boss. Occasionally, a tussle would erupt between two of the animals, while their handlers worked them in the gym or on the grounds in front of the program's unit. All it usually took was the sound of Hampl's displeased voice or her mere presence, stepping to the door to see what the commotion was about, and the disturbance ground to a halt, an attentive hush spreading across the prison's canines.

"I don't get it," an inmate trainer would complain. "We're with these dogs all day. They don't react that way to us."

"Dogs understand the pack setting," Hampl replied. "They know I'm the leader of the human pack here, and if I'm leader of the human pack, I'm naturally the leader of the dog pack."

PETER HAMPL, JEANNE'S HUSBAND

If anything, Jeanne is a perfectionist. When it came to the Prison Pet Partnership, she was a drill instructor. And the girls knew that.

She had certain rules. There was no swearing. The girls had to dress up nicely. The girls that met the public had to wear makeup and comb their hair. A lot of women had tattoos, tattoos they were not too proud of now that they were sober. She looked into having a plastic surgeon come in and laser burn them off. She said if you're going to get a job on the outside, you cannot shake someone's hand with the word "fuck" written across your knuckles.

When she was working as a nurse, she was a surgical nurse. She liked to go in and stop the bleeding and get to the pus and let's get on with it. That's the way she attacks anything she has a real fervent mission for or desire for. When she gets an idea in her head, do not get in her way.

THAT OCTOBER, Jeanne looked Bruce over and scheduled him for neutering with a local veterinarian.

Out on McNeil Island, the drug dogs were rarely sterilized. With the females, Sgt. Davenport found, it made little difference one way or another. But the males lost their edge after the surgery, showing a distinct drop in intensity, the very life-blood of a good sniffer dog.

Service dogs, however, were another story. The less frenetic energy the better. What's more, amorous distractions were simply unacceptable in an animal that had to be out in public.

In Bruce, Hampl had a good-sized, strong animal. If he made the grade, she reasoned, he could pull a wheelchair, roll a stricken person over, or serve as support when they lifted themselves.

This was also a highly aware creature, sensitive to his surroundings and much attuned to humans and their goings on, which raised the odds that he might alert to epileptic seizures. It wasn't every dog that showed such tendencies, but Hampl always kept the possibility in mind. If nothing else, Bruce was definitely a good candidate to become a paroled pet.

Within a few hours of Bruce's arrival, Jeanne ran him through a series of small tests, like all of her potential service dogs. She would, for example, pinch the dog's flank or squeeze one of his paws, creating just enough discomfort to draw a reaction. Or she would give an unexpected yank on the dog's leash–to simulate the leash being caught beneath the wheel of a wheelchair.

Typically, Jeanne winked and said she did all this "because I'm not a nice person," but the truth was that she wanted answers about the dog's temperament: Would he impulsively turn and snap at her? One or two transgressions could be forgiven; after all, maybe the dog was never taught how to behave. But if such attacks continued, the animal had little hope of making it as a service dog.

Equally important, Hampl wanted to know if the dog forgave those pinches. Some tucked their tails between their legs and skulked away, shying away from her from then on. For Jeanne, that simply would not do. She wanted the ones who took themselves less seriously, who quickly forgave, forgot, and were ready for whatever came next. That, of course, was Bruce in a nutshell.

18

As every inmate must, Barbara Thompson found her own way to endure incarceration.

She was thirty-five years old when she entered Purdy, carrying a nine-year, four-month sentence for stabbing her boyfriend with a paring knife during a dispute at a Vancouver trailerpark.

For most of that first year, Barbara kept to herself. She tried to get a feel for the prison landscape and its inhabitants, determining on some deeper level what persona and behavior would best serve her over the long haul.

For her fellow inmates, she projected an aura that said stay the hell away. It helped that Thompson's face had a certain pugnacity to it, a weathered look wrought by a rough upbringing and years of labor under the searing sun as a brick-layer and roofer. And though her sullen expression and body language went a long way toward keeping people at a distance, she didn't hesitate, when the need arose, to outright tell even guards to go to hell.

Barbara side-stepped a handful of physical confrontations with other inmates, mainly by inflating her spare, five-foot-two, one-hundred-and-ten-pound frame to maximum size and roaring. "I'd come out screaming and ranting and raving like I was some big old bad biker bitch," she remembers, "and they would back down."

Thompson witnessed some remarkable happenings in prison, including a mentally disturbed convict from the Special Needs Unit heaving a hefty correction officer against a wall like a sack of laundry, then putting up a terrific fight with the five or six backup guards who came running.

Hollywood depictions of women's prisons aside, the threat of violence was not a major issue in day-to-day life. Petty bickering was a constant, however, and Barbara had her share of disputes. A number of other inmates, in fact, say Thompson went to authorities with complaints as retribution for one personal affront or another.

Thompson admits she was never wild about being around women all the time and was always cautious who she associated with in prison. Too many of the individuals around her, she believed, could only lead to trouble. As a result, she made few allies and if anything put other women off by keeping to herself.

Barbara had no outside visitors and wanted none. She had long been estranged from her family. Her boyfriend, meanwhile, was scratched off her visiting list early on; for the first time, Barbara took a hard look at their history together and concluded that she was better off without him. And though she accepted some outreach visits from a Christian woman in Gig Harbor, she soon told her to stop coming, too. The anticipation of her arrival–heaven help if she was late–combined with the pain of goodbye was just too debilitating.

For awhile, Thompson did exchange letters with one or two male convicts, whom a fellow inmate told her about, but eventually she cut them off, too. "It was just ridiculous," she remembers. "After a month or so, they're writing, 'I love you' and 'You're my wife.' They tell you shit they think you want to hear, but they weren't in any better position than I was."

WHEN IT CAME down to it, Barbara discovered a potent antidote to the stresses of prison life and the wounds she suffered in the outside world. She found an outlet that promised never to betray her, manipulate her, or abuse her in any way. From a single source flowed most everything she needed: affection, trust, comfort, self-confidence, even a sense of feeling a little special in a place that reminded her every day of her sins. Barbara, after all, had her dogs.

She first heard about the Prison Pet Partnership when she was in Clark County lockup, awaiting trial. She loved dogs, was crushed at having to give up her two at home, and knew this would be the most rewarding way to fill the months that stretched before her.

To get into the program, one had to be almost a model prisoner. So it was that after an initial indiscretion–smuggling LSD into the facility from the county jail–Barbara steered clear of drugs and trouble in general. About a year and a half after she arrived, she was accepted as a dog handler.

Like many of the women around her, Thompson had a lot of pent-up anger. The dogs didn't eliminate that rage, but they smoothed its edges. Early on, when the animals failed to listen to her, Barbara would get so frustrated that she'd shout at them. Then one day it dawned on her that the dogs weren't being bad; they just didn't understand what she was trying to convey. What was achieved by yelling?

She joined the program in the spring of 1993 expecting to train dogs. Ironically, she found them teaching her. Lesson number one was patience.

By the fall of 1994, Barbara had worked with three dogs, all of which ended up in private homes but not with the disabled. Cinnamon, her first, was a headstrong keeshond. Working with him, Thompson learned training basics and built self-confidence. Her subsequent charges, Levi and Cheyenne, both German shepherd mixes, were nice but turned out to be ill-suited for service dog work. Both were adopted by a good-hearted correction officer who'd taken a shine to them.

Barbara rarely called attention to herself. She was never among the inmates highlighted when film crews or reporters showed up to do a story on the dog program. She left that to those who were more outgoing and telegenic. She also remained indifferent to most of her fellow inmates, including those she worked with every day. Some considered her surly, a complete bitch, according to one who later became a friend.

With her dogs, however, Barbara let down her defenses. Even years later she spoke as if they were children she had raised and sent out into the world. And why not? She'd spent virtually all her time with them. Some nights they even curled up beside her on her narrow prison bed.

From the very beginning it was understood that eventually she would have to give up the dogs; that was the purpose of the program. Still, it was painful when the moment of parting actually arrived. Cinnamon's owner regularly kept in touch, sending pictures and updates and bringing her in for grooming, which eased Barbara's heartbreak a bit. Also, the correction officer who adopted Levi brought him back every now and then–ostensibly for boarding–to allow Thompson a weekend with him.

Then that fall, Bruce arrived.

He was amiable and handsome. But being of Rottweiler stock, he also had a macho look that appealed to a number of the inmates. Barbara felt she had to have this dog.

Luck was on her side: Having recently placed Cheyenne, Thompson was available to train a new dog and Bruce, for his part, was ready for a handler.

They spent their first days together becoming acquainted and getting Bruce used to his new home. Thompson remembers him as wary at first, tentative around the other dogs and the eighty or ninety inmates that called Unit G-2 home.

Half yellow brick and half brown stucco, with some shrubs and grass outside, G-2 was a medium security building. It was a one-story structure and could almost be mistaken for a college dormitory. That is, of course, if one could ignore, right in the entryway, the guard station, or "cop shop" as the inmates called it, with its bulletproof glass windows. Not to mention the blue-uniformed COs, who prowled the two corridors of small, double-occupancy cells.

Those inmates with dogs–a half dozen were in the program that fall–were housed at the far end of the hall to the left, among the other convicts. Although handlers enjoyed the privilege of having their dogs-in-training with them almost constantly, they were for the most part bound by the same restrictions as the rest of the prison population.

Barbara watched Bruce particularly closely those early days, keeping him on his leash and limiting his interaction with anyone. (Others could pet the dogs, but only after asking permission, a rule that applied to inmates and guards alike. Because the dogs were in training, the handlers had the right to say no, that now was a bad time. In a world in which power so disproportionately resided with the officers, some inmate-handlers took great pleasure in this role reversal, as minor as it may have seemed to outsiders.)

It was hard to say why, but like all of Barbara's dogs Bruce had diarrhea his first days on the unit. Stress was probably a big part of it.

After all, this could be a clamorous place. One former resident of G-2 likened the atmosphere to that of "a really run-down hotel." Murmuring from televisions and stereos in prisoners' rooms, despite regulations about their volume, often wafted down the hall. A loudpeaker blared instructions from the guards. The younger inmates in particular lacked consideration, yelling and laughing past the cells at all hours of the day or night, as they headed to the bathroom, job assignments, or other programming.

Even under the best circumstances, the pressure of prison life was almost palpable, and a dog as alert as Bruce surely sensed the negative vibrations.

Every woman here carried a cross of some kind, be it separation from children and loved ones or the shame of being cast out of society. A handful went so far as to mourn the deeds that brought them here. At night you could often hear someone wailing for what their life had become.

Some convicts disliked their cellmates or had an enemy or two down the hall, which kept the cauldron churning. And though some got along better than others, guards and inmates were natural adversaries. Ratcheting up the stress were the random urinalysis tests and unannounced searches for contraband, which had the prisoners whiling away the hours locked in the gymnasium while correction officers–or "cops," as the prisoners called them–rifled through their most intimate possessions.

(Sometimes, too, the drug dogs were called in, which for awhile brought extra heat onto the inmates in the Prison Pet Partnership. The sniffer dogs, no doubt startled at picking up the scent of their canine brethren, often reacted just as if they found narcotics. The result was an intensified search, which usually turned up nothing, and some insinuating questions.)

For the most part, the inmate-handlers renamed their dogs shortly after the animals arrived. Usually it was just a matter of personal taste.

Barbara looked down at this good boy waggling at her knees and wondered why anyone named him *Bruce;* he wouldn't even come when she called him by that name.

She took a few days to get to know the dog better. She liked how he reveled in having his lustrous black and tan coat stroked, his ears scratched, and how he leaned into her, soaking up the attention like a happy sponge. Barbara smiled at his swagger. This was a tough but sweet dog, she decided. "Just a little stud," was how she put it.

Finally, it came to her. For some reason, this dog made Barbara think of Charles Bronson, the tough-guy actor of *Death Wish* fame. And so Bronson he became. Given what a pushover he could be, the name had a certain tongue-in-cheek quality as well. "It just clicked," Barbara would later say. "And it didn't even take him a day to realize I was talking to him."

DONNA DURNFORD, FORMER DIRECTOR, PRISON PET PARTNERSHIP

When I interviewed Barbara for that job, I was very impressed because she seemed genuine, and she was nervous. She gave a good presentation and presented herself well, but she was nervous. My read of it was that the job mattered very much to her. She struck me as someone who once she decided that she would place her trust and respect in someone, then their good opinion of her mattered.

She was also different temperamentally from the other two inmates. Barbara certainly had a temper and could get riled up easily, but she also seemed to keep her own counsel. I saw that as being important because the program was so small and we depended on each other to get our respective jobs done; it was important there wasn't a lot of collusion. That's probably not the most politically correct term I could use. But I just wanted to have three distinct personalities, for each person to be her own person in her own right.

I knew about her crime and what had gotten her there. She would talk sometimes about living on the street and the bad things that would happen. I don't know if this was my imagination, but it was like she decided that I was a lady and that I needed to be protected from knowing about some of the harsher things she had gone through.

Has she ever talked to you about her mother? I've worked in human services for a number of years and she's the only person I've ever heard in my life say what she said about her mother: "The bitch who gave birth to me." I think that says volumes.

We could be having the most grounded conversation and she would say that. Her face wouldn't change at all. There would be no affect change. She wasn't saying it to get a laugh. And she wasn't saying it necessarily out of any harshness. She had just summed it up that that's the way it was. That was just a matter of fact with her.

The dogs made a world of difference with Barbara, just like they did the other women in the program. There was such a cemented bond with her and her dogs. That was her outlet, her emotional outlet. That was somebody to safely love and care about, and she knew that would be returned unconditionally.

Barb was real protective of her dogs, whereas some inmates would be a little more outgoing and maybe let some of the others play with their dogs. She would let some of the COs interact and play with her dogs, but she really would not let the other inmates. Which was okay with me, as long as the dogs were socialized and well behaved.

At the same time, there was a change that I could see going on within her. I don't mean that having a dog suddenly made her Miss Personality or Miss Gregarious with everybody, but I could see an interchange going on within herself where she was more open. She certainly smiled more. She laughed more.

MARGUERITE RICHMOND, FORMER TRAINER, PRISON PET PARTNERSHIP

I worked with the program when Donna Durnford was executive director. I came in as a part-time inmate trainer, to teach the inmates how to train the dogs.

It was really intimidating at first because I'd never really been in a prison before. But the women I worked with in the dog program I never found intimidating. You see the movies about prison and you see hardened criminals and tough people, but I didn't find that there, at least not with the dog inmates. You could come in and just be talking to them and not even know you were in a prison. You never would have guessed that these were all a bunch of inmates.

They really tried hard to get into the program and once they were there the worst thing they could think of was to be kicked out of the program or to not be in the program anymore. It gave them status among the other inmates and, gosh, they had a companion, a dog that loved them, twenty-four hours a day, in their cell, with them all the time, which was just incredible.

Even the human companionship you might get in prison is not going to be consistent. It's probably not even going to be very friendly most of the time. But here you've got this dog just lavishing love on you. Most of these dogs came directly out of the shelter or out of a situation where they didn't have anybody paying attention to them

either. So you have a dog and a person who are both starved for affection and compan-
ionship. You put them together and they both just really benefited.

Barbara Thompson was wonderful. She was one of my favorite trainers. She was a
very kind, very generous person. Once she caught on, she did have kind of a natural
ability to train dogs. Some people, you can train them and train them and if they're
not a dog person they're just not going to get it. They're not going to get the timing or
they're not going to get the rapport with the animal. But Barbara picked that up right
away.

As I remember it, she had suffered quite a bit of abuse. It always amazed me how
incredibly gentle she was with the animals because usually somebody who suffers a lot
in their life has a hard time learning how to be nurturing and how to be kind. But I
found her just exceptionally patient and kind with the animals.

PATRICIA TOOMEY, FORMER INMATE-DOG HANDLER

How would I describe Barbara? Angry. Vindictive. Selfish. But at the same time, ded-
icated. Hard working. Determined. To be honest, I thought she hated me in there. To
this day, I have no idea why.

She had a lot of anger, and because I worked closer with her for the longer time, I
was one of the ones that felt it often. At one point, her and I almost got in a fistfight.
Everything I did, Barbara ran and told, even when it was wrong and she made up a
lie. That's why I went over to kick her ass! She got my room searched four different
times saying there was drugs in there. She was trying to get my job, my good time, and
everything taken from me.

She wanted nothing to do with none of us. It wasn't until the end that I found out
why. It was because she didn't think she deserved any friends or anybody to have any-
thing to do with her because she was beat so much by men.

One of the very last things I said to her, the very last time I spoke to her, I probably
shouldn't have said it, but I meant it. I said, "No wonder you were beat by men! You
deserved it!" Now that's a really raw statement for a woman to make to another
woman. It was a bad thing. I regret saying it. But I just wanted her to leave me alone.

Believe it or not, I had some great times with Barbara. She worked really hard.
She would work twelve hours right next to my side to build something, or to fix some-
thing, or to paint something. She was as dedicated as the day is long. Not everyone was
like that, so a lot of the work fell to Barbara and me.

If I needed someone to help me build a house I would ask Barbara because she
would do it right and she would work as hard as me. Now, the question is do I want
to put a tool in her hand to hit me with?

FOR MOST of her life, Barbara Thompson pushed her family to the recesses of her memory. As Donna Durnford saw, Barbara spoke of that part of her past not with obvious anger or sorrow so much as cold remove.

Barbara, who had a twin brother, was born in Pennsylvania, the last of four children. Her parents separated while she was still a baby. Her mother took the kids to Southern California, where she married a school system groundskeeper.

Family life was tumultuous, and Barbara speaks of a childhood wracked by beatings and molestation by her stepfather. The sexual abuse began, she says, when she was eight and ended three years later when she told one of her older sisters. The sister went to a minister, who in turn contacted authorities.

Investigators came to the house but nothing could be proved, and her stepfather, who has since died, was never criminally charged. A family maelstrom followed, however, with Barbara at the center. Well acquainted with alcohol and drugs before she was a teenager, Thompson ran away. She ended up in a state juvenile home, then a foster home, where she stayed until completing high school. She fell away from her family, speaking to none of them for years. Her mother she held in particular contempt for accepting the word of her husband, who dusted off an old Bible and swore upon it that he never abused the child, over her own daughter.

As an adult, Barbara learned that her reproductive organs had been damaged, apparently by the abuse, leaving her unable to have children. She also seemed to be on the fast track to the penitentiary, if not a more tragic end. She worked on and off as a street hooker, making a small pile of cash then burning it on "drugs and drinking and all that good stuff."

When she was eighteen or so, Thompson began helping a prostitute with whom she was living to smuggle heroin to the woman's boyfriend in Folsom prison. Barbara, in the process, met his best friend, Charlie Hayes. She was young and reckless, Barbara says, and found it hard to resist what she saw as Hayes' soulful eyes and tattoos from neck to feet. When he was released a year or two later, Charlie hooked up with Barbara. Before long, she was living with him.

It was a crazy life, Barbara recalls. She herself would be arrested at one point, outside of Los Angeles, for reasons now forgotten. The officers at the jail got a load of the "100 percent honky" tattoo on her upper chest and the swastika on her arm, and decided to try something of a social experiment, tossing her into a cell with some black suspects.

"The cops just wanted to mess with me," Barbara says. "So they put me in a cell with all these niggers, because they knew I didn't like them. A couple of them jumped me and they put my head down the toilet and were beating the shit out of me while the cop stood outside my cell and watched. A cop gave one girl a broom handle and she was beating the crap out of me with it. The next thing I knew, the hospital people were there."

Life with Charlie, meanwhile, was nothing if not an adventure. Barbara was nineteen when they got married in a spur-of-the-moment Las Vegas wedding. The next night they were back at his sister's place in California, resting on a water bed, when they got into a disagreement about something. Out of the blue, Charlie grabbed a knife and stabbed at her, but as he did, Barbara spun away and he sliced open the water bed, nearly flooding the place. And though Barbara fled, she returned later that night and stayed with him another nine or ten months. "Until he threw me out of a second story window," Thompson says. "That was the last I saw of him."

She took to the road after that, hitching rides around the country, taking odd jobs here and there, then moving on. The highway finally led back to California, where she found a new boyfriend, a brick mason, whom she stayed with for five or six years. Barbara remembers him as a kind, respectful guy who loved her and would do anything for her. She found such sentiments odd, almost unmanly. Once, she bashed him over the head with an ashtray–"for no reason, just because." She finally ditched him, saying she was going to visit friends in Utah and never looked back.

The late eighties found Barbara in Pensacola, Florida, where she took a job in a garden and nursery supply warehouse. That's where she met Dale Thompson, who worked there unloading trucks. He was a couple years younger and not exactly her type, she says, but they ended up going out, then sharing a place together. And though they never officially got married, Barbara began using his surname.

Dale was a roofer and taught her the trade. When Hurricane Hugo struck in the fall of 1989, they made their way up to South Carolina, where work was plentiful. When the demand finally began to ebb, they headed west, to Vancouver, Washington, where Dale's brother had his own roofing business and needed some help.

They'd been in Washington just a few months, living in a camper hooked up to an old Datsun pickup. The couple had a contentious history, but on the evening of January 24, 1991, fueled by Milwaukee's Best, matters got completely out of hand. As usual, words were exchanged and push led to shove. But this time, Dale wound up with a sucking chest wound.

By the time the police and medical personnel arrived, both Barbara and Dale had come down to earth. Worried, and realizing this was serious business, they concocted a rickety tale about how Dale's car had broken down when he was coming home and how two Mexicans attacked him. The cops nodded, but quickly saw through the ruse.

Dale was air evacuated to a hospital in Portland, Oregon, where emergency surgery saved his life. Barbara spent more time that night worrying about rounding up her dogs, who'd the police accidentally let escape from the camper, than protecting herself legally. She saw no problem with the cops searching the trailer, where they promptly found the bloody knife. She then brushed off her right to an attorney and gave investigators a detailed, self-immolating account of the whole affair.

DEPUTY DON POLEN, INCIDENT REPORT, CLARK COUNTY SHERIFF'S OFFICE, JANUARY 25, 1991

Barbara said that she drank about four beers before Dale got home from work. She said Dale had come home from work at approximately 9:30 p.m., and he had been drinking also. She said that Dale finishes work at about 5:30 p.m., and she had cooked dinner for him. Barbara said that Dale always comes home late, and she is "sick of it." Barbara said they started to argue because Dale acts like coming home late is a joke. She said that they each opened a beer, and continued to argue.

Barbara said that Dale then started calling her a "cunt." Barbara said that Dale knows that she hates to be called that name, and she asked him to stop. Barbara said that Dale continued to call her a "cunt," and then hit her in the chest. Barbara said, "He hit me in the tits to be exact." So Barbara said that she told Dale that she'd like to "kill him," so he reached into the nearby silverware drawer and pulled out a knife. Barbara said that Dale handed her the knife and dared her to do it. Barbara said she took the knife from Dale, and "like an idiot" stabbed him. Barbara said that all she was trying to do was to "hurt him" so that he "got off" her.

Barbara said that she then put the knife in the sink. She said she grabbed a rag and placed it over the wound, but Dale was not bleeding very bad. Barbara said that Dale looked like he was in pain, and when Dale started to cough, blood bubbled out of the cut. Barbara said that Dale told her that he was having a hard time breathing, and Barbara said she knew that she had hurt Dale. Barbara said that she left their trailer and went and called 911.

At 2235 hours, I placed Barbara under arrest for the assault.

Subsequent statements, by both Dale and Barbara, tell of her using a second knife, not the one originally proffered by Dale, to stab him. Different blade, same big trouble.

A judge set bond at twenty-thousand dollars, to prevent her from skipping town. Hearing this, Barbara wanted to laugh: She couldn't have posted bond if it was a hundred bucks. Impoverished and ignorant of the workings of the legal system, she sat in jail until her trial in August. Then a bad situation got worse.

It would be hard for authorities to ignore a domestic stabbing, but Thompson's case clearly had mitigating circumstances. Both parties had been drinking. Dale conceded that he provoked her. And though Barbara did have a winding trail of run-ins with police departments around the country, they were generally minor affairs that revolved around alcohol.

For reasons that remain unclear, Barbara's attorney, paid for by Clark County, apparently rejected the prosecution's offer of a plea bargain. She instead went to trial for first degree assault and was convicted lickety-split. Under mandatory sentencing guidelines for the State of Washington, she was then body slammed with a prison term that spanned the rest of the decade.

Barbara's punishment was so severe that she remembers seeing court bailiffs with tears in their eyes as she was led away in manacles. And arresting officer Polen recalls going home and sharing with his wife how terribly unjust the punishment seemed, given Barbara's circumstances.

Thompson insists her lawyer never told her about a plea offer and says she certainly would have accepted it. For what it's worth, Polen and the prosecutor were prompt to return telephone calls and discuss the decade-old case for this book, but her attorney at the time, Arthur Bennett of Vancouver, failed to reply to numerous messages left with his office.

At such a distance in time, it is hard to say what exactly went wrong. Whether Barbara's attorney or anyone else was to blame, she clearly received more prison time than she deserved, particularly in comparison to many of those convicted of more heinous crimes.

KIM FARR, FORMER CLARK COUNTY DEPUTY PROSECUTING ATTORNEY

That was a terrible case. You know, I've thought about that case several times since then. The reason it was terrible was that we had proposed an offer by which she could have served six months.

I just thought it was such a travesty because I wasn't sure whether the attorney had ever adequately informed her, or adequately informed her of the risks if she failed in court, or whether that was really her idea that she didn't want the deal–because some people do want to run the chance of going through a trial. I couldn't talk to her, so I always was concerned whether she really understood what the offer was and whether that was a real knowing rejection.

That case stuck in my mind for two reasons. One was that I don't think I would give someone a knife and dare them to stab me when we were in the middle of a fight. I thought that was pretty stupid, because they were both drunk. But secondly, my bet was that he'd been abusive to her repeatedly, that she was stuck in an abusive and bad relationship. It just seemed like one of these ugly, downwardly spiraling relationships that tragic things like this happen to. So we thought we'd break the cycle, give her six months, get her cleaned up, maybe get her out of that relationship.

This was a case where we gave a reasonable and I thought a very good offer, given the fact that she stabbed somebody. And it was rejected. I've pondered this case for years wondering whether it was that attorney or whether it was her.

It was just really sad. When we went to trial I felt like I was shooting a duck out of the water. We had all the evidence. There was really nothing to dispute. I couldn't figure out why we went to trial on that case.

19

Most of the inmates liked having the dogs around, or at least didn't mind them. In large part, the animals were a calming force, a pleasant reminder of life outside, as beautiful and as rare as fresh-cut flowers, the smell of the ocean, and countless other pleasures most of the outside world takes for granted. Even those inmates who were not handlers, if they asked nicely, could sometimes pet the dogs, scratch their bellies, or toss them a ball.

Yet not everyone was enthusiastic about the creatures. Some prisoners–often those from the inner city, who grew up knowing dogs only as fierce weapons– were deathly afraid of them. Others considered them dirty, flea-infested, or otherwise inappropriate for large group housing. Living in damp Washington, the dogs did get wet, which led some people to complain about their musky odor.

Most of the COs were supportive. Certain others opposed the program because it went against their vision of prison as punishment. To them, these inmates, some of them murderers, were enjoying themselves far too much and were receiving more public attention than they deserved.

Some guards considered it a matter of preferential treatment. In the limited and small-minded world of a prison cellblock, there was an element of power in possessing something others could not.

Indeed, to have a dog when other prisoners were denied so much as a goldfish was a tremendous privilege. Some of the inmate handlers lorded it over the others, especially those who longed to be in the program or who had been removed.

"Male prisoners are more violent than women as a rule," says former director Donna Durnford. "But at least they're upfront and kind of get it out of their system, whereas women do all this weirdness with each other.

"They would kind of strut and say, 'Oh, I'm in the program,' or 'Oh, look at my dog'. If an inmate that had been terminated from the program happened by they would really pour it on thick with their dog and how cute their dog was. And then after the person got out of earshot they would knock it off. Can you see it? It's like twelve-year-old girls."

Inmate handlers were granted more freedom of movement around the prison than other prisoners. If need be, they could even take their animals out to do their duty after Unit G-2 was locked down for the night. Some, like Barbara

Thompson, took advantage of the opportunity—even fabricated the need—to enjoy a cigarette or just breathe the night air, hours after anyone else was allowed. When a meteor shower or other astronomical event took place, the bladder of virtually every dog in the program appeared to be working overtime.

Some officers didn't mind the extra work this demanded of them. They, too, liked an occasional change of scenery and a smoke, and at times would even mosey down to one cell or another after hours and ask, "Your dog needs to go out, right?"

On the other hand, some guards saw it as a pain in the ass to unlock doors and stand in the chilly night as Bowser circled around, looking for the most perfect of locations to relieve himself. From their viewpoint, the dogs were just another thing to worry about, an element of unpredictability in a place where control was king.

Thompson, and everyone in the program, answered any criticism of the program by saying she worked hard at her job. Like all the handlers, Barbara had a variety of duties—tending the boarding kennels, grooming, and booking appointments—in addition to training. At three-hundred dollars a month, it was the best paying position available to prisoners, followed by kitchen duty at twenty-five cents an hour.

Training, however, was a round-the-clock effort in which the dogs learned not only specific skills, like pulling a wheelchair, but how to behave in the human world. The only way to stop extracurricular barking, for example, or possessiveness, or jumping on people, was to confront the problem as situations arose.

Sometimes the handlers worked with their dogs alone; other times they helped one another, offering suggestions or serving as an extra body to make a training point. Jeanne Hampl provided instruction as issues came up, then met formally with the convicts in the gymnasium for specific lessons.

Added to the mix that fall was a simmering tension between Jeanne and Barbara, which the other inmates saw and Bronson and the other dogs surely sensed. Hampl had a mission when she came on as director—to breathe new life into the dog program—and nothing was going to stop her. If some inmates' feelings got hurt along the way, so be it.

For their part, the prisoners who were in the program before Jeanne arrived had largely made up their mind about the new director before they really knew her. Thompson, foremost of the unwelcoming committee, bridled at Hampl's imperious manner, likening her to "Sgt. Carter" on the old *Gomer Pyle* television show. She felt Jeanne looked down upon the prisoners, showed no interest in what the handlers already knew about training, and considered her training techniques too harsh.

Both women were strong willed. Potshots came from both sides, according to one inmate onlooker, with Barbara in particular rarely letting pass an opportunity to express her opinion of her new boss.

The tension made for considerable discomfort among the trainers and, at times, the program's community volunteers. Everyone could hear the time bomb ticking between the two and knew it couldn't continue forever. Until it finally went off, however, everyone went about the work at hand.

Barbara started Bronson with the basics, making sure he was house-trained and helping him get comfortable with his plastic crate, used for transporting dogs but which also served as safe haven and bed. She also set to work on your everyday "sit," "stay," "down," and "come" commands.

The inmate noted that Bronson seemed to cower or sometimes even drop flat on the floor if she raised her hand around him or moved it too quickly. Barbara suspected he had been abused somewhere along the line. Whether that was true is open to question. But this certainly was far from a fearful animal. His general deportment, in fact, was confident and happy-go-lucky.

Although no one knew where Bronson would ultimately be placed, Jeanne had him pegged as a potential aide for someone with disabilities. As such, Barbara began teaching him tasks like picking up objects from the floor, retrieving a telephone, opening doors.

The driving force behind modern dog training, Thompson learned from the beginning, was positive reenforcement. No bullying or shouting at the dogs. And certainly no striking them. Dogs wanted nothing more than to please their people. Like humans, they did best when their good behaviors were emphasized and their bad ones quickly corrected and forgotten. Praise and encouraging pats worked wonders, as did food rewards. It helped immeasurably to make the lessons seem like play.

Bronson, Barbara soon discovered, loved peanut butter. She'd buy it for him at the canteen as a special treat and enjoyed watching him eat it, eagerly smacking his lips and working the sticky stuff with his tongue and jaws. Squeeze cheese was another favorite.

Often, Barbara would incorporate one or the other into his training, to pique his interest. She might smear some peanut butter or squeeze cheese on a wooden dumbbell, for instance, wait as he licked it off, then praise him to high heaven when he eventually picked up the item. Connecting the action to a command, she fortified the behavior.

Soon, Barbara would smear some peanut butter on a door knob and have Bronson climb up and start licking. Invariably, his paws would get behind the knob, as he tried to hang on. With a lot of encouragement, repetition, and spreadable treats, he went from licking to turning the knob to actually getting the door open a few inches. It was a gradual process, with each small step winning him high praise, until he finally managed to open the door all the way.

One day, Thompson saw a fellow handler teaching her dog to turn on a light—a big help to a disabled person who might have trouble getting up—and decided to try it with Bronson. She put some peanut butter on the switch in her room, summoned the dog, and tapped the wall plate. Up he went, front paws against the wall, and commenced licking. The light, of course, went on and Barbara showered him with compliments. Similarly, Barbara taught him to extinguish it. Bronson had the tasks down in just an hour, and Thompson moved on to other matters.

Late that night, the inmate was roused from her sleep by the flicker of the bright fluorescent light of her room coming on. A few seconds later, it went off. Then it came on again. Then off. On, off, on, off. Wrapped in the cobwebs of sleep, Thompson had no idea what was happening. Then it hit her: The dog was working the switch.

"Finally, he left it on," recalls Thompson. "I turned around and I said, 'Bronson!' Well, he's got this little blue rubber ball in his mouth and his tail was wagging so hard, his whole little butt was moving so hard, it was like he was saying, 'Come on, let's go out and play!'"

Barbara was proud of Bronson's prowess, yet her heart ached with every new achievement. She'd grown used to having her dogs as long as a year. Now, not only was Hampl breathing down the convicts' necks to prepare the animals within six months but here was Bronson, whom she adored, rapidly absorbing every lesson. Sometimes he learned a new skill in just two or three attempts, then would look at her merrily, anticipating whatever was next. She was running out of things to teach him, which would only hasten his departure. Or as Barbara put it years later: "He was getting too smart for his own damn good."

Intelligence, playfulness, and a gentle nature were all positive traits. If Bronson was to be a service dog, he also had to be unflappable. He couldn't be distracted when he was with his owner in public. Besides putting his person at risk, it was unacceptable to cause a commotion in a restaurant or shop, where dogs were normally forbidden. The goal was to be unobtrusive as possible.

When Barbara first came to Purdy, she thought the incessant noise would drive her insane. And though she never really got used to it, she now sought it out, as a test of Bronson's resolve. She brought him out by the tennis court, for example, where the special needs prisoners had their recreation period, always a raucous affair. Or, she'd walk him outside G-2, where a group of prisoners might be decompressing, cutting loose a bit in gales of laughter or hollering at one another. And though he was wary at first, Bronson seemed to quickly gain confidence.

Often, Barbara and the other handlers took turns putting their dogs in a down-stay, then stepped back as the others worked to distract them. The women skipped by, leaped over them, yelled, tossed doggie treats before them–anything to draw a reaction, which in turn would be immediately corrected. Thompson remembers Bronson as a rock, looking to her with hopeful eyes, but never budging until she said okay.

Thompson credited Bronson alone for his training success. Indeed, he was one of those dogs who appear periodically, when the stars are in proper alignment, who's so bright and excited about learning that his trainer seems diminished.

Yet with service dogs, it was critical, no matter how smart the animal, to work as part of a team. Barbara deserved praise for planting those seeds with the dog, as well as for nurturing, encouraging, and otherwise fostering his development.

Constantly together, Barbara and Bronson became a familiar team around the prison, the dog on his leather leash, padding amiably by her side. "Here comes the tough guy," someone would say of Bronson, as they strolled down the corridor.

Except on the rarest occasions, Thompson refused to leave Bronson by himself. Dogs were banned from the cafeteria, but Barbara rarely ate there, preferring instead to buy canned items, such as chicken, tuna, or soup at the canteen and have them in her room. And because the library prohibited dogs, Thompson limited her trips to once a month, stockpiling her reading material weeks in advance.

Their room–or "house," as the inmates put it–was a tight fit. Eight by ten feet, with concrete block walls and a cold linoleum floor, it was starkly furnished with a pair of bunk beds, a desk, and a dresser. Prison regulations required that the dogs not sleep on the beds with the inmates, though how strictly that was enforced depended on the guards on duty, whether they got along with the inmate in question, liked dogs, or were sticklers for such rules.

For the most part, Bronson slept in his crate, its door wide open, comfortable on soft blankets, not far from Thompson's head. He also had a pillow under the desk if he wanted a change of location.

Usually, the inmates in the Prison Pet Partnership had a say about whom their cellmates would be. After all, if a newcomer had an aversion to dogs, or a disregard for them, or if the person got along poorly with the handler, it would only impede training.

But now and then, the handlers had to take whomever the prison gave them. Before she had Bronson, Barbara briefly shared a cell with a practicing wiccan, or witch, who was in on drug charges, but finally convinced the powers that be to house the woman elsewhere.

Thompson hit it off better with thirty-one-year-old Tami Croft, who was doing a short stint for attempted robbery. Tami had been sent down to talk with Barbara, to see if the two prisoners could get along and if she could handle sharing a cell with a dog.

As it turned out, Barbara said okay. Tami had never been to the penitentiary and constantly worried about her parents, particularly her father who had emphysema and an eighteen-acre farm to run. She only lived with Thompson a couple months, but in that time they became friends, a real achievement considering Barbara's disdain for most of the inmates. It helped that Thompson was seven years older and by then knew the ways of prison life inside and out. While others only saw Barbara's anger, Croft considered her a respectful, stable presence, even a comfort.

As was Bronson. Tami, who loved dogs, was initially wary of the Rottweiler cross, but soon found what a nice animal he was. "Bronson was just a big lover," she would recall years later. "He was so smart. I feel that he could almost read your mood, whether you were happy or if you were worried or if you were depressed.

"I remember sitting at the desk writing letters home and he'd come and put his head on my leg and just look at me with those big brown eyes. It was just like he was giving me a big hug."

Along with privileges, the dog handlers were given a considerable degree of trust. They regularly met with outsiders, for example, who came to the prison to work with their future service dogs or to have their own pets groomed or boarded—no small accommodation in a place where suspicions of everyone who entered the gates ran high. The inmate-handlers also had access to an outside telephone line. And though it was for scheduling appointments, not personal use, just the opportunity to speak to someone different for a change was like a gift from heaven.

As with any job, there were unspoken perks. Barbara, for instance, won the friendship of certain COs who were dog lovers, which occasionally resulted in unauthorized favors. One guard who boarded his pet brought along a slab of cooked prime rib. He handed it over to Barbara explaining that it was for his dog, though it was understood that the inmate should enjoy the lion's share, for taking good care of his best friend.

It was in that spirit that Thompson once told the guard that his dog sure loved avocados and next time around found her favorite fruit among the canine's effects. "My God," she recalls. "An avocado! You'd kill to get stuff like that in prison."

For all the pleasure such kindness brought, Barbara knew that freedom remained years away. She resisted even thinking about it, shaking her head at the women who tortured themselves by marking the days off on their calendars or who sat around and boasted of the sexual exploits they would enjoy when their release finally came.

Still, on those nights that she took Bronson out to do his business, Thompson occasionally gave herself permission to ponder a different existence. Under the Pacific Northwest sky, in the stillness of the prison yard, she took a drag on her cigarette, and let her mind wander.

Barbara liked to imagine Bronson as her own dog, out in the real world. In some of her reveries, she'd take him to a river, where he could chase balls and swim to his heart's content. Other times, it was the beach. In every scenario she saw herself spoiling the dog rotten and loving every second of it. But in the end, Thompson always cut off those fantasies before they got too far along, snuffed out her cigarette, and headed back inside.

"Why depress yourself?" she said.

BARBARA THOMPSON

From the time I first saw Bronson I thought he was gorgeous. Perfect coloring. That look in his eye. He was very alert. He was very aware what was going on around him.

Bronson and I clicked right off the bat. I was close to my other dogs, but not like I was with Bronson. He really took a piece of my heart. He used to smile at me all the time. Like show his teeth, but it wasn't the mean kind. He was always happy. I don't remember him ever waking up in a bad mood or anything.

Have you ever met a person that you instantly like? That's Bronson. To me, he's like a person in a dog's body. He's got a personality. He's funny. He's a happy dog and he's pretty affectionate. It seemed like he would go out of his way to make people feel comfortable. He just seemed like a really caring dog, like he picked up on something out of each person.

I remember when they denied my appeal. I wasn't crying or nothing but I was really disappointed. It was, "Oh, my God, what am I going to do now?" Just down in the dumps. I'd be sitting on my bed and Bronson would come over and he would push my hand up with his nose and want to be petted and want to play. I'd be like, "Get away from me." He would be very persistent. In fact, he came up on my bed a couple times and tried to put his big body on my lap and he'd lick me and stuff. I'd say, "Okay, okay, I'm getting out of my slump."

Now, the dogs in the pet program do have to be nice. You don't want them walking around outside in a crowd of people, or even inside the prison, growling. That's a big no-no. You cannot have a dog with aggressive behavior out there as a service dog.

It has happened that dogs have growled at guards. First you reprimand the dog. You tell him no. Then what we would do is get the dogs to know the officer, because some dogs don't like the uniform. Sometimes the officer would bring in little treats or something and you allow them to give your dog a treat and to pet him.

Bronson got along with all the COs. But I think there was one time ... Well, there was a big black cop, Harris, who was an arrogant asshole. Bronson was really good with everybody. But one time Harris walked by me or said something to me and I was like, 'F-you,' because I talked to the cops like that if I had to, and he got on my shit.

Well, Bronson started barking at him. Of course I wanted to say, "Good boy!" But you can't do that. I had to correct him in front of the cop. And you know, after that Harris and I became friendly and Bronson was okay with him. I think Bronson picked up a lot of that from me.

When I was training Bronson and he learned something new, I'd feel proud. I had to go and tell everybody and show everybody. He progressed so fast. People were amazed. They'd say, "God, Barbara, you're doing really well with the dog." I'd say, "Thanks, but it's really not me; it's the dog." I had a small bit to do with it because I led him there, but he did all the work.

Of course, I didn't want him to learn that fast. I wanted him to be like my other dogs. Not that they were dumb. They were just a little slower. With Bronson, you could show him one thing once and he would do it. It was nice, but it was like, "Do you have to be such a little smart aleck?" I would have loved to have had him at least another year.

Somebody told me one time that they thought Bronson was the runt of the litter. That could be it, that he's overcompensating. I don't know. I just think he's got a wonderful personality. I think that's just how he was born.

Some of it is being a dog, but a lot of it isn't. For awhile there I thought Bronson had human parts in him. Really, I did. I've met a lot of dogs and I've had a few, even before I went to prison, and Bronson was the best, I swear.

20

Yvonne Eileen Wood, who was doing forty-six years for directing the murder of her husband, was not your typical prisoner.

Most women who came to Purdy were hard edged. The penitentiary was hardly a place of perfect smiles and stylish haircuts. Difficult lives were often etched on the women's faces. Bad decision-making brought virtually every inmate here, along with poverty, lack of education, and dysfunctional, often violent, upbringings.

Yvonne, however, was over six feet tall, good looking, well spoken, with a disarming sweetness to her personality.

She grew up the youngest of three daughters in a middle-class family in California's San Joaquin Valley. (She and one of her sisters were adopted, she reports.) Her father was a manager in the fruit industry, her mother a housewife. Yvonne even had a couple years of college at UCLA behind her before she got married and began the itinerant life of a military spouse.

Wood says her husband, a first lieutenant out at Fort Lewis and a former MP, would physically abuse her, sometimes clubbing her with his service baton. She used that accusation, in fact, as well as the promise of proceeds from a $150,000 life insurance policy to convince her Army Ranger lover to enter the couple's home one night in May 1987 and slay her husband. The plan, which was also known to others, was to set up the killing like a burglary gone wrong.

At first, Yvonne, then twenty-six, appeared to be a sympathetic figure, the grieving widow. But when the case broke wide open and she went to trial, prosecutors painted her as cold-blooded as they come. Richard Wood was shot five times, but is believed to have died only because his wife intentionally held off before summoning help. All this happened while the couple's four year old was asleep in bed.

Besides her appearance and background, Wood was also set apart in prison by furious grand mal seizures, which struck an average of twice a week. She claims they were the result of her husband's beatings, though given the prosecution's portrayal of her as an expert manipulator and liar, it's difficult to know for sure.

Yvonne's seizures were fearsome to witness and perilously long lasting. No sooner than she recovered from the cotton-headedness and full-body soreness that followed one event, she would inevitably be lashed again.

Her medications helped little, if at all. And being confined to prison meant that almost every seizure was a public one, often before dozens of women, and usually involving emergency transport–whether necessary or not–to the clinic. Like a lot of people with uncontrolled seizures–myself included–Yvonne says she wondered how much more she could endure and whether she even wanted to continue living.

Her perspective began to change when one of the inmates from the Prison Pet Partnership told her about seizure dogs and their knack for warning that a person was soon to go into convulsions. Yvonne knew dogs were capable of some astonishing feats, but she never heard of this.

What she discovered was that seizure dogs were among the most elite service animals working with the disabled. Around the country, only two or three reputable organizations that train traditional service dogs also turn out seizure dogs–both for their alerting abilities as well as post-seizure response work, such as rolling a person over, or summoning help. Most groups refuse to get involved, simply because the stakes are so high. With their person unconscious, a seizure dog's work can truly become a matter of life and death. Adherence to training becomes critical, with little room for error.

One day, one of the prison program's dogs–Petey was his name–started getting antsy around Wood, pacing around her and seeming distressed. When the seizure hit, it was clear that the dog had been alerting.

That whet Yvonne's interest. She enrolled in some classes in dog grooming and basic obedience that Tacoma Community College offered at Purdy, did well, and found a place with the Prison Pet Partnership.

So it was that Wood, in addition to the duties she shared with everyone in the program, became the human acid test for dogs that showed potential to seizure alert. Those animals that seemed to behave strangely around Yvonne before or even after a seizure would be temporarily transferred over to her, to better monitor the dog's reactions.

What sounded like a simple job–hang around and wait to have a seizure–was in reality fairly demanding. Jeanne Hampl had to constantly implore Yvonne to pay attention to what the dogs were telling her. It was all consuming, to always be watching and waiting.

It also wasn't easy to know when the dogs were alerting, for the changes that came over them, especially early in the process, could be subtle. For example, in detecting oncoming seizure activity–whether it was a change in odor they were picking up or an electrical discharge from the brain–a dog might disobey basic commands and refuse to settle down. Who could blame Yvonne for thinking this was just a young dog feeling feisty? Yvonne needed to learn to read the dogs, and what's more, to trust them.

Hers was a risky job. Not every dog responded in a predicable manner when they saw someone writhing about in convulsions. Some ran and hid. But others heard a primitive call and out of fear or an instinctive need to cull the weak from the pack, tried to attack her. On more than one occasion, fellow inmates diverted dogs with bad intentions away from Yvonne's flailing body. And though she didn't let it consume her, Wood had legitimate cause to be cautious when she was alone in her cell with a new dog.

Wood regarded the program as a blessing. She understood what people with epilepsy were going through when they spoke of the seizures beating them down and how much they loathed the drugs and their forced dependence on others. By working with the dogs and in turn the recipients, Wood could direct her own painful experience with seizures toward helping others.

Bronson was a case in point.

The Prison Pet Partnership had an office within the confines of G-2, kitty-corner to the guard station, right down the hall from the inmates' cells. Once a sewing room, it was now equipped with all the basics–an old computer, desks, and some phones. (Jeanne Hampl's office was an adjacent cell.) All of the inmate-trainers came by the office at some point, to say hello and chat, book appointments, or follow up with clients.

Some time around mid-November, Yvonne came in, apparently to grab something for the dog she was training. Barbara Thompson and Bronson followed. And though Barbara had been warned that flickering lights could set off Wood's seizures, she simply wasn't thinking as she went over and flipped the switch.

The fluorescent lights blinked on and instantly Yvonne dropped to the floor in spasms. Thompson had never seen Wood–or anyone for that matter–have a seizure, but she knew enough to quickly get her away from the furniture, so she wouldn't hurt herself, and gave her some room.

Bronson, in the meantime, rushed over, clearly concerned. He brought his front paws up and rested them on Wood's torso as if to hold her in place and urgently licked her face. Even when the emergency team carted her off on a stretcher, the dog refused to leave Yvonne's side, determinedly following all the way to the clinic.

Bronson's entire focus became Yvonne. Even when the clinic staff said no dogs were allowed, normally obedient Bronson was having none of it; Barbara had to forcibly pull him away.

Obviously, something significant was going on in the dog's mind. Bronson gave no warning of the attack–it happened too fast–but his intense concern made Hampl wonder just how aware this dog might be to her condition.

When Wood was released from the clinic, Jeanne instructed her and Barbara to exchange dogs for about a week. Their cells were but a few doors away from one another, so Thompson could still visit with him. But this would be a good test of the extent of Bronson's talents.

Yvonne says she was skeptical. She adored Bronson, having a personal taste for Rottweilers and this friendly young dog in particular. Up until now, however, the only dogs that picked up on her seizures were the more typical breeds that came through the program, such as golden retrievers and Border collies.

Yet Bronson did come to forewarn of Yvonne's seizures. It took a couple of times for her to be sure, but as he circled her with a certain urgency and the seizures in fact swept over her, it seemed apparent he was on to something.

It was right around this time that I happened to telephone Jeanne Hampl yet again to see if my chances for obtaining a dog had improved. She told me now there might be good news. She said that Bronson, whom she had mentioned previously, was showing indications of seizure alerting. I still had a long way to go–Jeanne had yet to even meet me–but now she said there was a chance that this might, just might, be the dog for me.

YVONNE WOOD

I have probably trained about twelve seizure dogs, eight of which were placed and four that didn't make it for other reasons, whether it be health reasons or they made it and didn't certify afterward.

I'm not really sure why some dogs alert to seizures. I've met with researchers who have come out and they were asking, "Well, is it a chemical imbalance? Is it something you put off?" I'm really not sure. But I know that it's accurate. Whatever it is, it's consistent. Most of the dogs we put out were running like ninety-eight percent accurate.

The time span that they alert differs from dog to dog. I had one dog alert forty-five minutes before a seizure and to me that's a little too far in advance, because you sit there and say, "Okay, when is it coming?"

If you talk to seizure-dog recipients, or even just service-dog recipients, and I include myself in this, you'll find they say things like, "This dog has given me back my world," or, "This dog is like my left arm." To recipients, these dogs are a body part.

Being able to go out of the house on their own, these dogs give people a level of independence that even Jeanne Hampl sometimes forgets.

JEANNE HAMPL

I probably gave Yvonne more seizures than other people. We did have to be careful. I remember we had an alarm system go off one time, which had a strobe light, and I couldn't get it to go off. Yvonne went down like a stone because it was just flashing away. And when we would go into the gymnasium, I would have to tell Yvonne to stay out until I got the lights on, because they were those old fluorescents that shot down the tube back and forth.

Yvonne would seize and three-quarters of the dogs in the program would just go about their business. They didn't even care that she was on the floor. The dogs that went on to seizure alert were dogs that were like, "Oh my God, we need to take care of this."

It's really an interesting phenomenon, but I had inmates come and tell me that their dogs were responding to their migraines or to another inmate's migraines, and all of those dogs also seizure alerted.

Usually if you get non-trained response behavior to a seizure, most of those dogs will seizure alert. Now, what I mean by non-trained is that I haven't told this dog a thing; I haven't said to this dog lie down, be still, anything; the dog just assumes what to do and is appropriate in the presence of a seizure.

When they did alert, we would put the dog on a down-stay. We would reward the dog while the person was seizing. A lot of praise.

And then of course when the person started to wake up, and the dog would become more interactive, starting to nudge or lick, we would encourage that and tell the dog how wonderful it was. That's how we would encourage that intimate response behavior. You reward the dog for doing that, but you can't teach it.

The other response behaviors—get the phone, get help, help me stand up—all of those things are trained. We don't even have to teach the dog how to do it with someone seizing. They just put two and two together.

BARBARA THOMPSON, like all of the inmate-handlers, had a powerful attachment to her dogs that incarceration only heightened. Being a loner no doubt contributed to Barbara's need for an understanding, true-blue companion. So strong was her connection that even when Yvonne was seizing and all the commotion was erupting, Barbara felt a stab of jealousy. This was her dog, her pride and joy; yet in an instant Yvonne seemed to be all he cared about.

Most of the inmates had similar stories. Yvonne herself tells of a Border collie she trained that was so attached she would rarely leave the prisoner's side. Then one day the man the program was considering to receive this dog came into the prison. "Brigitte acted like she didn't even know me," Wood says. "She walked away from me, walked by him, sat by him, was perfectly content and happy, and never looked back."

Dogs, of course, have their reasons. Bronson had his own drives, primal in nature and apart from human experience. Perhaps, as Jeanne Hampl suggested, all dogs have their role within the pack and Bronson saw his as caregiver. On the other hand, maybe it was just his personality. Maybe Bronson wasn't much different than those humans who devote themselves to helping others.

Barbara understood she shouldn't take it personally, but it still stung. Nor did it make it any easier when Jeanne wisely asked her and Wood to exchange dogs for awhile. Or later, when a volunteer would take Bronson away from Thompson for day trips, to work on and test his skills in shopping malls and other public places.

It all served to remind her that Bronson would soon be out of her life. Knowing this, Barbara made sure to have his photograph taken, as she had with every dog she trained.

One day that November, Thompson had a fellow inmate employed by the prison take two pictures of Bronson, at a dollar-twenty-five each.

Taken one after another, the photographs show the dog sitting on the grass with some bushes and Unit G-2 directly behind him.

One shot is poorly composed, slightly askew, showing mostly lawn. It is taken from too far away and includes the shadow of a pole running across the dog's hindquarters. The second is better. Bronson is at center stage. He looks proud. He's wearing a thin choke chain, his mouth is closed, his ears alert. A certain spunkiness is evident, too, as he gazes at the camera like he can hardly wait to be released so he could romp around with the other dogs.

Just before Thanksgiving, Barbara took the nicer of her Polaroids and along with a brief letter, sent it to me so I could see what the dog looked like. When that snapshot arrived, completely unexpected, it was like a gift from above. Bronson was so beautiful. I held the snapshot and my eyes just welled up with tears. Michael saw that and thought the letter was bad news or that Barbara had written something that hurt my feelings, and I had to explain that these were a different kind of tears. I was crying because I was happy, I said.

IT HAD BEEN a tough autumn. Harry was away in Panama. The seizures and flashbacks persisted for much of October, striking particularly hard at the end of the month. After the MPs at Fort Lewis found me in a field near our quarters, "combative and unwilling to answer questions," with a bloody gash on my forehead, I ended up spending a week on the psychiatric ward at Puget Sound Hospital in Tacoma, because no beds were available at the VA.

For obvious reasons, patients tend to get more attention at private hospitals than at the Army facilities and the VA. There's often more staff and a greater choice of activities, including occupational or art therapy. But Harry's military health plan only covered about two-thirds of the bill, which meant the meter was running to the tune of two or three hundred dollars every day I was at Puget Sound. For a family of three living on a soldier's salary, that was no small worry.

Also gnawing at me was that Grace McCardle had recently revealed that she planned to retire within the next year. Her children were grown and she wanted to travel, visit her family and friends and see the country a bit while she was still able. Finding a counselor that I felt comfortable with and trusted had been so difficult. Where would Grace's departure leave me?

Of course, I had more immediate troubles. For much of my Puget Sound hospitalization I had lapsed back into the world of private Proctor. Early on, I asked a bewildered staffer why I hadn't been included in formation that morning. At another point I fell into seizures, having a run of four before the medical team could get them under control.

The doctors thought my condition sufficiently troubling to contact Harry's superiors, who summoned him back from Panama, which only increased my anxiety. Harry was trying to get his military career back on track and disruptions like this didn't help. He wasn't happy to be singled out to return home. (He later had a change of heart, however, for while he was gone the Cuban refugees in Panama rioted. In restoring order, which Harry undoubtedly would have been in the thick of, more than two hundred American soldiers were injured, some quite seriously.)

I was hospitalized for a week. Six days after my release, I was brought back, this time by a Washington State Patrol officer who came upon me early one morning along the side of Interstate 5, which ran by Fort Lewis. Most likely, I had a seizure at home and in my postical state simply started walking.

Although much of the incident is a blur, I could recall bits and pieces. I remember walking along the side of the highway, in the same direction as traffic. A cream-colored pickup stopped at one point and the man behind the wheel called to me, asking if I needed a ride. He frightened me and I backed away until he finally drove off.

When the state trooper found me I was several miles from home, sitting on a wall near an overpass, trying to pull together my thoughts. He asked my name and all I could tell him was Leana.

The officer, courteous and concerned, helped me into his car and brought me to the nearest hospital, which happened to be Puget Sound. At first, the staff had no idea that I'd been there just a week before or what my problem may have been, whether I was a psychiatric patient, on drugs, or what. While I was sitting in an observation room, however, I was lashed with a series of seizures, which brought the staff running and helped explain my earlier confusion and disorientation.

I was only hospitalized two days, but my postical wandering now had me more concerned than ever. The danger of trudging onto the highway without control of my mental faculties was obvious. And though being run over was the biggest danger, I was also defenseless against any human predator who might have happened upon me.

I debated whether I should tell Jeanne Hampl about the incident, but I never did. I was sure she would consider me too much of a risk to have Bronson. I had come too far to lose him now, I told myself, and I needed him too much.

21

A current of excitement coursed through the program, as it always did when an extraordinary animal revealed himself. With Bronson's quick intelligence and solid temperament, it was evident almost from the beginning that he had the makings of some kind of service dog, no small feat in itself. But now that he showed signs of seizure alerting, his future was coming into focus.

Specifically, Jeanne Hampl thought he might be a good match for me. Not only might he warn me of oncoming epileptic storms, but he was a sturdy animal who could be a great help after seizures, whether it was rolling me onto my side to keep me from aspirating vomit or towing my wheelchair when the Todd's paralysis hit.

Nothing, of course, was guaranteed. Bronson had bridges to cross before he was assigned to any recipient. And who could say what Jeanne would think when she finally met me and got a closer look at my circumstances?

Barbara Thompson would teach Bronson the basics of working with a person in a wheelchair. First, she got him used to wearing the harness. Then, she sat in the chair, initially just allowing him to get comfortable around the contraption. Before long, she started him on pulling on command, stopping, as well as heeling and sitting calmly at her side.

Come December, Thompson also introduced Bronson to his service pack, which she now strapped on him before every formal training session. It was bright red, with pouches that went on both sides of the dog, and a patch that said Prison Pet Partnership.

For the most part, seizure-alert dogs need few accessories like a harness or pack. Usually, their humans are able-bodied and can carry their own extras. Still, Jeanne Hampl thought that in public it was best for assistance dogs to at least wear the pack. That way, the general populace, storekeepers, and others could clearly see that this was not your everyday dog. Plus, the pouches were a safe place for medications, medical records, and wallet.

"Okay," Barbara would tell Bronson, "it's time to go to work." And the dog would stand obediently before her as she outfitted him.

With the pack, Bronson was transformed. Clearly he understood this was his working outfit and that it called for his undivided attention. His body language, even his facial expression, became a picture of readiness and utmost seriousness. And when it was removed, he was a playful dog again, ready to chase a ball or relax.

Once or twice, when Barbara put him in one of the kennels while she worked, grooming a dog or tending to some other task, she forgot to remove the pack. Returning an hour or so later, Thompson's heart dropped to see Bronson seated there, that same determined look on his face as when she left, refusing to play or even ease up until it was removed.

For Bronson, these were busy days. Barbara and her fellow trainers began honing his post-seizure response work. They started him, for example, on rolling a would-be stricken person to her side. One of the women would lay on her back, with a toy beneath her, then Bronson would nudge her with his head, driving to recover the plaything, until she rolled over. High praise followed each successful repetition.

Bronson's training was soon to step up in other respects as well. After Christmas, Rachelle Lunde, a volunteer from Gig Harbor, was scheduled to begin taking him from the facility and into the community once or twice a week, starting the transition from prison to family life.

For Barbara, this would be her only Christmas with him, and she wanted to make the most of it.

The holidays could be gloomy enough for prisoners. Not only were they separated from family and friends, but incoming gifts were restricted, as packages were year-round. And though officials did make certain efforts to acknowledge the holiday, the hard facts of incarceration remained unchanged.

The highlight of the season for Barbara tended to be ordering from the prison-approved Hickory Farms catalog and having a cheese and salami holiday package to nibble on for a week. Some years, she pooled her Christmas snacks with some of her fellow inmates and enjoyed a small get-together.

In the dog program, handlers showered what Christmas cheer they could muster on their animals. Several photographs would be taken of Bronson that Christmas, including one in which he wore mock antlers and another in which he was crowned with a Santa's cap as he lay on a white drape spangled with gold stars, a foot-high decorative Christmas tree behind him.

Around the same time that Barbara began to hear the clock ticking toward her farewell to Bronson, I was going out of my way to welcome him, throwing hope ahead of any guarantees that he would be mine.

After Thanksgiving, I bought him a wicker bed, for which I would make a comfortable quilted pillow, as well as numerous toys.

On one of our trips to the pet store, Michael asked if he could buy Bronson a Christmas present. We picked up several packages of treats–pig ears, rawhide bones, you name it–for all the dogs in the program, and a special squeaky toy for Bronson.

Michael was confused and concerned about the dog. He was excited about the prospect of Bronson joining our family, but he wasn't sure what his own relationship with the dog would be.

I explained that Bronson's job was to help Mommy. And though Michael could play with the dog and help exercise him, this was not to be the typical family pet.

To help him come to terms with Bronson's impending arrival, I encouraged him to write the dog a letter, figuring it would help him express his feelings, and included it with the package we sent out in early December.

> Dear Bronson,
> Hello! My name is Michael Shane Beasley. You are going to come live with us real soon. You will help my mommy. You sure are pretty. We can be friends.
> I asked my mommy if you can sleep in my bed with me but she says no. But you can still come in my bedroom if you want to.
> I wish you could come to my house for Christmas. Santa brings neat presents. I will ask him to bring you some too.
> Can we be friends? I LOVE dogs. Mommy and Daddy say you have to go to school some more before you can come to be in our family. So you be good and get A's in school like me.
> Mommy says the teachers at your school have you on a special food. But if (you're) real good your teacher can let you have a dog candy. But you have to share with your dog classmates. I bought them with my own money for you.
> Merry Christmas Bronson.
> I love you.
> Michael S. Beasley
> XXXOOO

Not long after that, Michael decided he also wanted to write to Bronson's trainer. I passed that note along in a letter I sent to Jeanne Hampl.

> Dear Barbara,
> My name is Michael. I am nine and a half years old. I want to say thank you for helping my mommy. My mommy started to cry when she got Bronson's picture. But she said they were happy tears, so I am not mad at you no more. Thank you for making my mommy happy. Will you please give Bronson a big hug for me and tell him not to bite me. I love dogs, so him and I can

be friends. I had a cocker spaniel but she died. We have not had a big dog before. I hope he likes me. Daddy said Bronson is going to be my mommy's dog. But is it okay if I play with him on his days off? I am going to hang up a stocking for Bronson, so Santa will bring him some toys, too.
Love,
Michael
XXX000

Within a week or two, a letter came back from Barbara, thanking us for the gifts and telling more about Bronson and his care. (Like all mail that left the prison from the program, it was read and cleared by Jeanne Hampl.) She was particularly concerned about bloat, a twisting of the stomach that often kills deep-chested dogs like Rottweilers, and advised us not to feed him for an hour and a half before and after exercise.

She mentioned Michael's letter to Bronson, saying she had gotten teary-eyed when she read it, and showed it to practically everybody.

Soon afterward, a letter arrived for Michael—this one supposedly from Bronson. Included with it was the Polaroid of the dog in his Santa hat and a neatly typed letter on Prison Pet Partnership stationery:

Dear Michael,
    Hello! Thank you very much for your letter and my Christmas present! I really enjoyed the bones and I did share them with my doggie friends. YES, we can be friends! I would like that very much. Don't worry. I won't bite you but I may lick you to death!
    Do you like to play ball? I love to play ball and Frisbee, so when I'm not working, you and I can play together, okay?
    I am doing very good in school and I am learning many things.... I had my trainer, Barbara, send you a picture of me that I had taken just for you. I have a Santa hat on and a Christmas tree behind me.
    It would be nice if I could spend Christmas with you but I think I should spend this one with Barbara. I am still in school and, besides, I think Barbara would like to spend this one Christmas with me before I come to live with you. But you and your mommy and daddy and I can spend all of the other Christmases together, okay?
    Well, Michael, I must go to school right now, but I hope to hear from you soon. Be good and have a VERY MERRY CHRISTMAS!
    I love you too.
    Love,
    Bronson
    XOXOXOXOXOXO
PS–I had Barbara type this for me but I told her what I wanted to say.

22

Bronson had been in confinement, in one form or another, for months. His circumstances had improved since his days at the humane society and even the drug dog program, but prison was still prison. As with humans, dogs can show signs of strain when they have been in an institution a while. Close living conditions, lack of variety, and the ever present tension in the air take a toll. Depression is possible, as are stress-related physical problems.

So the dog had to be thrilled that Tuesday morning, two days after Christmas, when Rachelle Lunde arrived to take him for his first excursion outside the razor wire.

Rachelle was one of the Prison Pet Partnership's top volunteers. A wife and mother of two small children, she had been with the program more than two years, first with the old regime and now under Jeanne Hampl.

In her early thirties, Lunde was slender, with an open, friendly face, and long light-colored hair that draped across her shoulders. She was attractive, but what people tended to remember most was her determined cheerfulness and willingness to help.

Rachelle spent most of her life in Gig Harbor. Her father was in the Navy, so the Lundes moved around when she was small. The family settled down around the time she hit sixth grade, when her dad, a chief fire control specialist, was stationed at the naval shipyard in Bremerton.

Growing up, Rachelle spent a lot of time by herself. The family's house was somewhat secluded, down by the water, a fair distance from any neighborhood kids. And though Rachelle had three siblings, they had a big age disparity. Her sisters were seven and five years older than her and her brother was nine years younger. Then, when she was twelve, her father became severely disabled following surgery for a brain tumor. It was wrenching and confusing to see her once-strong father laid so low. His need for caretaking absorbed everyone's time and attention even further.

Not that Rachelle complained. She made do with the friends she found. It should be noted, however, that many of them she literally found. They were dogs.

As an adult, Rachelle would be hard pressed to remember where they all even came from. There were so many over the years–purebreds and mixes, big and small, handsome and ugly. A lot followed her home. Or people released them on the property. They got there one way or another. And because of her mother's soft heart for creatures, these visitors often became boarders.

Rachelle liked to outfit the dogs, tugging a sweater onto them or perhaps her dad's boxer shorts. They'd follow her to the beach and nose around, or sit with her as she did her homework. Rachelle and dogs just seemed to have a mutual understanding.

That rapport was obvious when she started helping with the prison program. Rachelle knew considerably less about training than someone like Jeanne, but her gentle manner, patience, and empathy went a long way toward winning an animal's favor and instilling a desire to please.

Lunde was loyal to Hampl and the program. She also knew her place on the totem pole. And while she had respect, indeed affection, for many of the inmate handlers and the disabled people she met, it was the dogs to whom she was most devoted.

She kept a photo album of the canines she worked with over the years and recalled them with the fondness of old friends. If there was even a hint that one of the animals was being treated improperly or neglected in any way–by a recipient, inmate, or whomever–the usually sunny Rachelle became more like a thunderstorm. The humans could speak for themselves, she figured; these creatures could not.

Lunde's most vital role for the program was taking individual dogs away from the prison for anywhere from a few hours to a weekend. While the inmate-handlers did the heavy lifting part of training, Rachelle worked out the kinks. She exposed the dogs to the world they would soon be entering, introducing them to everything from grocery stores to movie theaters. She field tested the animals, and where need be, threw in some instruction of her own.

As she drove with Bronson from Purdy that first day, Rachelle watched his reaction to being in her minivan. Yet the dog, a veteran of more than a few trips into town when he lived on the farm, was undaunted. He was excited, Rachelle noted, and moved around quite a bit. Experience–and Lunde's anchoring him by his leash–soon eliminated that problem.

They spent the better part of their first get-together at Rachelle's home, becoming acquainted.

The Lundes lived in a nice suburban development in Gig Harbor. Rachelle had been an administrative assistant for a bank before she had kids, and her husband worked in computer operations for Boeing. They had a spacious backyard, with an expanse of lawn, some bushes, a shed, and a sizable wooden fort for the kids, complete with a slide. All this was enclosed by a picket fence, which also contained her dogs Cougar, a Great Dane, and Jessie, an elderly cocker spaniel mix.

That day, Bronson romped with the dogs as well as Rachelle and her kids, Jacob, age four, and Rebecca, two and a half. He showed particular affection for the little girl, merrily trailing wherever she led.

Bronson had his own version of hide-and-seek. He would hurry behind the slide or a bush, peek out, and wait for Rachelle or the kids to find him. When they did, he waggled his hindquarters with such uncontrolled joy that one would think a spring had busted loose.

And, if the children climbed the ladder to the upper reaches of the fort, six feet above terra firma, Bronson galloped up the slide to join them.

By the time Rachelle brought him back to the prison, she was smitten.

The following Saturday, New Year's Eve, Rachelle brought him with her family to brave the holiday crowds in Seattle. They cruised the Children's Museum, Pacific Science Center, some shopping malls, and a food court. Crowds, even hordes of children, failed to throw off Bronson. He marched through one clamorous setting after another like he was running for office.

Before the day was out, Bronson would fearlessly pad across grating and sit serenely, though curious, through the mayhem of an automatic car wash. It may not have been derring-do, but similar challenges have sent many a wonderful dog into panic.

Which is not to say Bronson was flawless. He boarded the monorail with the Lundes, but the instant the train moved he took a leap into Rachelle's lap that would have made Marmaduke proud. He returned to the floor when she commanded, and stayed there. But the unease in his eyes suggested it was more out of deference to her than any assuredness that this was a very good idea.

At Westlake Center, a shopping mall, Bronson encountered his first escalator, and wanted nothing to do with it. He hugged the floor, as a matter of fact, and tried to scramble away. Given the crowds, Rachelle's husband Rolf finally had to carry him onto it to get to their stores.

Such excursions produced a steady stream of experiences and lessons for the dog–and Rachelle.

Bronson was skittish at his initial exposure to a grocery store. The electronic doors were unnerving, the shopping carts rackety. His paws also slipped out beneath him on the polished tile floors. It took a few minutes, but with Rachelle's encouragement–and steady pulling–he soon found his sea legs.

When they toured supermarkets, she attached Bronson's leash to the shopping cart handle and tempted him with all the goodies the store had to offer. She made sure they came within sniffing distance of the delicatessen meats, ground beef, cheeses, and what seemed to be particularly enticing to the dog, the fresh fish. If he went to smell, or looked ready to grab a bite, Rachelle gave a quick snap–or "pop," as trainers often put it–of his leash and leather collar and issued a stern, "Leave it."

Bronson wanted to obey, but at times his inner turmoil revealed itself to comic effect. They would stop before one delicacy or another and he staunchly refused to even look in that direction. Yet his body betrayed him: His nose twitched, or the drool came down in strings, or he trembled. He was trying so mightily to be good that Rachelle had to grin. She bent down, gave him a good-boy pat, and handed over a treat for a job well done.

At times, as they walked along with the empty cart, Rachelle would intention-ally take a sudden turn to the left or right. The maneuvers surprised Bronson and sometimes the wheels caught his toes, which sent him leaping back. And though Lunde endured more than one glare from animal lovers who thought it a nasty trick, she wasn't harming him; she was sending the message that it was his job to pay attention and steer clear when need be. (Trainers, in fact, will use a similar technique when teaching a dog to walk on a leash, changing course without warning, making sharp turns, even going in the complete opposite direction, until the pupil learns to pay heed.)

At the register, Rachelle usually handed Bronson something–her purse, keys, even dollars–to hold in his mouth. When the time came, she had him present the cash to the clerk, just as he might under certain circumstances for a disabled per-son.

This process became so engrained that after awhile if Rachelle neglected to give him something, Bronson lifted an item off the candy rack when she wasn't looking and held that. He particularly liked gum, for some reason, and M & Ms, which he never ate but comforted himself by grasping from the corner of the package. And while Rachelle snuck more than one item back to its place, she usu-ally just paid for it. At home, a drawer began filling with candy she had no inter-est in eating, even if it had never seen the inside of a dog's mouth.

In the stores, folks asked about Bronson, or shared stories about their own pets. Most were friendly and Lunde took this as an opportunity to educate people about assistance dogs. But that got wearing at times, even for someone as kind as

Rachelle. Sometimes she just wanted to rush in with Bronson, pay for her carton of milk, and get home.

And though the pair became a familiar sight around town, store employees often had no idea of the dog's purpose. Occasionally, a worker said dogs were prohibited, but when Rachelle explained, most had no problems. (Under the Americans with Disabilities Act, a disabled individual with a service animal cannot be denied access to public accommodations. Technically, though, the law did not cover service-animals-in-training.)

Once, Lunde happened to be wearing sunglasses when she went to pay at the supermarket. With her hands full, she emptied her change onto the counter. But as she counted out the amount due, she noticed the clerk being a little too solicitous.

"This one's a quarter," the woman said, as if speaking to a child. "And here's a dime."

Rachelle looked at her, puzzled. "Excuse me," she said, "but do you understand that I'm not blind?"

"You're not? But isn't that a seeing eye dog?"

Public restrooms, meanwhile, were a major hurdle for Bronson. Indeed, few dogs were comfortable with the hard, porcelain surfaces and the raucous sounds of toilets flushing and hand dryers blowing. The acoustics only made matters worse.

When tested, Bronson walked in with no problem. Getting him into a stall, on the other hand, was a battle of wills. No amount of cajoling on Rachelle's part could convince him that this tight, uncomfortable compartment was any place he cared to go. He sank to a sitting position, tossed his head back defiantly, and refused to budge.

Between pleading and pulling, Rachelle finally got him in. But when she closed the door, he'd crouch down and try to back out, commencing the tug-of-war all over. Bystanders heard the commotion and looked on with wonder at the scramble of paws and feet beneath the stall door.

When Rachelle finally convinced Bronson to remain in the stall, she still had to position him. In this, the least desirable of locations, she found herself jumping over, straddling, and climbing onto the toilet, first to get him where she wanted, then to make him lay down and stay.

It got better with repetition, but Rachelle was never completely satisfied with Bronson's restroom etiquette. Eventually, he agreed to lay down where she wanted. But rather than rest on his belly and chest, he had a tendency to loll onto his side. More often than not, half his body spilled over into the adjacent stall.

Rachelle then had to slide him back, pulling all four feet like he was a sheep about to be sheared.

Sometimes, too, the dog simply got curious, and when Rachelle looked away, poked his head under the partition to investigate the doings next door. An unassuming patron would be taking care of private matters, only to glance down and see a Rottweiler staring back. Rachelle knew something was amiss when she heard a loud gasp from the next booth.

Once, Bronson even reached under the partition and came back holding someone's purse by the handles, just as he had been taught to carry Rachelle's.

The volunteer returned the booty, of course, and tried to reassure the stunned woman. "He's not being trained as a thief," she said.

Bronson was nothing if not an independent thinker. He learned what humans had to teach him, then explored its outer limits.

One day, out at the house, he and Rachelle were playing in the backyard when the telephone rang. She hurried inside to answer it, leaving him there with her dogs. When she returned a couple minutes later, she saw no sign of Bronson.

Rachelle scanned the yard, bewildered.

She looked to Cougar and Jessie, half expecting an explanation, but mum was the word.

She rushed to the children's fort and peered inside, then to the shed.

"Oh, my God!" she said. "He jumped the fence!"

Clearly, that's what happened. Reminiscent of his days back on the farm, the dog had vaulted over the picket fence and by now had to be half way to Yakima.

"Bronson!" Rachelle shouted, her panic rising. "Bronson!"

Her fears cascaded in as she charged into the house. This dog was a runner, she told herself. How would she ever find him? What it he gets hit by a car? How could she return to the prison without this dog? She thought of everyone she let down–Jeanne, the program, the needy person who might have received this dog, even poor Bronson himself whose mangled body was probably lying in the street that very moment.

Rachelle yelled to Rolf and the kids that she had to leave, that Bronson was loose. She flung open the front door, ready to race up the street in pursuit, but sitting there before her–so near the door that she almost flopped over him–was Bronson. He gazed up with a happy expression, as if to ask, "What took you so long?"

RACHELLE LUNDE, FORMER PRISON PET PARTNERSHIP VOLUNTEER

Bronson is a very dignified dog. He is very self-confident. He always has been. He's very self-assured and he looks it. He's got a look on his face that says he knows he really is a neat guy. He just exudes that he is one cool dog.

Bronson was known as a little street fighter. He's really good with other dogs now, but let me tell you.

There were two dogs in prison at that time that wanted to be in charge: Spencer and Bronson. Spencer happened to be a Rottweiler mix as well. He was older. He was in the program longer, since before Jeanne got there. And Bronson, who was fairly young at the time, was just a punk. Now he's a good-sized dog but at the time he was very thin. And he looked more like a lab than a rot.

Every time he would go by Spencer he would do something to nettle him. He would just nettle him. Or he'd snap at him. It got to where you couldn't put the two dogs side by side.

You'd try putting Bronson with other dogs and eventually he would do the same thing. He just wanted to irritate a dog. I don't really think it was anything malicious. There wasn't any all-out fights where the fur was flying and all. He was just a little punk when it came to other dogs. He wanted to be top dog and he didn't own the right to be top dog.

Then, he came over to my house and learned a lesson or two.

Bronson would get a little bit rough with my Dane, Cougar. He would start chewing on an ear. Or he would grab the neck a little too hard and nip. Or he would try to take a ball away from him. Or Cougar would have one of his bones and Bronson would go up to take it away.

He was much shorter than my Dane, but he would try to put his neck over my Dane's back, which is a very dominant sign.

Well, Cougar would pick up his leg and put it on top of Bronson and just hold him down. There were a couple times when Cougar would just kind of half stand, put a leg on top of Bronson, flatten him, and not let him up.

Or he would put his mouth over Bronson's neck. He didn't hurt him. He never bit down. But Cougar held him on the ground and Bronson would squirm and his butt was stuck straight up in the air. He wanted to get out. But Cougar was holding him and you'd hear this whining and this horrible noise from Bronson, like he was in so much pain, that horrible stuff was happening to him, like he was being chewed up alive.

Cougar would finally let go, and Bronson would get up and kind of shake and walk off. It took about ten times of really being put in his place to learn that he just couldn't run the show with everybody.

His improvement started when he figured out he couldn't be top dog. When he decided where his place was in the pack, that he wasn't going to be the alpha dog, from then on out things went much, much smoother for him.

"BROTHERS AND SISTERS, I bid you beware," wrote the poet Rudyard Kipling. "Of giving your heart to a dog to tear." Few could appreciate that admonishment any better than the inmates of the Prison Pet Partnership. Their dogs were their lives. The animals provided companionship on friendless nights, a listening ear when no one else cared to hear, and a sense of pride and accomplishment in women who since the day they were born had precious little that said they mattered. Life, in fact, had handed most a much darker message about their worth, which being behind bars only seemed to confirm.

From the beginning, however, the relationships with their dogs were doomed. The day would never come when the inmates watched their animals dash through some woods, or romp at the shore, or poke their heads from a car window to face the breeze. The handicapped individual receiving the dog might return now and then for brush-up training instruction. If they were kind, they'd drop a card in the mail at Christmas with some snippets of news and a snapshot. But for the most part, these dogs were forever gone.

Parting always stung. Indeed, an unspoken reason behind Rachelle and the other volunteers taking the dogs out for increasingly longer stretches was to commence the separation process and allow the women to steel themselves for the inevitable.

Barbara Thompson liked Rachelle. Admittedly, the inmate felt a pang of heartache at Bronson's glee when the volunteer picked him up for each new adventure in the free world. At the same time, she appreciated Rachelle's detailed reports at the close of each outing, that she took time to get to know the dog, and that she always found something positive to say.

Still, when the volunteer mentioned that she planned to take Bronson for an entire weekend, the inmate curtly told her no. "What am I going to do without my dog all weekend?" she demanded.

Rachelle shrugged. She knew Barbara wasn't sent to Purdy for being a debutante and had no intention of crossing her. Still, this dog needed outside work and Thompson was in no position to refuse much of anything.

Soon after, it would be Jeanne Hampl who issued the edict: Bronson would go with Rachelle that weekend. End of conversation.

As it was, concern was growing about Bronson. On one or two occasions, while inside Rachelle's house, he had urinated–dribbled more than anything–while just walking along. He seemed not to even realize he was doing it.

Rachelle brought him to the local veterinarian that the program used. He could find no physical problems, but raised the possibility that this was stress related, perhaps from the penitentiary environment. Certainly some dogs showed signs of aggression or developed severe diarrhea because of the tension. Uncontrolled urination was not out of the question.

While less an issue for Bronson, some prison dogs showed behavior changes once they got a taste for life outside of Purdy. Some became downcast at the end of a trip. Others resisted leaving the car to go back inside the prison. Once they had returned, some stared blankly at the doors of their cells, moping. When the handlers asked Jeanne Hampl what she thought was going on, the director said it was obvious: "They're sick of prison. Just like the inmates are sick of prison." In other words, their time there was rapidly reaching its end.

Bronson's malady passed, but Rachelle still found quirks that needed attention. One was an aversion to hats, of all things.

The first sign was when he refused to stop rumbling–even after a collar correction and reprimand–at a man wearing one in the elevator of a medical building. This behavior stumped Rachelle, but she started putting two and two together when she came downstairs one day in a baseball cap and the dog went wild barking at her, as if she was in mortal danger.

There was no telling what it was with hats. Maybe he never saw them before and they startled him. To Rachelle, it only made sense that Bronson would be sensitive to his environment. This was common in seizure-alert dogs: If something was unusual or amiss, they let you know.

All the same, it would be unthinkable to send him out with a disabled person growling and barking at folks because of their headgear. Jeanne suggested that acclimation was the answer. So off Rachelle went for a Goodwill store, where she purchased a variety of old hats for about a quarter each.

Now, everywhere the dog looked around the Lunde house someone was wearing a hat, from a glittery New Year's Eve top hat to a preposterous straw model with flowers drooping over the brim. The dog might be relaxing somewhere and in would parade Jacob and Rebecca, hats a-flopping left and right. Friends dropped by and Rachelle would issue them a hat before coming in.

Once she even enlisted the UPS man. He begged off at first, but proved no match for Rachelle's enthusiasm. No doubt contemplating the peculiarities of his job and the customers he encountered, the deliveryman that day carried a package the entire stretch of the Lunde's lengthy driveway, made his delivery, and greeted Bronson, all while wearing the red and white signature chapeau of the Cat in the Hat.

At home, Rachelle reenforced Bronson's lessons in picking up items such as keys, or rolling her over on the floor, or retrieving the telephone. In fact, she wrapped and taped a diaper around the telephone receiver to make it easier for the dog to grasp it in his mouth, then forgot about it. One evening another couple was over and about halfway through dinner the wife seemed distracted, as if a burdensome problem was gnawing at her. She slowly set down her fork, then came out with it. "I'm sorry," she said, "but why is there a diaper on your telephone?"

Rachelle, a devout Christian, also brought the dog to the Gig Harbor church where she and her family worshipped. As with everywhere they went, Bronson was to remain inconspicuous. Rachelle was always proud when she and Bronson departed from a restaurant, for example, and overheard someone exclaim that they had no idea a dog was present.

So it was with both humor and embarrassment that Rachelle recalled the affair that brought Bronson lasting renown among the faithful at Harbor Covenant Church.

The Reverend Steve Grubb had decided to take an unusual approach in his sermon that fateful Sunday. His message was going to be that you never knew what life would throw at you but whatever it was, you had to catch it and use it to your best advantage. To emphasize his point, he had wadded up some paper, with a Biblical verse written on it, into a baseball-sized ball and unexpectedly hurled it out toward the flock.

The symbolism was obvious: Who would catch life's opportunities and who wouldn't?

That's when Bronson appeared out of nowhere and before God and Man launched himself six feet straight into the air, snatched the projectile in midflight, then just as suddenly disappeared back under the pew next to Rachelle, savoring his prize.

In unison, the congregation gasped. Most had no idea a dog was in their midst. Had they really seen what they thought they saw?

"It was just total silence," Rachelle would later recall. "The piano stopped playing. About three or four seconds went by, and then everybody just started laughing.

"Our poor pastor. He was just standing there dumbfounded because he hadn't known Bronson was there. He said, 'I can't even remember what I came up here to say.'"

As time went by, Bronson became something of the church's mascot. He joined Rachelle for her women's Bible study group and was remembered by fellow participants even years later for the impeccable timing of his snores during a prayer or reading of a passage.

When hymns were sung, be it in church or Bible study, Bronson often participated, by howling. Rachelle hushed him when the choir performed during services. But if the entire congregation was raising the roof, she usually allowed the dog to chime in. Most people could hardly hear him, she figured. And if they did, his voice was far from the worst of the crowd. (More unsettling for Rachelle was the howling's effect on her children: Jacob couldn't stop giggling and Rebecca was mortified as people turned to look.)

Bronson had little interest in "up tempo" hymns. He preferred those that started slow and had a wide range. He could always be counted on to contribute to "Amazing Grace." Another favorite, perhaps because of the moving flute introduction, was "All Hail King Jesus."

Rachelle never understood exactly what set him off, be it the high notes or some ancient urge to howl with the pack. She decided this was just Bronson's way of praising his Creator and let it go at that.

23

I have had some cleaning binges in my day, particularly when Harry was away and I needed to keep my hands and mind occupied. But for duration and single-mindedness none matched the torrent Jeanne Hampl unleashed a day or two before the end of 1994. After months of telephone conversations and steadily rising hopes, I had yet to meet her. Now she was calling to arrange a home visitation—a major step on the road to obtaining a service dog from the prison program—and she planned to bring Bronson.

For the next ten days, in preparation for Jeanne's arrival, I worked to subdue every last reminder of dust, dirt, and disorder to invade our military housing unit on Fort Lewis.

I scoured every wall and floor in every room. I stripped the old wax off the tile floors, then waxed them again, while our furniture sat outside on the lawn. I scrubbed the windows, inside and out. Every piece of furniture and knickknack was wiped clean. No cranny or corner went untouched. Every surface that could be polished was polished. All of the sheets and bed coverings were laundered, as was every article of clothing. I worked the yard to make it presentable, bleached the concrete on the porch to whiten it again, and the night before Jeanne showed up, I even gave our cat Sam a bubble bath.

Nothing was left to chance. I stayed awake that entire night, worrying and double-checking to make sure the place looked perfect. By morning, all that was keeping me going was nervous energy, caffeine, and cigarettes.

I worked myself into such a state that I feared I might go into seizures right in front of Jeanne. As it was, I had several episodes in the week leading up to her visit, twice needing emergency room treatment. The day after Jeanne set up the appointment, in fact, I cracked my head against our television stand and needed a CT scan, which came back negative. After another event, it took several hours before I regained consciousness, a matter of some concern to my doctors and family.

I'd thrown everything into the hope of obtaining this dog, to the point that I neglected sleep and proper eating. To my thinking, my future, perhaps even my life, hinged on this evaluation. Nothing mattered more than making a good impression for Jeanne.

Harry took a brief break from MP patrol duty that morning, and we sent Michael to school late, so the entire family could be home.

Around ten o'clock, Jeanne arrived, joined by Bronson and Cindy Mack, a volunteer and friend of Hampl's who as a military wife knew Fort Lewis and the issues that might confront my family. I ushered them in and we sat at the dining room table.

Jeanne intimidated me from the start. It was nothing she said or did, but more her to-the-point, authoritative manner. Although I would come to respect her as much as anyone I've known, my immediate reaction was that this was not a woman I wanted to tangle with. That she controlled my fate made her seem all the more commanding.

Cindy, smaller that Hampl and bespectacled, was quiet, less intense, and initially stayed in the background. I half-wondered why she was there.

I did my best to pay attention to my human guests, as we made small talk over freshly baked cookies and coffee. But it was difficult to keep my eyes off this gorgeous dog, still on his leash, at Jeanne's side.

As an adolescent, Bronson was still fairly lean. He weighed no more than sixty-five or seventy pounds. He had the coloring and markings of a Rottweiler, but his face was more narrow. His ears, while floppy, tilted back a bit, revealing their underside.

The upper half of his head was a sleek black. It cloaked his face like Batman's cowl, with a thick strip that continued down his muzzle to his nose. Tan ovals above his eyes resembled eyebrows. The rest of his snout and his throat were also a rich tan.

What impressed me most about the dog was his kindly face. He simply looked happy. The contours of his mouth and muzzle were such that he seemed to smile when he panted. And his eyes, burnt orange in color, were the warmest I'd ever seen–in a dog or a person. He gazed so steadily and intently in my eyes, I almost felt like he was searching my soul. From the moment I greeted Bronson I knew I wanted him.

Jeanne asked if he could be let off his leash and I said of course. I got him a bowl of water and he lapped his fill. Yet he paid little attention to me at first. He was too busy exploring, almost as if he was considering whether this was someplace he wanted to call home.

He padded over to Michael to say hello. My son, who'd been bitten by a dog the previous summer, was excited by the prospect of Bronson joining our family but uneasy at how big he seemed up close.

Bronson also detected the scent of the cat–who was away from the hubbub, upstairs on my bed–and sniffed around for him. (Bronson would eventually meet Sam during that visit, but not long afterward the cat was euthanized. He suffered from feline immunodeficiency virus, a feline version of the AIDS virus, and had been deathly sick for weeks.)

Bronson was further intrigued by the squawks of our parrots and Michael's two parakeets. Although he never barked or made a move for their cages, Jeanne was uncomfortable. If I were to receive Bronson, she said, I might have to keep the birds caged or find them new homes. In the meantime, she would work on getting him used to being around birds. (None of us knew it at the time, but chasing chickens was what started Bronson's troubles back in Orting, and there was no telling how well he could suppress his natural prey drive.)

As we got down to the purpose of their visit, Jeanne and Cindy surely detected my nervousness and how hard I was trying to say and do everything right. They tried to keep the discussion friendly rather than make it an inquisition.

Jeanne's first concern was basic dog care. Much like a responsible breeder who assesses a prospective buyer of her puppies, she wanted to make sure our home would be a safe place for Bronson. We discussed other animals I'd owned over the years, in particular dogs. Was I willing to endure the minor disruptions that a dog brings, whether it was shedding or possibly jumping on the furniture? Would the yard be fenced in? Was I aware of the leash requirements on the base and in the community?

Although I wouldn't have to pay the program for Bronson, it was important that we had enough income to at least provide him with the basics, such as dog food and veterinary care.

Jeanne wanted to know what accommodations we would make for Bronson. Where, for example, would he sleep? Who would take him out and feed him if I was too sick to do so myself? What were my expectations of him?

Hampl had learned to take nothing for granted. Some people claimed to want a service dog but had no comprehension of the commitment and teamwork it demanded. Others were clearly uncomfortable around dogs, which raised the question of why they applied in the first place. One candidate, who failed to make the cut, raised Jeanne's eyebrows by declaring that she only wanted a white service dog–to go with her white carpeting.

But the home visit was more than questions and answers. Jeanne came to see for herself where Bronson would live and to meet me on my own turf. She wanted to get a feel for how I functioned, whether I could handle the needs and demands of a dog, and how I reacted to having a dog around the house. She also wanted to meet my family, see how we behaved toward one another, and get a sense for daily life at our place. More than anything, Jeanne wanted to be assured that Bronson would fit in, that everyone was behind having him there.

For the most part, everything went smoothly. The only time I really became unnerved was when Harry and Michael departed for work and school. I had come to rely on my husband to watch out for me in the event of a seizure or any physical problems that might linger from the coma. But he also guided me through social situations. His presence boosted my confidence. And if I was baffled about what to do or say, he would jump in and take the lead. If anything, he was overprotective. So when he said goodbye to return to work, my anxiety soared.

My greatest fear was that I would be unable to adequately answer Jeanne and Cindy's questions. Even nine months removed from the coma, my short-term memory remained spotty. If, for example, one of them posed a question then went on to explain why she was asking, my thoughts would slip away from me and I'd forget the original question. Several times, I had to ask what they meant, or if they could rephrase their questions.

They stayed about two hours. Before leaving, Jeanne mentioned that she would like me to come to the prison for training with Bronson. She promised to call in a day or two to schedule a time.

With their departure, my accumulated stress was cut loose and I sank into a chair, quaking. Later, as I picked up the dishes, I replayed snippets of conversation and berated myself for saying this or not saying that. Even my neglecting to put napkins out with the coffee and cookies became a major point of self-reproach.

When Harry asked how I thought it went, I said I didn't know. They asked a lot of questions, but I had no feel for what they thought of me or my answers, whether I'd be a good match for Bronson, or a likely candidate for any service dog. That I was moving onto the next stage, going to the prison to work with Bronson, seemed to promise nothing. I was hopeful, of course, and went about life as if the dog was soon to be mine. But truth be told, I simply didn't know.

Shortly after, I wrote a thank-you note to Jeanne and a letter to Barbara Thompson, filling her in on the visit and thanking her for her kindness to Michael at Christmas. I figured she was anxious to learn how Bronson and I got along.

My ability to put my thoughts down on paper had improved considerably since the coma, though the writing itself was painstakingly slow and measured.

Dear Barbara,

We met Bronson at our home on the ninth. We all were taken by him. My husband was very pleased and even said for the first time since my seizures started he can see light at the end of the tunnel for us.

Our son, Michael, was quiet and sat still on the sofa. This behavior was odd for Michael. At one point Bronson put his front paws on Michael's lap and gave Michael a big wet kiss. Michael was afraid at first but Jeanne and I told him it was a big kiss and Michael relaxed some.

Of course I fell in love with Bronson right away. My husband says that Bronson has me wrapped around his little toe already. Ha ha. But Harry is right.

Bronson is a very beautiful dog. I was impressed with his behavior in my house. He made himself at home but was respectful also. My birds excited him but after he was told "Leave it," he didn't bother them.

I really liked Bronson's eye-to-eye contact. He shows self-confidence and strong self-will. That's a good trait. I am usually afraid to go anywhere. With Bronson at my side he would give me the self confidence I need.

It has already started, although I don't know if Jeanne noticed.

During their visit, Michael went back to school and Harry went back to work. Soon after I could feel my chest shake inside and my hands start to shake. I tried to hide my anxiety by smoking but it didn't make it stop. Then Bronson walked by, close to me, and I looked at him and I stroked his back. It really surprised me but my shaking slowed a lot. After awhile it started again and Bronson came to me again. I stroked him longer this time and my shaking stopped. I'm not sure, but I think Bronson knew.

When they were getting ready to leave I showed them the upstairs. This is when Bronson met our cat, Sam. When Bronson tried to sneak in a sniff of Sam he got batted on the nose. Bronson came to me for sympathy. The expression on Bronson's face was priceless. He had a look as if to say, "Your cat hit me!" I stroked him and said, "Oh, did that kitty hit you? Well, that kitty is a 'leave it.' You're all right." And then I patted him.

Bronson loved all the toys we got for him. He seemed to really enjoy his doll. It's a fuzzy sheepskin doll with a squeaky toy inside.

We bought an oval rug for him to lay on downstairs and I got some material to make him a thick, quilted bed. Last night we got Bronson a few more things and a toy box. We still need a baby gate, but we have time for that. Harry called around for prices on fence supplies and this weekend we will go look at them. We want something strong, not this chicken wire our neighbors have. But this year the military is supposed to fence in each yard really nice, so we may not have to do it ourselves.

Thank you for the letter to Michael from Bronson. He loved it, and the picture. You have a real special touch. Thank you.

Sincerely,

Leana L. Beasley

24

That the dogs were trained at Purdy was a given. But I never imagined that I myself would have to enter the penitentiary. When Jeanne said that was the next step, I was stunned. The more I thought about it, the more it filled me with dread.

In the aftermath of the coma, all of my problems, both physical and emotional, collapsed upon me. Even when the seizures were at their worst, I'd always been otherwise healthy. Now, with my damaged lungs, the lingering effects of the Todd's paralysis, and all else, I was defenseless against anyone who might want to harm me. I was also emotionally fragile, wounded by even the hint of a harsh word, and wary of the world's dangers, real and imagined. That a seizure could strike at any time, anywhere–and kill me, as almost happened, in a hospital of all places–only stoked my fears.

I was too scared to venture outside to tend my flowers. Now I was going into a prison? Maybe the convicts in the dog program were considered safe, but what about the others? Some women there had committed unconscionable, brutal acts, often as a matter of habit. A prisoner with nothing to lose might take great satisfaction in cracking a former cop in the face. What's more, Washington state prisons had seen a number of disturbances around that time. Why not this facility? Why not now?

I went overboard in expecting the worst. In truth, the inmates knew next to nothing about my personal life. Women's prisons were also less violent than the typical men's facility.

Still, I was far from alone in my fears. Being around criminals made a number of volunteers and staff from the dog program uneasy, to the point that some left to work elsewhere. Even my husband, who was healthy and in the prime of life, was nervous about being inside the barbed wire.

When the day finally came, I remember standing in the prison gymnasium with Jeanne Hampl, waiting for Barbara Thompson and Bronson to arrive. The other handlers, dressed casually in jeans and sweatshirts, had already begun to work their dogs. It was peculiar to see animals in a penitentiary, but uplifting as well. (One inmate, who was not in the program, said she was thrilled to see dogs upon her arrival at Purdy. She assumed they were prisoners' pets from home and figured her dog would soon be able to join her.)

Barbara and Bronson appeared five or ten minutes late. I thought little of it, but Jeanne was clearly irritated. Some problem or other had come up with the strap on Bronson's backpack, the inmate said, but rather than reply, Jeanne just gave her an icy look. It was obvious something was in the air between the two women, though I figured it was none of my business.

At the moment I had my own stressors. I was so nervous and spoke so quietly that people could hardly hear me. Yvonne Wood, who I talked to briefly, later said I reminded her of "a scared little child."

Seeing Bronson again helped. He greeted me like we were old friends. And though he appeared massive and threatening as he galloped toward me during our first exercises, I soon gained my composure. Patting, stroking, and praising him after the successful completion of each exercise probably benefited me more than the dog.

Although Bronson's main purpose would be his seizure work, he was also to assist with tasks that my poor health made difficult, like getting the telephone or picking up items from the floor. If he was to be with me everywhere I went, his obedience training had to be impeccable.

Barbara Thompson had done a great job, especially considering that this was her first service dog. Bronson's training was almost flawless. He responded to every command with the precision of a well-drilled soldier. Harry, who had gone through the military's special K-9 program and worked extensively with patrol dogs, sat off to the side amazed. He said he never saw such a disciplined animal, that this was the ultimate "push-button dog."

Yet Bronson was far from a robot. He was intelligent, enthusiastic, and affectionate. Our bond began to form that very day, in fact, as did my protectiveness of him.

During recalls, in which the dogs ran across the gym to us, one of the inmate handlers kept reprimanding Bronson, apparently because he was whining as he awaited my call. I had no idea who the woman was or what was bothering her—whether she disliked Bronson for some reason, or if she had a running dispute with Barbara, or if she was just an angry person—but I finally got fed up.

"Stop scolding my dog!" I snapped.

The outburst surprised even me. The mouse had roared—at a convict no less.

Jeanne came over to make sure everything was all right, then the lesson resumed. What would strike me was how quickly I became attached to Bronson. In my mind, this was no longer Barbara's dog or the Prison Pet Partnership's dog.

This was *my* dog. And I was willing to defend him, no small leap considering how reluctant I would have been to defend myself.

BARBARA THOMPSON

Leana seemed real timid and shy. When we were training at the gym her contact with me was really short. I think she was afraid. Because she didn't know me. I could have been an ax-murderer for all she knew.

Bronson, on the other hand, was never timid. He was just always a friendly dog. So it didn't really surprise me that he went over to her right away. I think she was a little bit apprehensive because of his size and the way he looked.

But three minutes later it was like they just clicked. It was just a natural thing. It's like he sensed that she needed him. And I think she sensed that this was a pretty smart dog.

When I saw them, Bronson and Leana, I just knew they were supposed to be together. She needed him and he needed her. That kind of broke my heart, but I had to tell myself, "Barbara, that's what this is all about."

I was jealous. I was told, we all were told, don't get too attached to the dogs. Now how in the hell do you not get too attached? I did anyway, with every dog I had. And it never got easier as you lost more dogs.

I remember Leana telling me she was pleased with Bronson's mix—and her husband was glad, too—because if she was out by herself, people would see this Rottweiler and wouldn't mess with her. Even though he wasn't no bad dog.

BARBARA THOMPSON would have been wise to say goodbye to the dog program the day that Jeanne Hampl became director. The inmate had been hired under a previous boss, loved her job, and by all accounts performed well. With the arrival of Jeanne, the atmosphere changed.

As new bosses do, Hampl had her own manner of conducting business. Operations became much more professional, orderly, and strict. Jeanne's approach to training differed from how Barbara had been taught. And the new director's demanding personality ran headlong into Thompson's refusal to be pushed.

In any business–in or out of jail–the collision of such temperaments only spells disaster. When it comes down to an employer and worker, it's not hard to predict who at the end of the day will still have a job and who won't.

Barbara was a low-level employee, a prisoner no less, who earned a few hundred dollars a month. And though she did have certain employment rights, she had virtually no power. So Barbara did what the powerless often do when they're unhappy–she griped.

Specifically, she tried to undermine Hampl by telling others that Jeanne "beat" and "abused" the dogs, a potentially ruinous allegation given the nature of the work. The prisoner made such remarks to a number of people, including the volunteers. Among them was Rachelle Lunde, who found the comments not only untrue but highly inappropriate. Ultimately, Thompson even took her accusations to a prison administrator, who essentially wrote them off.

Granted, Barbara's life experience made her sensitive to the potential mistreatment of any creature. But those who know Jeanne, including other inmates in the program at that time, roll their eyes at the picture Thompson was painting. "Half-truths" is how fellow inmate Leslie Hays, characterizes Barbara's statements. Handler Patricia Toomey calls them "a pure lie."

When she first started as director, Jeanne was not above pinching a dog's ear to convince him to open his mouth to hold an object, or issuing a quick disciplinary slap on the rump with a leash, or flipping a would-be dominant dog onto his back to make his place in the pack crystal clear. Like the discipline of dog training itself, Jeanne has evolved to the point that today she uses only positive reenforcement as a trainer.

Nonetheless, Barbara harbored a hostility that went beyond Hampl's training methods. "Jeanne and I hated each other from day one," Thompson would say years later. "It wasn't like one week we got along good and a week later we had a falling out. The hate was mutual. And it was strong."

It is doubtful that Hampl, with her businesslike approach to the program and a life outside of the prison, was equally invested in their differences. Still, that January a series of events played out that finally brought everything to a head.

For Barbara, it was becoming increasingly obvious that Bronson would soon be gone from her life. She really had no more to teach him. All that was left was fine-tuning.

Moreover, the dog's affection was being divided. Rachelle was taking Bronson now with more frequency and for longer stretches. That the volunteer and he had become fast friends was undeniable. Then, at mid-month I showed up for training and really hit it off with the dog. None of that could have been easy for Barbara to witness.

The inmate's relations with Jeanne, meanwhile, were only getting worse. Rather than fall into step, Thompson continued to buck and rear at Hampl's authority. She never seemed to understand that Jeanne's resolve was indomitable. One way or another, the program would run as Hampl saw fit. If it took the termination of an inmate-employee who by now was becoming a major pain, so be it.

That winter, Thompson collected a number of formal reprimands. Most were minor affairs, but they added up, as they often do when someone is soon to be fired. But there were more serious matters, too. Her back-biting about Jeanne, for example, made Rachelle Lunde uncomfortable and an incident report was filed. Barbara was also counseled about her work ethic and increasingly negative attitude.

Then one day Hampl asked Barbara if she could use Bronson, the program's star pupil, for a demonstration during training. Thompson, who had no ownership rights to the dog whatsoever, outright refused. She said Jeanne would be too hard on him and use him as "a beat-up toy."

Jeanne was insulted. An argument ensued. Jeanne declared she was running the program and the class and if Barbara wouldn't cooperate she should return with Bronson to her cell.

Thompson did. She stewed over the incident, feeling she'd been sent to her room like a naughty child. That night, she says, she penned a letter to a prison administrator about Jeanne's supposed maltreatment of the animals, expecting it to be held in confidence, then dropped it in an in-house message box.

Perhaps she knew her days were numbered and was trying for a pre-emptive strike. Clearly, Thompson wanted to put Jeanne in a bad light with the powers that be.

It turned out differently, however.

The day after my first training session with Bronson, an incident occurred that under normal circumstances probably would have been discussed and quickly forgotten, but which now signaled the end of Barbara's tenure.

For the second time in a week and a half, Bronson ran after and frightened an inmate who was not in the dog program. Each time it happened to the same convict, in the same place, in almost the same manner.

Barbara and Bronson had just entered Unit G-2 after having been outside. The woman was at the guard station in the foyer. And though it was common knowledge that certain inmates were afraid of dogs, this one apparently was very much so.

In the first instance, the woman claimed Bronson "charged" toward her, which sent her fleeing down the hall, the dog chasing behind, barking.

The woman, who let loose a shriek, undoubtedly overreacted. Bronson was young and exuberant, but not aggressive. He was probably just excited. But running from a dog when you're afraid only makes matters worse.

That said, people's fears must be respected, especially in the close quarters of a prison. Bronson was Barbara's responsibility. And though this was hardly the only dog in the program ever to walk around untethered, he should have been under control.

Barbara did little to defuse the situation. She rounded up Bronson that first time, and rather than apologize, snapped at the inmate: "You didn't have to scream, you bitch!"

The woman was seething. But when it happened again–the convict this time seeking refuge in the guard station–she fired off a letter to Hampl. Ironically, she never accused Bronson of trying to harm her, but wrote of her concern that in fleeing him, someone could "run smack into something and knock themselves out."

At times, overseeing prisoners was like presiding over school-children. Hampl was hardly joking when she said that getting her own two kids through the teen-age years was good preparation for working at Purdy.

In Barbara's case, enough was enough. Six days later, Thompson was summoned to the program office. With Hampl that day was the inmate's prison counselor, whose presence the inmate knew was the kiss of death.

Jeanne wasted little time, telling Barbara she was dismissed effective immediately. She cited Thompson's negative attitude, the comments to Rachelle, and the failure to have Bronson under control.

To this day, Thompson suspects Jeanne saw her letter to the prison official, and believes that was the true reason she was fired. Hampl insists that letter came afterward, as part of Barbara's failed effort to overturn the dismissal.

None of that mattered. This had been building for months and everyone knew it. When Thompson was finally discharged, she tried to buy some time. She insisted that Bronson's training was incomplete, that he still needed work.

Jeanne pulled her up short. "He's ready," she said curtly.

Barbara had a half hour to pack her belongings. She was being moved out of G-2, away from the dogs and the program.

The walls of her life tumbling around her, Thompson wanted to bash Jeanne in the face, if not worse. She'd also been around long enough to know better. The "goon squad," as she called the guards, would be on her in seconds, and before she knew it she'd be in segregation, contemplating the walls and getting her meals through a slit in the door.

Instead, the prisoner beat back her rage. She slumped away, feeling like she'd been walloped in the stomach. She returned to her cell, hugged Bronson, and broke down weeping.

Soon, inmate-handler Leslie Hays, thrown into the least enviable position, knocked and said Jeanne wanted her to take the dog. Barbara asked her to wait outside for a minute or two. Then she stroked the dog's sleek coat. "Bronson, I'm so sorry," Barbara said through her tears. "I hope you'll be good and have a good life with Leana."

Thompson surrendered Bronson's toys, backpack, and equipment to Hays, then the dog himself. As Bronson legged down the hall at Leslie's side, Barbara watched from behind. "I love you," she called.

25

It only made sense for me to finish my training with Bronson away from the prison.

I could never adjust to the heavy clank of the gates slamming behind me and the anxiety that set off. In the wake of Barbara's firing, meanwhile, Bronson was removed from the prison. Rachelle picked him up that very night, and would keep him at her home until his placement was completed.

So it was that Harry and I met Rachelle and Bronson in a small park in downtown Gig Harbor one Friday, to begin working with the dog in public.

Quaint and on the waterfront, this was a popular stop for tourists. There were gift shops, nice restaurants, and a promenade to stroll and gaze out at the boats in the harbor.

In many ways, it was an ideal proving ground for Bronson and me. Besides being relatively near the prison and Rachelle's home, the area was also fairly contained. That made it easier to work with the dog in a variety of environments—from a medical building, to a knickknack store, to a dock—in a short time.

Most people around Gig Harbor were less than thrilled at having a prison in their backyard, yet the dog program had strong local support. Jeanne, Rachelle, and many others had been good ambassadors, and with Bronson in his telltale backpack we would be greeted that day by a number of friendly faces. For me, all but a shut-in the past few years, that alone made the trip gratifying.

This was my first meeting with Rachelle, who I took to immediately and whose open, friendly manner quickly put me at ease.

Bronson, too, seemed happy to see me, and anxious to work.

For the first hour or so, the volunteer took us through the paces. She gave me Bronson's leash and observed how I handled the dog.

Rachelle knew the town inside and out. She led us to through a few stores and other buildings, trying us out on a flight of stairs, and an elevator, among other settings. Along the way she coached me, pointing out Bronson's tendencies and suggesting how best to correct problems, like navigating doors or narrow passageways.

After awhile, she told Harry and me to take him off by ourselves while she waited in the car. This way, Bronson could give me his undivided attention and not be looking over his shoulder for Rachelle.

Like a teenager on her first solo drive with the family car, I was excited about taking charge of the dog. Yet the responsibility weighed on my mind. In my fragile state, visions of disaster loomed large. I pictured Bronson escaping and dashing off, and of me going to jail, or being sued, for failing to take care of this invaluable creature.

"If I lose this dog," I told Harry, "I'm dead."

I knotted the leash around my wrist as an extra precaution, like a child might, then Bronson, my husband, and I set off on a tour of Gig Harbor's waterfront.

Given my isolation in recent years, it was an adventure. We window-shopped for a while. Then one merchant who was familiar with the program waved us in and wanted to know all about Bronson. Afterward, we took a break for a soda, then strolled around the marina to admire the boats.

All the while, we tested Bronson's behavior in different situations and on various surfaces, from carpeting to gravel. We stepped out onto a floating dock and I got so anxious when it swayed that Harry took my hand and reassured me. The dog, however, never missed a beat, staying at a perfect heel.

Bronson, in fact, performed flawlessly. He was so military, so intent on his job, that I began to doubt whether he was even a very happy dog. I had yet to see him at play. And no one told me about how he transformed himself from happy-go-lucky to serious as a surgeon the moment his backpack came on.

When I handed him back to Rachelle at the end of our session, I was exhausted. The walking was more than I was used to. And though I was now all but certain Bronson would soon be mine, I continued to put depleting pressure on myself.

Although I was pleased at how well things had gone, I had a lot of questions for Rachelle and even took her up on her offer to call her at home with more. What should I do if a store owner says I can't come in with the dog? What items would Bronson need when he finally came to stay with us? Where should I take him for veterinary care? What if he needs emergency care after hours? I'm sure Rachelle wondered if my questions would ever end. Still, she took it as a positive sign. It was the recipients who asked none at all, she said, that made her nervous.

I wasn't just inquisitive, though, or diligent: I was consumed with fear that everything could still fall apart. With my porous memory, I worried I would forget some important aspect of Bronson's training or otherwise prove inadequate.

Rachelle brought the dog to meet us twice more over the next week, at the Tacoma Mall and on Fort Lewis. Those trips were much like the first, as we focused on Bronson and me working as a team.

At the mall, Rachelle allowed me to have Bronson for the better part of the day. Taking our time, Harry and I hit J.C. Penney, a card shop, and a number of other stores. All the while, I was wary that the dog might bump into a display or that his backpack might catch a shelf and break something, though it never did. On the military base, Rachelle, Bronson, and I visited the PX and the commissary.

To be honest, I felt uneasy walking into a place of business, especially restaurants, with a dog. During those early expeditions, I always expected someone to refuse us entrance, but that never happened.

In every new situation, I grew more impressed by Bronson's training, intelligence, and determination. One of the biggest eye openers came when Harry and I stopped with the dog for a snack at the mall's food court. Among his lessons in prison, Bronson had learned never to eat anything without permission, especially off the floor. Not only was it bad manners to be gobbling crumbs and other droppings, but who knew what was down there, be it medication someone may have dropped, rancid food, even rat poison.

With Bronson tucked properly beneath our table, I decided to test his willpower. First, I dropped a French fry by one of his front paws, but he seemed so indifferent I assumed he didn't notice. In trying to land a second one closer, so he'd be sure to see it, I accidentally plunked him on the head.

Bronson looked up in mild surprise and the French fry rolled to floor. He gave it the once-over, glanced again at me, then set his head between his legs and returned to his private thoughts.

My husband and I looked at each other and laughed out loud.

"I've seen a lot of dogs in my day," said Harry, "but I've never seen one like this."

FRIDAY, FEBRUARY 3 could not arrive soon enough. That was the day that Bronson was coming to our home for what was supposed to be a trial weekend. The way Jeanne explained it, Rachelle would drop the dog off at our place on Fort Lewis; he would stay for the weekend; then I would return him on Monday.

I was bubbling over with excitement. Everything I had prayed for seemed finally to be coming true.

Bronson may have been an adult now, but I puppy-proofed our quarters nonetheless, tucking in loose wires behind cabinets and making doubly sure any hazardous household products were out of reach. And though I did clean a little, I was too weak to GI the place again. Recently, I'd started having uncontrolled coughing fits that struck while I slept. The attacks, a result of my lung damage, caused me to choke and left me fatigued and enfeebled.

After Jeanne's visit in January, Michael and I gift-wrapped the presents we'd gotten for Bronson. We put them in a new milk crate, which would serve as his toy box, and attached a big bow. In addition to his wicker bed, I also purchased a large travel crate for the dog, which I now put out as well.

In the meantime, Michael and I made a banner that read, WELCOME HOME, BRONSON. My son used crayons to fill in each letter of the first two words with a different color, for a rainbow effect. The dog's name was then colored all in red, with a black border. I stretched the banner across our front window, surrounding it with balloons.

Out on the Olympic Peninsula, meanwhile, Rachelle got Bronson ready. Before the dogs leave the program, they're washed, brushed, and brought completely up to date on their shots and any other veterinary matters.

Between the kids, the dogs, and all her other commitments, the volunteer was busy from the moment she woke up. Still, she couldn't help but feel melancholy.

Rachelle told herself she was a bridge for the dogs she worked with, not a destination. But Bronson, like only one or two of her charges before or since, had touched her deeply. She fantasized about refusing to let him go, but figured that Jeanne or the authorities would eventually come knocking and the jig would be up.

Loading Bronson into the minivan that morning, Rachelle understood that he might not return. Although no one told me, it was not unusual for recipients to do so well with their dogs during the weekend visit that come Monday Jeanne allowed them to stay.

Typically, setting it up as a short visit took pressure off the person receiving the dog. For many people, those first days can be overwhelming. It can also be sobering to discover that for all a service dog can do to make life easier, the animal needs caretaking, too. Some people fail to understand how much that entails until the creature is staring them in the face.

Rachelle tossed a box of Kleenex on the passenger seat, knowing she was going to need it, then departed for the military base. Unfamiliar with Fort Lewis, she had a hard time locating our quarters. That is, until she turned a corner and saw the banner. She grinned and thought, "You'd think they were adopting a child."

Rachelle brought Bronson in and visited awhile, getting the grand tour of our quarters and going over some final details. I took snapshots of her and Bronson on our porch. As always, she said, I could call if I had any problems. When it was time to leave, I could tell Rachelle was a little sad.

RACHELLE LUNDE

Most of the time when I've delivered the dog to their recipient, when I'm leaving, I will start to walk off; they have the dog in hand; and the dog will try to walk with me because they don't really know this other person that well. They've met them. They've worked with them a little bit. But the dog knows he's supposed to be with me, and so I have to tell them, "No, stay." And I'm usually trying really hard not to cry at this point.

Most of the time, if I don't turn around, I get probably ten to twelve yards out the door, and sometimes I'll hear a bark, like, "Hey, wait, what are you doing, come back here."

Bronson didn't do that. It was kind of odd. I just expected it. That's usually what happens. He did go to the door when I left. I turned around and he was watching me, but he didn't bark and he didn't jump up on the door or do the normal reaction. All of a sudden he had somebody new and he just seemed to know that's where he belonged, that that's where his home was.

In truth, Bronson was hesitant after Rachelle drove off, but I did my best to keep him occupied with toys and plenty of pats.

As it turned out, we had a peaceful, wonderful weekend. Harry, Michael, and I went to the PX with Bronson and picked up a few items; Mona and her family came over to meet him; and some of Michael's friends paraded through to get a look as well. Mostly, we just took it easy, giving the dog a chance to settle in at home.

I grew attached right away. What won me over more than anything that weekend was that Bronson never let me out of his sight. If I left the room, no matter how briefly, he followed, even if he had been sleeping or enjoying a toy.

His gaze, in the meantime, was just so affectionate, trusting, and loving. Because Jeanne had been insistent that a service dog should never climb on the furniture, I got down on the rug with him and pet him as he lay his head across my lap.

I felt I had found the truest of friends. Now I saw the loneliness of my days, when Harry was at work and Michael was at school, falling away. And though the dog had yet to fully demonstrate that he would alert to my seizures, I was anxious to find out.

The prospect of going back to life without him—no matter how briefly—was too much to bear.

By Monday, I became so upset about him going back to the program that I began sobbing and shaking. Ever the soldier, Harry urged me to follow the rules as Jeanne had spelled them out: If she said the dog was supposed to go back, he had to go back, no questions asked.

Still, I felt I had to try. When I called Jeanne at the prison, I reported that the weekend had gone great, maybe too great. I'd absolutely fallen in love with Bronson, I said, and just couldn't bring myself to return him. I would if she insisted, of course. "But, please," I begged, "can't he just stay?"

There was a long silence on the other end of the line. That wasn't like Jeanne and it worried me. Yet I could tell she was weighing all I'd said.

When she finally said okay, that she could probably work with that, I smiled wider than I had in years. Bronson was home to stay.

PART III
TEAM

"Thee it behoves to take another road,"
Responded he, when he beheld me weeping,
"If from this savage place thou wouldst escape ..."
                    —Dante Alighieri
                        The Divine Comedy, Inferno,
                        Henry Wadsworth Longfellow
                        translation

26

It didn't take long for reality to set in. I loved Bronson and I was proud to have him, but that didn't change my physical condition. Only a year had passed since the events that led to the coma and my ravaged lungs. As the initial excitement of having Bronson began to subside, doubts crept in. Could I really trust my life to a dog? I almost died because of the seizures in a *hospital*. Now an animal was going to keep me safe?

Neither Jeanne, Rachelle, nor anyone connected to the program said specifically what Bronson would do to alert to my seizures. They simply told me to stay on guard for unusual behavior. Dogs react differently to different people. Just like any owner learns his pet's unique way of saying he wants to go out or would like some attention, I'd have to get to know Bronson's method of warning me that trouble was rolling in from my temporal lobe. That would take time. Doubting the dog would only make the process more difficult.

In the early days after Bronson's arrival, the attacks stayed at bay. The dog's comforting nature had a lot to do with that. We ventured out of the house a bit, going to the PX and around base. We accompanied Michael to school because he wanted the other kids to see mommy's great new dog. And we visited with Mona, who was pregnant with her third child, due that spring, and one or two of our neighbors.

At home, this was an adjustment phase for everyone. Bronson had to find his place in the household as a working dog with high standards of behavior yet still have the freedom to be himself, with a distinct personality. Everyone in the family had to respect his presence and understand that life was going to change, and not always in ways everyone expected or preferred. Bronson wasn't a pet, after all, but an extension of me. Accommodations would have to be made.

The dog and I took it slow. He made life easier for me around the house, retrieving the telephone, for example, if I had trouble getting up. Or if I was cleaning, he might bring over a rag I'd left across the room.

To reenforce that he should stay with me, I followed Jeanne's advice and even in the house often kept Bronson connected to me by a leash I attached to my belt.

I'd talk to him as we moved through our day, saying we'd have lunch now or go for a walk in a little bit. How much he understood, I can't say. He tried diligently enough, though, cocking his head quizzically and keeping his gaze fixed on me.

Bronson brimmed with personality. If I dampened his enthusiasm by saying he had to wait a minute before we could go somewhere, he'd emit a truculent groan. When he completed a task to perfection, he held his head high and strutted about as if he knew how talented he was. With the coming of Bronson something returned to our home that had been in short supply over the past year: smiles.

Michael kept his sports balls on a lower shelf in his bedroom, and in the mornings when I'd go to wake up my son, Bronson would zero in on the black and white, leather soccer ball and make off with it. Stuffed toys, a baseball mitt, and all other kinds of balls–including a red, white, and blue soccer ball–were within striking distance, but he only wanted the black and white one. I'd turn to say good morning to Michael, then hear the ball thumping down the stairs, the dog thundering behind. Bronson would joyfully pounce on it, mouth it, and push it all over the place.

We were amused at first. But soon Michael grew irritated. Bronson was stealing his ball at every opportunity. I put it up high, but then my son couldn't reach it. (Eventually, I surrendered and bought Bronson a soccer ball of his own.)

But this mania ran deep, as I saw one day when we were visiting my friend Theresa and her children. Theresa and I were in lawn chairs, sipping our morning coffee, and watching our kids and some neighborhood youngsters romp around the backyard. Bronson lay on the ground beside me. He was out of his backpack, taking it easy. Just to be safe, I slipped the loop handle of his leash around one of the front legs of my white plastic chair.

It was all was quite pleasant until the kids began playing soccer. At the very moment I took a swallow of coffee, Michael booted the ball in a high arc right before us. Up came Bronson's ears, his head, and before I could speak, the dog himself. As sudden as a karate chop through a board, he burst forth, snapping off the leg of my chair with his leash, and surged across the lawn.

Coffee flew everywhere and I sprawled face down into the grass. I looked across the lawn and saw Bronson snatch the ball as the kids raced toward him.

"Bron-son!" I sputtered.

He trotted back, bearing his trophy and dragging his six-foot leash, the chair leg still entangled in the loop, as the pack of giggling children chased along behind.

He spat out the ball near my head, gave my face some swipes with his tongue, then looked at me quizzically, as if to say, "Gee Mom, what are you doing on the ground?"

Theresa found it so hilarious that she was almost in tears.

"What are you laughing at?" I said. "He broke your chair."

"It was worth it. I haven't laughed so hard in months."

She had a point. Obviously, someone was going to need more work on staying put, but Bronson had been off duty, no real harm was done, and when I looked at myself there on the ground, I had to admit it was pretty funny.

Around this same time some mysterious happenings were occurring involving our refrigerator. I didn't know who, but someone kept leaving the refrigerator open and it was driving me crazy. Every day I barked at Harry and Michael: "If you're going to get something to eat out of the fridge, shut the door! You're letting the cold air out and you're wasting electricity!" And every day I heard the excuses: "I wasn't even in the kitchen," Harry would say. "I shut the door," said Michael.

Still, it continued. I was convinced one of them was having a little fun at my expense. So, I repositioned my living-room chair to give me clear view of the refrigerator. Then I bided my time and furtively monitored my husband and son as they went in and out of the kitchen to make a sandwich or to grab a glass of milk.

One morning, I noticed Bronson strolling into the kitchen. Casually, he went over to the refrigerator and with his teeth grabbed the dish towel I'd draped through the handle of the door, and yanked it open. His canned food was in there as well as a lot of other stuff a dog would find appetizing. But he never disturbed anything. He just sat there, wrapped in the cool air, and stared inside.

When I mentioned this to Jeanne she let out a laugh. She said Bronson had probably gotten some lessons in prison on how to open refrigerator doors for the disabled. She also pointed out that at Purdy he ate in the morning and early evening, while I only fed him at dinner time. She figured he was opening the door because he was hungry.

Now that I knew, I made some adjustments, removing the dish towel, for one, and feeding him twice a day.

Some problems required more delicate handling.

Jeanne made it clear from the start that it was essential to restrict Bronson's activities with Harry and Michael, to ensure that he developed a strong primary relationship with me. For the first two or three months, everyone else was to do their best to ignore Bronson. I was the only who should feed him, take him out, brush him, bathe him, and issue commands, ground rules that in large part would continue for as long as Bronson and I were a team.

When new service dogs come into a family setting, it's natural for the animal to be drawn away from the disabled person they came to help and gravitate toward those who can romp with them, especially children. But if it happens too much, the person who needs the dog tends to become less important in the animal's eyes and loses authority.

Michael, then nine, refused to accept that Bronson wasn't a pet, though I explained this time and again. My son wanted to play with the dog. He asked to take him to the park by himself or to play fetch. Repeatedly, he was told to leave the dog alone.

When I tried to work on Bronson's training, Michael constantly interrupted. He'd ask questions when he should have just been watching. If I instructed the dog to pick up something and he failed to do it right away, my son would jump in and do it for him. When I encouraged Michael to go out and play with his friends, he resisted.

"I didn't know he was going to be taking my job!" Michael cried one day.

"Your job?" I said. "What do you mean taking your job?"

"Now that you've got Bronson you don't need me to help you anymore."

Michael was wounded. He reacted to Bronson like a big brother who was jealous of a new baby. When Bronson approached, he'd push the dog away, saying, "Don't touch me! You're not supposed to touch me!" Or he'd complain, "I have to pick up my toys. Why does he get to leave his stuff all over?"

I'd been regularly calling Rachelle with questions, updates, and reports of Bronson's doings. She understood that the dog needed to establish a strong bond with me, but saw that some concessions for Michael were going to be necessary. She conferred with Jeanne, who agreed.

The solution we came up with was to set aside specific times, usually at the end of the day, when Michael could play with Bronson. I worked out modified versions of softball, in which Bronson played the field and retrieved all of Michael's hits, and soccer, in which they took turns dribbling the ball and chasing one another. Hide-and-seek was another favorite. I'd command Bronson to sit and stay, while Michael made himself scarce. After the dog sniffed him out, Michael rewarded him with a food treat.

I also tried to involve Michael as much as practical in the dog's training and exercise. Bronson needed work on his "stay" command, for instance, so just as the inmates did for one another's dogs at the prison I had my son and some of the neighbor kids cavort before him, trying their best to crack the dog's resolve.

Bronson, who adored children and sorely wanted to play with them, was really put to the test. And Michael felt proud that I trusted him to help with such a special animal.

But it isn't only children who have conflicting emotions when a service dog joins a family. Spouses, too, have to reconcile themselves to some changes. Michael Goehring, who runs the Great Plains Assistance Dog Foundation in North Dakota, tells a story of one husband who lashed out at him for providing his wife with a helper dog. The couple's relationship had been constructed around the wife's disability and the man's helping her. With the dog, she needed him a lot less. The offshoot was that that gentleman showed up at Goehring's place one night threatening to kill him and to poison every dog in his kennels.

Harry wasn't that way, but Mona and other friends did notice that my husband sometimes seemed a little put out by all the attention the dog received. He made small jokes that belied a certain jealousy. For example, Bronson had to be well groomed when we went out in public, especially if I had an appointment at the VA, so I bathed him regularly, about every two weeks. And everyday, I rinsed his coat. Because I was still somewhat feeble, it was usually just easier to run spray the dog after I finished bathing myself. Which led Harry to comment: "The dog takes more showers with my wife than I do." At other times, he'd remark, "You're more married to the dog than you are to me." Seeing that I was with Bronson every moment, that wasn't entirely wrong.

Harry also had to get used to Bronson's presence in our bedroom. With the dog's wicker bed stationed on the floor next to ours, he shared the most intimate secrets of our marriage. During one romantic interlude those first few weeks, Harry turned around to notice Bronson sitting there intently watching us.

Our sex life could be touch and go as it was. Now, my husband put on like this was another burden he had to carry in the bedroom. "I can't even make love to my wife without feeling I'm being critiqued by the dog," he muttered, which had us both in stitches.

27

The most intimidating part of having Bronson was the contract I signed with the Prison Pet Partnership. I was the dog's owner and was liable for his behavior. But the document also listed numerous terms and conditions, which were unnerving when seen in black and white, in legal language. Even though it was largely intended for Bronson's welfare, such a commitment scared me to death.

Among its demands, the agreement called for proper care of the dog right down to flea control and clipping the nails, maintenance of his training, restrictions against using the dog under the influence of alcohol and drugs, home owner's or renter's insurance to cover any damage he might cause, and allowance for home visits by program officials.

In reality, most of the requirements were simple to meet. But with my battered self-confidence, I doubted I could live up to expectations, especially legally binding ones. What I feared most was that if I failed the program reserved the right to "revoke recipient's ownership of said dog and reclaim the dog."

The document scared me. In my mind, every problem that came up, every mistake I made, might have Jeanne Hampl banging on my door, demanding Bronson's return.

All my life I'd gotten the message that I wasn't good enough. All my life I lost the people, creatures, and dreams I cared about most: My father when my parents divorced; my childhood pets, which were sold or taken away; my stepfather Les Weaver; my career; my health; and in the end, almost my life.

The contract said the prison program was to be informed about any problems involving the dog. I overcompensated, constantly calling Rachelle, and to a lesser degree Jeanne, with every issue that arose, no matter how small, and drove them half crazy. What kind of shampoo should I use on the dog? What kind of food should I feed him? I called with daily updates, training questions, and cute things he did. Then, because of my short-term memory lapses, I'd forget their advice and have to call again.

Other times, I was afraid to telephone, figuring this would be the mistake that convinced them I was unfit for such a dog. When Bronson broke out in what appeared to be hives less than a month after his arrival, I was in tears when I called Rachelle. She reassured me, and because Harry was away drove to Fort

Lewis that night and took us to an emergency veterinary clinic. (The doctor said Bronson had an allergic reaction to something, though we never did learn the source.)

Toward the end of February, Harry, Michael, and I took a trip to eastern Washington to see my mother and my sister Kathy, who had her own place. A full year had passed since the events that led to the coma and I wanted them to witness for themselves how far I had come in my rehabilitation as well as meet Bronson.

Although my family obviously knew I had medical problems, they seemed to want to put those difficulties to the past, refusing to accept that I was disabled. I looked fine, they seemed to be saying, so what was the problem? They doubted I needed a service dog. My sister even refused to allow Bronson into her house, telling me to tie him up on the porch if I wanted to come inside.

This had more to do with age-old tensions between us, I believe, than the dog. All the same, I had no intention of leaving Bronson tied out. To do so would have violated everything I promised the program when I accepted him. After all, this was an animal whom if he was trained in the outside world would have cost upwards of ten thousand dollars. I'd have a lot of explaining to do if Jeanne Hampl ever learned that I'd treated Bronson with such disregard.

I was responsible for the dog and his safety. No one else. What's more, to separate from him, unless it was absolutely necessary, ran counter to what I was teaching him about staying with me. Above all, this was a seizure-alert dog. How could he do his job if he wasn't at my side?

My sister shrugged when I told her Bronson had to stay with me. "Oh, well," she said, then went inside with my mother, while Harry, Michael, and I were left on the porch to chat with my stepfather and Kathy's boyfriend.

I thought my prayers had been answered when Bronson entered my life. But as the weeks passed owning him seemed to become a burden. The dog was becoming the focal point of more problems, conflict, and work than I ever expected.

On the most basic level, caring for a dog takes effort, especially when you're struggling to care for yourself. Bronson needed to be bathed and brushed regularly, his teeth brushed, his toenails trimmed. Every day, he had to be fed, taken out to potty, exercised, and kept up on his training. Taking him with me in public, meanwhile, required as much preparation as venturing out with a two-year-old. I had to make sure he was clean, then decide whether he should wear his backpack or, if it was warm, just his leather walking harness. Did I have his water bowl? Bags to clean up after him? Treats?

As it was, Bronson continued to reveal nothing I could understand to be seizure-alerting behavior. Jeanne said he exhibited signs on my first visit to the prison, the day I had seizures on the Narrows bridge, but we had no assurances he would do it again. And if he did, what exactly would he do? Jeanne didn't know for certain. There was no manual to consult.

For weeks, Harry and I waited and watched for the dog's acknowledgment of an oncoming attack. It was baffling to try to read behavior in a dog that could have meant anything–or nothing.

Inevitably, seizures did arrive, creating their familiar chaos. In one instance, after an attack at home, I recovered enough to try to make my way downstairs to telephone my husband, but lost my balance and crashed down several steps, detonating more seizures. Another time, the convulsions hit when I was in the car with Harry.

After these and other incidents, I wondered why Bronson failed to alert. Then when my head cleared Harry and I thought back and tried to determine if we missed something the dog did that was indicative of oncoming trouble. My short-term memory being in shambles only made the process more difficult.

We did notice some behaviors that showed up more than others before seizures, but because they weren't so unusual for a dog of Bronson's age we didn't know what to think. He would be calm, for example, then suddenly become energetic and playful. Or, he'd bring his toys to me like little offerings. Other times, he sat before me and licked my hand or snuggled close. Sometimes he just stared intently at me, a common trait in Rottweilers.

Still, none of this seemed particularly urgent. At times we guessed that Bronson was trying to tell us something and Harry had me lay down on a blanket away from any furniture. But even when a seizure followed, we remained uncertain if the dog knew ahead of time.

Being on Fort Lewis only heightened my stress. The military atmosphere, especially the constant presence of men in uniform, kept my PTSD simmering. This made life particularly hard as the anniversary of my rape neared. If not for Bronson and the powerful sense of responsibility I felt toward him, I might well have checked myself into the psych ward at American Lake or Western State, as I had in past years.

A week or so before the anniversary, the flashbacks stalked me. As had happened time and again, I'd be taking a shower and grow frantic as I saw the water rushing down the drain seemingly turn to blood. One night, I had a dissociative episode in which I ended up out on a playground near our quarters, wearing just a T-shirt and shorts. I wondered later why Bronson failed to accompany me when I left our place, though I suspect that in the state I was in I failed to recognize him—if in fact I ever saw him—and closed the door before he could follow.

As it was, Fort Lewis was hardly the most welcoming place for an assistance dog. In the civilian world, the disabled have the right to be accompanied by their service animals in public accommodations under the mandates of the Americans with Disabilities Act of 1990. On military bases and other federally funded facilities, it's the Rehabilitation Act of 1973. Yet none of this seemed of any concern to people we encountered on base. Repeatedly, we met with rejection and denial of access.

Part of the problem was that a military base tends to see few handicapped people, let alone service dogs. Most soldiers, after all, are young and physically fit. The seriously injured or otherwise disabled are promptly shipped out.

There was also the military mindset to contend with. In the rigid, close-cropped world of an Army base, anything out of the ordinary is eyed with suspicion, often in defiance of common sense. When unusual situations arise, like the appearance of a woman with an assistance dog but no visible disability, self-preservation kicks in. No one wants to make even a simple decision without consulting a superior or a manual for proper procedure.

At first, I didn't mind the roadblocks. During one of Rachelle's training visits we were refused entry to the commissary, where I did my grocery shopping, but she spoke with the manager about the law and what Bronson did for me and no one bothered us again. The dog and I were also stopped a couple times at the PX. But those were mainly matters of lower-level workers being uninformed and were quickly remedied.

What gnawed at me were the unreasonable confrontations. Bronson and I would be in the mall area, where the PX was located, minding our own business, and a lieutenant or captain would bark at me to get the hell out of there with the dog. I'd try to explain, but officers were so used to having people jump at their commands that they would have none of it. It was frustrating, to the point that I'd sometimes start crying. And while I was no longer in the military myself, I knew that Harry could be punished for failure to control his dependents if I pressed my case too passionately.

When we were out, Bronson invariably drew the attention of children. It was hard enough when mothers allowed their kids to approach the dog without asking me, running fingers sticky from ice cream and candy all over his coat. But what do you say to a parent who's yelling at you because her child is terrified of dogs yet your dog has done nothing wrong?

Sometimes Bronson and I would be ordered out of the base's smaller shops by storekeepers. All I knew to defend myself was to show my Prison Pet Partnership identification card and the laws regarding service dogs that were printed on the back. It could have been the Boy Scouts pledge for all they cared.

Still, we had our victories.

One time I was in a convenient store near our quarters when another customer, a giant of a man, lit into me about the dog being there. My friend Theresa, a tough lady in her own right, saw this and hurried over. She got on her tiptoes, right in the guy's face, and said, "Back off! She's disabled and she has every right to be here with this dog!" That emboldened me to put in my two cents as well, and pretty soon the guy was sounding retreat.

Then, there was the night that I brought Bronson to a roller-skating party for Michael's fourth grade class at the post skating rink. No one noticed the dog when we entered, but just after the dog and I settled in at a table with the principal and teachers, the woman manager came roaring over and demanded I remove the dog from the premises.

Even though it's not required by law, Bronson was wearing his backpack, which was clearly marked SERVICE DOG. I showed her my ID with the laws and attempted to explain that we had the right to be there.

She replied that because the establishment served food animals were forbidden. Again I told her she was mistaken, but this only got her more agitated. Back and forth we went. When she finally threatened to call the MPs, I shrugged and told her she should feel free, because I wasn't going anywhere. Secretly I was smiling, because I knew Harry was on duty.

HARRY BEASLEY

I was the patrol supervisor that night. I was the guy in charge of all the different road patrols. I'd make sure my people were doing their patrols, doing their logs, and whenever an incident occurred go and check to make sure they were handling the situation right.

Leana told me when I was getting ready for work that they were having a thing over at the skating rink for the kids and she was going to take Michael and have a good time. I said, Okay, no problem, and went to work.

About six-thirty, seven o'clock, as I'm driving around on patrol, training this new guy how to be a patrol supervisor, a call comes over the radio dispatching a unit. It was, "Unit Twenty-one, proceed to the skating rink reference a woman that's creating a disturbance with a dog."

I looked over at the guy and said, "That's my wife."

He looked at me and said, "You're kidding, right?"

"No, that's my wife."

So we headed over to the skating rink and we got there. I knew there was a conflict of interest, so I wasn't going to handle this. I put my hand on the guy's shoulder and I said, "This is the situation: My wife has a medical dog. That medical dog has all rights of access as a seeing eye dog. Now, have fun and deal with it."

I just hung in the background and watched as the other MPs dealt with the lady and my wife and the guy I was training dealt with the lady and my wife.

It went on for awhile and then finally, he asked me some question like, "Sgt. Beasley, how old is your wife?" He needed the information for the report log. But he asked right in front of this rink manager. When she realized Lee was my wife, it was just unreal. The look in her eyes was like, "Uh oh." Doom and gloom, despair and misery.

After she was made to realize that she was the one breaking the law, I received a tearful apology as well as a promise that she would educate her employees about service dogs.

That was satisfying, but it hardly eliminated the pressure. Adding to my constant worry that the program would reclaim Bronson, the dog's presence seemed to kindle a run of conflicts and controversies, which all took their toll.

Once, one of my neighbors summoned the MPs because she thought Bronson was attacking some children, when in fact he was playing with them. Another time, I was told it would be better if I no longer brought the dog to church.

On and on it went, until it all became too much. On more than one occasion, I was crying and told Rachelle that maybe I should give the dog back, that I couldn't handle it anymore. She was firm with me but kind. If need be, Rachelle said, I could return Bronson, but I also made a commitment and if for no other reason than the dog's sake, I needed to try to stick with it. A lot of problems, she felt, were less significant than I made them out to be.

She was right, of course. I hung in there, and little by little that spring, life did improve.

Grethe Cammermeyer from the VA and Jeanne wrote letters on behalf of me and Bronson to authorities on Fort Lewis, which eased some problems.

Cindy Mack, who'd been with Jeanne for the home visit, began meeting me on base and gave me pointers on training and how to handle certain situations. I learned a lot just by observing her body language and her self-confidence when we walked into a business establishment with the dog. In many ways, I had been so timid and uncertain when I went places with Bronson that I was setting myself up to be stopped.

Harry, for his part, did his best to make sure his fellow MPs knew the law regarding service dogs. He wrote a lengthy report about me and Bronson and our legal rights in the MP pass-on book, which details significant recent events on base and is widely read by the law enforcement officers. He also spoke at a briefing with his own company and reached out when possible to those in the two other MP companies.

At the briefing, Harry told his colleagues that they might see me and Bronson around base from time to time. Most of the MPs already knew that I had seizures, but now I was accompanied by my seizure-alert dog, he said. He spoke about the law and what function Bronson served.

They would be able to identify the dog, Harry explained, by his red backpack.

"Yeah, he's got on a red smoking jacket," chimed in one of the guys, drawing some laughs.

And that's how, in certain circles at least, Bronson became known as "the dog in the red smoking jacket."

RACHELLE LUNDE

Bronson probably is the most prayed-for dog in the history of all dog-kind. At Gig Harbor Covenant, the women in our Bible study group got used to seeing Bronson when I brought him with me during his training. In fact, if I showed up and I didn't have Bronson, it was immediately, "Where's Bronson? Where is he?"

In the weeks after he went to Leana, I remember asking the women, "Would you just keep it in your prayers that Bronson and Leana will develop a strong bond?" There were an awful lot of people that weren't even in our Bible study group that I asked, "Would you pray for Bronson and Leana?"

God can work through a whole bunch of different mediums. For us, the hope was that God would work through Bronson. We were hoping that there would be a real softening to Leana's character, that she would feel the need to take care of him, and that possibly that would give her the strength to stay out of Western State, the mental facility here, and that this relationship would work for her self-esteem, and that it would help her to start feeling like she was capable.

You see, Leana was very excited at first. You get a new dog and it's a lot of fun. Then after everybody in your neighborhood has met him and now you've just got to take him out and go for a walk, it's not as much fun anymore. The honeymoon is over. For Leana, a lot of it was that she could see there was a lot of work involved. Plus, she was having problems on base taking the dog anywhere. I think she was starting to ask why she should go through all this trouble to make it work when all she was getting was a bunch of hassle for it.

I was concerned about Bronson. If he came back to the program, where would he go? Was this going to cause him to be more insecure? We know that the more placements a dog has, the longer it takes to settle down into each home. Bronson was certainly an easy dog to place, but how was he going to react to the next situation? Each time you run more of a gamble.

We wanted it to work between Bronson and Leana. But I really felt that she needed prayers for some mental stability, that she would not be so worried about everything. I would get four calls a day sometimes. I would get a phone call, for example, if she thought his collar was too tight. I'd say, "Well, loosen it up." She wasn't really calling me about that, though. I think she just was terrified of taking Bronson and that she felt she couldn't do it.

It was like walking on eggshells. She was so concerned that if she did anything wrong that Jeanne was going to fly out of the sky and take Bronson away. I kept saying, "Leana, she doesn't want to take the dog away. That is not the purpose of the program. We'll work with you. She doesn't want to take him back. We want it to work."

28

Like most programs that provide service dogs, the Prison Pet Partnership asked its recipients to build on their training skills after they settled in with their animals. Jeanne usually encouraged them to find a trainer in their area. It was impractical to return to the prison for regular lessons, but Jeanne also wanted the new teams to develop an independence apart from her and their former trainers.

Like me, most people receiving assistance dogs are novice handlers. They've learned the basics, but have to follow up under the eye of a professional to improve and to hammer out inevitable problems. Sad to say, too many allow training to slide. That can cause the dogs to regress and in some instances actually become a hazard to their owners. Often, people neglect to contact the program until the situation has seriously deteriorated, which over the years has resulted in a number of dogs going back to the prison and being placed with new owners.

I met with one outside trainer–one of the founders of the prison program, in fact–but felt unwelcomed. Among other things, she said she was afraid that the fluorescent lights at her place would cause my seizures to kick in, and that it'd probably be best if I looked elsewhere.

Finally, I signed on with Jeanne, who in addition to her job as director taught basic and advanced obedience for everyday dogs out at her home in Gig Harbor. It wasn't quite what Jeanne preferred, but I found comfort in having the program well aware of my situation and that we could resolve problems early.

That April, Bronson and I started with a beginner's class, a level that reflected my abilities rather than the dog's.

Harry and Michael accompanied me, but to participate in a class with eight to ten strangers, none of whom had disabilities, was still a giant and nerve-wracking step. My classmates would have no idea of what I'd been through. All they would see, I worried, was a woman in her thirties who behaved like an insecure child. With my memory impairment, I feared they'd think me retarded or stupid. I thought I'd be unable to keep up with the class or that with my poor balance I'd stumble and embarrass myself.

Everyone turned out to be was friendly enough. We were all there to learn, after all, and had a common interest in dogs. Bronson being in his backpack allowed for conversation, too, without my having to say too much about my problems. All the same, I mostly kept to myself.

It was at this point that I started to see Jeanne from a new perspective. She and her husband Peter had a gorgeous three-bedroom Cape Cod with a water view, on one and a half acres. She usually held her classes in the yard but if it was inclement moved them into her oversized, three-car garage.

Away from the prison, Jeanne seemed more human to me. At Purdy, among the inmates and guards, she carried herself with an almost military bearing. Now, she remained a commanding figure in the role of teacher, but came across as more relaxed and friendly.

Her sense of humor, which leaned toward the ironic and took me a while to catch onto, seemed more evident, too. One day, for example, as Michael was romping with some of the dogs after class, I heard Jeanne mischievously call out: "That's it, kill the kid! Kill the kid!"

I met her dogs, an independent-minded Welsh corgi named Foxy, whom I learned suffered from seizures herself, and Blaze, an intelligent golden retriever. Blaze, I soon found, was skilled in working zippers. It became a ritual every class for her dogs to raid my tote bag, which they knew carried Bronson's treats as well as one or two toys.

The sessions, meanwhile, covered the very basics of obedience: Sit. Stay. Down. Come. Heel. We did recalls again, summoning the dogs from a short distance. And Jeanne had me work on making sure Bronson paid strict attention as he walked on the leash, testing him with a series of sharp turns and about-faces.

Right from the start I struggled. With my memory problems, I couldn't always distinguish between my right or my left. Jeanne taught us that whenever we walked with the dog, we were always to step off with the left foot. Time and again, I led with my right, which soon became exasperating for me, and as time passed, for Jeanne.

The only time we should address our dogs by name, she said, was before the command "come." I couldn't get it, though, and I'd continually say, "Bronson, sit" or "Bronson, down," which caused him to lurch forward a few steps before following through with what I wanted.

Harry, whom I'd grown to depend on to help me navigate the world, tried to help by furtively hand signaling or mouthing instructions from the sidelines. As often as not, this only added to my confusion.

Once or twice, I came to class banged up from seizures I had at home. When I told Jeanne of being caught off guard by the convulsions, of still not detecting any signs from Bronson, she seemed little concerned about the dog's ability to alert and instead put the responsibility on me.

"Did you listen to your dog?" she asked. "It's not the dog's fault if you're not paying attention to what he's telling you."

"But I was paying attention," I insisted. Maybe Bronson was acting a little antsy, or licking a bit more, or holding eye contact longer, I said, but if anything it was subdued. He didn't seem worried or perturbed in any way. There was no indication he was warning me of anything.

Jeanne's reply was unwavering: Keep a journal of the dog's behavior. Take notes if you have to. But *pay closer attention.*

JEANNE HAMPL was never much of a bleeding heart, not as a young nurse at New York's embattled Bellevue Hospital and not now as director of a non-profit organization that brought together the disabled, convicts, and dogs rescued from shelters.

Back in the sixties, she met plenty of women who became nurses to save the world from pain and suffering. Reality slapped the idealists down like so many flies. The ravages of poverty, social problems, and mental health issues that their patients endured should have been fair warning. Then came the realization that the sick often failed to get better. Many died. Saving someone–somedays, any-one–wasn't always in the cards.

Bellevue's male prison ward, where Jeanne filled in as head nurse, was even more disenchanting. While some patients were truly appreciative of the nurses' kindness, the predators among them saw only weakness and opportunity to manipulate and take advantage.

Disillusioned, the bleeding hearts usually departed Bellevue, and nursing, for safer emotional shores.

Though unaware at the time, Jeanne had more selfish reasons for gravitating to the field. She did find reward in helping people, but if you ask Jeanne today why she became a nurse–or years later a dog trainer–she'll say that in large part it suited her need for control.

Hospital patients, especially those of forty years ago, tend to do what they're told, and in its own way that made Jeanne happy. Similarly, she found satisfac-tion in working with canines, who learned best in a structured, consistent, orderly environment.

Jeanne grew up in a cramped rent-controlled apartment in Jackson Heights, Queens. She and her sister Joan shared the only bedroom with their grandmother while their parents bivouacked in the living room.

The Martin family was far from rich, but the kids wanted for little. Jeanne's father John was a fireman. He retired at age forty-five, and with a determination to savor life's pleasures lived frugally and avoided steady work the rest of his days. Her mother Julie, for her part, was a fixture on the sales floor at Bloomingdale's.

If anything was lacking around the Hampl household it was pets. The family owned a dog for awhile when Jeanne was a toddler. And though her sister brought home stray cats periodically none of them remained long either. Jeanne liked dogs, but in the close quarters of apartment living her animal companions were limited to goldfish and turtles.

A graduate of an all-girls Catholic high school, Jeanne weighed joining a convent, but settled instead on the Bellevue and Mills School of Nursing, a highly regarded city school where her sister had gone. Ever the perfectionist, Jeanne graduated at the top of her class in 1965.

She worked at Bellevue as a nurse, and in her free time began to pursue her interest in animals. She owned a horse for awhile and boarded it–at twice the cost of her rent–in Central Park. While trail riding, the pinto periodically tossed her and clopped back to the stables alone. Jeanne slunk in ten minutes later to the cheers and good-natured ribbing of her fellow riders and the stable workers.

She met Peter Hampl, then an intern in oral surgery, at the hospital and they dated. In what began as inexpensive entertainment and became a tradition during their years together in New York, the couple took in the Westminster Kennel Club Dog Show. Strolling among the many breeds at Madison Square Garden, they were particularly enamored with the golden retriever's handsome appearance and friendly nature. Peter, a duck hunter, also thought a golden would be an ideal hunting companion.

In 1968, Jeanne and Peter were married. Son Timothy followed a year and a half later. And when her husband completed his residency, they moved to Washington State, where he'd been offered a job. As an added inducement for Jeanne, Peter promised that once they were situated he'd buy her a horse.

Life, of course, had its own plans.

When they got to Washington, Jeanne settled in as a stay-at-home wife and mother. She never did get her horse, but Peter talked to a golden retriever breeder who promised him first choice of a litter that was to be available around Christmas, about a month before the couple's second baby was due.

Ten days before Thanksgiving, tragedy struck. Jeanne was by herself, driving home from a dental wives meeting when an elderly man rolled through a stop sign and onto the highway. She slammed his car broadside. Remarkably, he walked away unscathed. Despite wearing her seat belt, Jeanne was less fortunate.

As she heaved forward upon impact, banging her head against the steering wheel, her placenta tore from the uterus.

Paramedics rushed her to the hospital. But with the uterine damage, Jeanne's entire clotting system shut down. Hours passed before doctors were able to control her bleeding and operate. The baby would die and Jeanne required a blood transfusion.

She spent two weeks in the hospital, then six weeks later discovered she'd contracted hepatitis and was back again. She also learned she had two broken kneecaps, which had been overlooked during her first stay.

With the demands of an infant son, Jeanne could afford little time for mourning. But her loss cut deeply, and for years afterward she spoke of events as occurring either before the accident or after.

While she was recovering, her husband asked whether they should still get the puppy. Already decimated by one loss, however, Jeanne was hardly going to let every dream go to ruin.

The golden retriever, whom they named Arrow, went a long way in helping her through a tough time. He was a pleasant distraction, a joy, and a healer.

Peter started the dog's obedience training with a class at the local community center. When Jeanne was well enough, she took over Arrow's training and at their instructor's urging entered him in some local competitions.

Jeanne was inexperienced in the show ring and mainly followed her instructor's directions. Arrow, on the other hand, was a natural. He won his Companion Dog title, the first in a series of AKC obedience rankings, and fell just short of the Dog World Award, an honor bestowed upon the best and brightest competitors.

After Jeanne had her second child, Theresa, the kids would occasionally bicker over whom their mother loved best. When they stormed in to demand an answer from their mother, she replied with her characteristic humor: Arrow was her favorite, she said.

That joke sailed over the little boy's head. Years later, Tim told her that he'd long thought she meant it, that Mom really did love the dog better than him.

"You know, honey," Jeanne replied, poker-faced, "there were times I did."

Success in the show ring fueled Jeanne's interest in working with dogs. She continued competing with Arrow, who earned further titles in obedience, tracking, and hunting competitions.

Then, when Peter got his own golden retriever for hunting and started taking an interest in field trialing, Jeanne followed suit with yet another golden, this one named Braggin. Unlike obedience work, field trialing played off the animal's instincts and breeding. Yet it was far more challenging in that it called for the dogs to find and retrieve game birds at distances of a hundred and fifty yards or more, with the handlers using only whistles and hand signals to direct them.

As the Hampls' passion for field trialing grew, their house filled with golden retrievers—as many as four at one point—and Jeanne's skill as a trainer steadily improved. Both women and goldens were disparaged in the sport at the time, which only added to Jeanne's satisfaction as she and Braggin collected one blue ribbon after another.

The Hampl children, meanwhile, grew restless watching their parents' dogs muck through field and stream every weekend. For the sake of the family, Jeanne and her husband eventually bought a boat, took up water-skiing, and left field trialing behind.

Jeanne's involvement with the Prison Pet Partnership, however, was taking shape. She had donated a golden who was falling short as a hunting dog to her friend Barbara Davenport and the state drug dog program. Davenport, however, found the animal too well trained for her purposes—he wouldn't jump on any furniture, for starters—and passed him along to the prison program.

Purdy was but five minutes from Jeanne's house. As she got more interested in the Prison Pet Partnership, she was asked to join the board of directors. She volunteered now and then as a trainer and took a number of dogs out of the prison to get them acclimated to working in the community.

When she finally took over as director in the summer of 1994, Jeanne was ready for a new challenge. Her kids were grown. And while she ran the business side of her husband's oral surgery practice for the better part of nine years, it reached the point that she finally had enough.

Her nursing background would go a long way in helping her assess the needs of the disabled who came to the program seeking assistance. And though she had limited experience in preparing service dogs, she knew she could draw on her expertise in other areas of training. The basic principles, after all, stayed the same.

It took time for the inmates to accept Jeanne's strong personality, but once they did many developed a lasting affection for her. Years later, after being released from prison, a number praised her as one of the most influential people in their lives.

They discovered—as I soon would—that if you had Jeanne as a friend you had someone who'd stand with you through the toughest of times.

For her part, Jeanne also experienced a softening during her years at the prison. As she got to know the women, she started to see the criminal justice system through new eyes. Before spending much time at Purdy, she was skeptical about rehabilitation. Now, she questioned the dearth of opportunities for the inmates to develop new skills and contribute something to society.

Jeanne also grew as a dog trainer. In many ways, preparing service dogs was a welcome alternative to field trialing and other contests. For as much as she enjoyed winning, there was always something uncomfortable about pushing the dogs day in and day out to satisfy the human ego. At Purdy, she felt the hard work had a useful purpose.

For Jeanne, the unique ability that dogs have to help people ultimately came down to the animal's down-to-earth, honest nature. They accept us, for the most part, for better or worse. And unlike people, dogs lack the capacity for deceit and subterfuge. To survive, they do what works. Bark at the mailman, for example, and eventually he goes away. Stare at your human at five-thirty and she gives you dinner.

And if a dog that seizure alerts has his owner trained well enough, he can get attention when trouble's coming.

From what she learned at Purdy, Jeanne became an authority on seizure-alert dogs. She would go on to educate assistance-dog groups and testify in court as an expert witness about the phenomenon.

Time and again during my first spring with Bronson, in an effort to make me pay closer attention to the dog's behavior and prepare for my seizures, Jeanne would implore, "Leana, listen to your dog!"

She belabored the point until her voice echoed in my dreams: "Trust your dog!" she said. "Dog's don't lie." The catch was that I had to learn that lesson on my own.

29

Though slow in coming, a transformation was underway. Even as I struggled to interpret Bronson's awareness that seizures were approaching, the dog was chipping away at the bleakness I saw in my life. He lightened my spirits. He brought routine and responsibility to my day, especially after my husband and son left for work and school. And the pride I felt in the dog and in myself as an ambassador for the prison program was obvious.

Grace McCardle was among the first to notice. Less than a year after I frightened her by swallowing all those pills in front of her, she noted in the records of my counseling sessions that Bronson was having a good effect on me. "Neat appearance," she wrote. "Talks easily. Good eye contact. Emotionally stable. Is more confident of herself since having the service dog. She has also become more feminine in appearance–hair curled, wearing earrings, and summer shorts. Previously she has told me she does not try to look feminine because she does not want to be attractive to men for fear of rape. She seems to be willing to take more risk in feminizing her appearance. She could be more confident with the dog accompanying her. I also believe she is recovering more with less PTSD symptoms and fewer dissociative episodes. She deals with here and now situations."

In April, just before Easter, Michael, Bronson, and I joined my friend Theresa and her kids for a trip to the mall. Inside, the shopping center had a section decorated with flowers and with a regal, high-backed chair, for children to have their picture taken with a fellow in an Easter Bunny outfit. The man had on an adorable white costume, complete with a fluffy tail and a big bunny head with a pink nose. With those ears, he must have stood seven feet tall.

It was too cute to resist. I told the photographer about Bronson and asked if the dog too could be photographed with the Easter Bunny. She chuckled and said sure, but when I asked Bronson to sit in the rabbit's lap like the kids, the dog wanted no part of it. He was even hesitant to put his paws up on this strange creature.

As shoppers stopped to watch, grinning and calling their children's attention to the dog, we decided to have Bronson occupy the chair by himself, with the Easter Bunny standing next to him. I held Bronson's gaze by dangling a biscuit behind the photographer, and the Easter Bunny struck a pose, draping his arm across the top of the throne, and crossing his legs as if he was waiting for a bus.

I loved that picture and sent copies to everyone. Rachelle Lunde, remembering Bronson's fear of hats, laughed out loud to see the dog's steadfast demeanor alongside this monstrous rabbit. Out at the penitentiary, Jeanne Hampl got such a kick out of the photo that she sought out Barbara Thompson, housed now in another part of the facility, and brought her a copy. Barbara, who had little love for Jeanne, still had to grin when she saw this image of her favorite student.

That same month, my friend Mona gave birth to her third child, a son named Aaron. I was supposed to be with her when she delivered, in fact, but ended up hospitalized for seizures instead. Harry and I were named godparents, a source of considerable pride on my part.

When I first saw the baby, I was hesitant to hold him. I worried about being caught off guard by the convulsions or that the Todd's paralysis, which sometimes caused spasms, might cause me to drop him. We finally decided that I'd sit on the couch and cradle the baby in my lap.

Bronson, who I doubt ever saw an infant before, adored Aaron. When the baby was in his carrier, the dog lay beside him like a friendly sentinel. If Aaron fussed, a concerned expression fell across Bronson's face and he looked to comfort him. If the other kids got too rambunctious around the baby, the dog reprimanded them with a low "wooo-wooo-wooo."

Later, when Aaron graduated to crawling, the dog hardly budged as the baby crept across him, tugged his ears, or gripped his fur for stability. If the baby lost his balance and fell, Bronson peered over to make sure he was okay, gave him a swipe or two with his tongue, then returned to his nap.

Obeying Jeanne's entreaties, in the meantime, I worked to pay closer attention to Bronson's behavior. One afternoon, while visiting a neighbor with Theresa, I noticed what I thought might have been a significant change in the dog's manner. Bronson had been playing with the children but suddenly stopped, wanting nothing more to do with them, and threw his entire focus on me. Jumping up, feet in my lap, he urgently licked at my face. I petted him, then ordered him down. Within seconds, he returned, softly whining, licking, sniffing, and shimmying.

Like previous episodes, this seemed ambiguous. Maybe Bronson was alerting, but maybe he just wanted attention. Not wanting to terrify the children in the event that I did have a seizure, I started to leave. But my friends convinced me to stay, insisting that Bronson probably wasn't alerting and even if he was I'd be safer with them.

A half hour passed. Forty-five minutes. An hour. I finally decided that the dog was just playing me for all the affection he could get and tried to ignore him.

Then, nearly two hours after Bronson began acting up, I slid out of my chair and onto my friend's dining room floor in full convulsions. Five or six seizures, in fact, hit before the paramedics could get there. One seizure that the EMTs witnessed wracked me for almost twenty minutes. To feed oxygen into my lungs, and ultimately to prevent brain damage, they had to nasally intubate me and ended up giving me a gushing bloody nose.

For two days I was hospitalized. And though Bronson was kept out of the ambulance because of lack of space, Harry brought him to the hospital the next day, and he stayed with me until my release.

SATURDAY, MAY 13 broke sunny and clear. Fort Lewis was holding its annual fair for National Pet Week, an event that attracted several hundred people. There were going to be exhibitions by military working dogs, presentations on grooming and first aid for pets, booths with free literature, and a vaccination clinic. Bronson was due for shots, so I made an appointment and looked forward to getting out a bit.

Harry slept in that morning after working late the night before and Michael begged off. So Bronson and I set out around nine o'clock. It would be the first time we'd be out together without family or friends watching over me. And though it was just a baby step in the healing process–the PX was but a twenty-minute walk–it did show my growing confidence in the dog and myself.

Behind the base elementary school was a wide trail, actually a dirt access road, that stretched through the woods toward the center of the base. It was beautiful back there, and if you paid attention you could often see wildlife, like jack rabbits or deer.

We were halfway down the trail, less than ten minutes from home, when Bronson broke from his heel position and began whining and dancing around me. Caught up in my own thoughts, I figured he was excited about being out on the trail. Maybe it was the rabbit we'd seen a little earlier that had him worked up, I thought, or any of a thousand scents from the woods.

As we went on, Bronson grew more agitated. Going completely against his training, he snatched a leg of my trousers with his teeth, tugging me toward him. Only when the nausea and the acrid smell of my aura came upon me a few minutes later did I realize that seizures were coming on fast.

Panic shot through me, and I broke for home. We only got as far as the school, however, when I realized I wasn't going to make it.

I lowered myself to the ground in a grassy area. Worried that the dog might wander off when I was unconscious, I knotted Bronson's leash to my wrist.

I have no how bad the seizures were or how long I lay there. Little that happened over the next six hours is completely clear. When the convulsions ran their course and I could get up, my mind was tangled in confusion. Apparently, I tried to go home, but instead of turning left, I went too far and took a right, trudging straight out of Fort Lewis's front gate. My next memory is of staggering along the side of Interstate 5 near the Tacoma Mall, some sixteen miles from home, where I headed north toward Seattle, against the whoosh of southbound traffic.

How I arrived there remains a mystery. It's even possible that I uncomprehendingly accepted a ride from someone, who then let me out either on or near the highway. The morning temperatures had been cool, so I had on jeans, two layers of shirts, and a bright pink windbreaker. It was mid-afternoon, and I was hot and tired.

At my side, away from traffic, was Bronson. At first I was unaware he was even there. When I did notice him, I was mystified as to who he was or why he was with me. The farther we traveled, small bits of memory surfaced. Slowly it came to me that this dog belonged to me, that I was in some way disabled, and that his job was to help me.

Mammoth rigs thundered past. As I struggled to make sense of my predicament, I was bewildered by the blank backs of the highway signs we kept passing. I never thought to turn around and look at their front sides, though I probably couldn't have understood them anyway.

By the time we reached the interchange for highway 16, which runs out to Gig Harbor, and Tacoma's 38th Street, I was distressed. My breathing had become heavy and I couldn't stop coughing. In the distance was a tower-like structure. (It turned out to be St. Joseph's Hospital.) Convinced I could get help there, I fixed that as my destination.

Bronson and I had already crossed the interchange for traffic going away from Gig Harbor. Now we were standing on a small asphalt island, attempting to cross against the flow that was charging toward that waterfront community. The cars kept coming, and Bronson who had been in a heel position kept stepping in front of me and leaning in, blocking me from moving forward.

When the unmarked state patrol car pulled in behind me, I was sitting on a concrete barrier, confused and upset. A man who looked to be in his mid-fifties, approached. Larry Raedel, a detective sergeant for the Washington State Patrol's drug task force, had just gotten off duty and was driving home when he spotted me.

Raedel had a friendly manner. He asked a couple questions, but I could tell him little more than my first name. I explained that I wanted to cross the road but couldn't. I began sobbing and he assured me everything would be okay.

Bronson, meanwhile, was by my feet. And Raedel, on the opposite side of the barrier, was surprised when he finally noticed the dog, in a red backpack no less. He radioed for assistance, then spoke to me a little about the dog, asking if he was thirsty. I said he probably was, and got Bronson's bottle out of his backpack and let him drink from it.

Shortly afterward, a second trooper, whom I later learned to be Robert Veliz, wheeled in. He was tall and dark haired, and like Raedel, dressed in the French blue Washington State Patrol uniform.

"Leana," Raedel said after they conferred, "this is officer Bob. He's a friend of mine. And he's going to help you get where you belong."

I hesitated when they told me to take Bronson and climb in the back of Veliz's cruiser. Childlike, as I often am in my postical state, I said that I shouldn't accept rides from strangers. They assured me that officer Bob was a friend, and I finally gave in.

Veliz radioed in to report that we were on our way to nearby Puget Sound Hospital. The plan was to bring me to the emergency room, where the staff could evaluate me, try to determine who I was, and decide what to do next.

Once there, we were met in the foyer by a security guard and two nurses, a man and a woman. The female nurse said no dogs were allowed and that I should tie Bronson to a pole outside. By now, my mind had largely cleared and I explained that that this was a service dog, that under the law he was allowed to come in with me. I was astounded that someone working at a hospital, of all places, was unaware of that.

"Are you blind?" the woman asked, sarcastically.

"No, I'm not blind," I shot back.

"Then you're not authorized to have a guide dog."

"This isn't a guide dog," I said. "He's a service dog."

Adding to my frustration, Veliz was ignorant of the very laws he was sworn to enforce. Rather than support me, he assumed she was right and said Bronson had to stay out. "She's breaking the law," I told him, "and you're letting her."

Back and forth we went until Veliz finally asked if I had any identification, and I found Bronson's Prison Pet Partnership ID in the dog's backpack, with the laws spelled out on back. I handed over the card as well as my medications, then explained that I had epilepsy and PTSD, how the dog assisted me, and that the VA had helped me to obtain him.

None of this seemed to matter to them, though it apparently gave Veliz the idea to contact the prison, then the VA, in search of someone to take responsibility for me. He went inside and after a few calls, I later learned, managed to track down Harry. My husband, who had searched all over base for me, was waiting by the telephone for news.

When the trooper and nurse returned, the tension escalated. At first, no one mentioned that Harry was on his way. Instead, they continued pressing me to leave Bronson outside. I finally told them that if they weren't going to allow me inside with the dog, I was leaving.

The nurse shrugged. If I refused to come in, she said, they couldn't force me, then went back inside.

I started to walk off, but Veliz grabbed my arm, pulling me up short. "You're not going anywhere," he said.

Bronson, in response, positioned himself before me, and as he did on the highway, pressed against me as if to push me back.

"I'll take that dog away if you try to leave," Veliz snapped, then motioned with his hand, as if to grab the leash.

"*You won't touch my dog,*" I said. It was an order, not a request.

Veliz seemed surprised but pleased to have produced such a reaction. He pointed to the wall by the ER entrance. "Get over there or I'll take that dog and you'll never see it again," he said.

My emotions and physical well being were already frayed from all I'd been through that day, but now the stress was taking its toll. To be in the right, to need help, but to receive only stubborn resistance from people who should have known better was maddening. My eyes teared up, but I refused to cry in front of this man.

"It's against the law for you to interfere with this dog's work," I said. "You can't take him from me."

"I'll take that damn dog anytime I want," he shouted. "Now get back there by the wall or I'll handcuff you and take that dog away."

The threat of physical restraint triggered old demons, and my anxiety soared. If not for my breathing difficulties, I'm sure I would have fled.

Frustration only fueled the fire. Not only was I being denied entry with my service dog, but now I couldn't leave either. I had done nothing wrong. I wasn't under arrest. As I saw it, Veliz brought me to the hospital as a courtesy. When they refused Bronson access, I felt well within my rights to go.

Veliz went to his car for something. Bronson, in the meantime, had to potty and a security guard, who'd replaced the one who met us on arrival, directed me over by some bushes. It was around that time that I attempted once more to leave. Veliz again seized my arm, saying I could go when my husband arrived, but until then, I was his responsibility.

By my third attempt to walk away, Veliz was visibly angry. Grabbing me hard, he spun me around to face him. In the process, Bronson, who I was holding short on his leash, got jerked as well.

"If you don't stay here, I'm going to call a mental health professional and have you committed to Western State for a seventy-two-hour hold. Then I'm going to take that damn dog to the pound."

"If I go to Western State, he goes to Western State," I replied. "You can't take my service dog from me."

Bronson, growing anxious, once again moved between us. I stroked his muzzle to calm him.

"I don't care what that dog was trained to do," Veliz said. "I'll take him to the pound and have him put down and you'll never get him back."

"You *will not* touch my dog."

"I *will*." At this, Veliz snatched the leash from my hand, stepped back, and yanked. Bronson, throttled by his choke collar, yelped as he left the ground, then thunked to earth at the state trooper's feet. The dog hunkered on his stomach, trembling.

"You hurt him!" I cried.

Veliz looked down at the dog, stunned.

"Let go now!" I said.

Veliz offered no resistance as I slowly reached over and took back the leash. As I led Bronson away from the trooper, I could see that the dog was in pain. I massaged his neck and the side of his head. The trooper, realizing he'd crossed a bad line, retreated a bit. "Now do what I said and get over by the wall," he told me, more subdued.

He then directed the security guard to keep an eye on me while he went inside to make a telephone call. A few minutes later, Harry pulled in. "There's my husband," I said. "I'm leaving."

Just as I was nearing Harry, the state trooper trotted behind me and again took my arm. This time, I ripped myself away and glared at him. "You said I could go when my husband got here. He's here, and I'm leaving."

"Not until I talk to him."

I tried to tell Harry all that had happened, how the nurse denied me access with Bronson, that the trooper backed her, and that he'd harmed the dog.

Harry was grateful I was safe. At the same time, he'd never seen me so angry. Unsure of what he'd walked into, he mainly wanted to get me out of there.

"We found your wife on the freeway, and, well, you know her history," Veliz told him, derisively.

"I know her history," Harry acknowledged. "Is she free to go?"

"Yeah, get her out of here."

At this, Veliz stalked off, and I lit into Harry. "That trooper hurt Bronson," I said, "and you didn't say a damn thing about it!"

"Let's just go home," he replied. "You can call Jeanne Hampl and tell her what happened. She'll know how to take care of it."

30

I knew Bronson was injured but had no idea of how badly until we got back to Fort Lewis. When we went to leave Puget Sound Hospital, he balked at getting into the car, which was strange given how thrilled he usually was to go anywhere. I had to lift him and set him on the back seat. Coming out at home, he was slow and stiff.

Bronson winced when I scratched him toward the back of his jaw, usually his favorite spot. At first I figured his collars were bothering him. So I removed the leather, buckle collar, but when I went to take off his choke chain, I found it taut rather than loose-fitting. I thought maybe it was knotted, but upon closer inspection was stunned to see that his neck had swollen almost two inches.

The dog was so uncomfortable when I went to remove the choke chain that Harry and I thought we might have to use a bolt cutter. As it turned out, I was able to gingerly ease it over one ear at a time.

Bronson was limping, clearly favoring his left front leg, when he went to get some water. I ran my hands across him, manipulating his shoulder and joints. He was in more pain than I initially thought.

By this point, my levels of anxiety and anger were dangerously high, given my potential for seizures or a full-scale PTSD attack. Above all, I worried that when Jeanne Hampl learned of Bronson's condition she would blame me, and again the prospect of losing the dog tore at me.

I made detailed notes of everything I could piece together from the confrontation at the hospital. Then, I called the Washington State Patrol to lodge a complaint. The man who took my call—I never got his name—refused to listen, insisting that the trooper did nothing wrong and that I should take my problem up with the hospital.

I was still upset ten minutes later when I called Jeanne Hampl at home and regurgitated the day's events. She heard me out, then urged me to calm down and direct my energy toward taking care of Bronson. In the meantime, she said, she'd make some calls.

The first individual she contacted, a supervisor at Puget Sound Hospital, refuted my account of events. When Jeanne then called the state patrol, the sergeant on duty readily told her that hospital personnel refused Bronson access. He denied, however, that the trooper grabbed Bronson or erred in any way.

Still, Jeanne had enough corroboration to know something was amiss. She spoke twice more that night with Puget Sound, and each time the accounts changed, until the ER staff was putting the blame on me, saying I refused to come in.

The next day, Jeanne fired off letters to the heads of the hospital and the state patrol, with copies for the state attorney general, among others. She scolded both organizations for their employees' ignorance of laws that have been on the books for years as well as their maltreatment of "a confused and disoriented individual." She also pointed out that "it is a misdemeanor to interfere or deny admittance to a physically disabled person and their service dog" and offered to educate their staffs. She closed with the hope that this "embarrassing and humiliating" incident would never be repeated.

I tended to Bronson at home. His shoulder was too tender for his backpack, so at Jeanne's suggestion I sewed him an identifying scarf. It was red, trimmed in white, with a white triangle on which I stenciled "Service Dog" and "Prison Pet Partnership Program." (Later, I designed a new backpack, with sheepskin-padded straps, that was easier on his shoulders and chest. Jeanne liked it so much that she asked me make more, for other dogs in the program.)

A veterinarian on base as well as Robert Ries, a private practitioner associated with the prison program, examined Bronson's neck and shoulder for possible nerve damage as well as a small tumor that now appeared on his left front ankle. The growth turned out to be a histiocytoma, which was benign, its cause unknown. We wrapped the leg to keep Bronson from gnawing the tumor and eventually it went away by itself. For the soreness, Dr. Ries said to continue with aspirin and to keep the dog's activity to a minimum.

Even before he was laid up, my pampering of Bronson had amused Jeanne and Rachelle Lunde. Not long after I got the dog, I told Rachelle that I gave Bronson a daily massage, to reduce the stress of being a working dog, and she had chuckled.

"He likes it," I said.

"I'm sure he does!" said Rachelle. "I'd like to get a massage every day, too."

Now, I lavished even more attention on the dog. I put his water and food bowls on crates, so he wouldn't have to stoop. I blocked off the stairs with a baby gate, meanwhile, to prevent him from climbing up to the bedroom. I brought down his wicker bed and slept on the couch to be near him, for both our sakes. When the dog had to potty, I helped him down the stairs to the yard.

The run-in with the state trooper left Bronson head shy, so I also spent a lot of time reassuring him and gently stroking him around the head.

As I reflected on all that happened, I realized how devoted and caring Bronson truly was. Sharing a crisis in many ways brought us closer. On the highway, the dog had taken it upon himself to prevent me from plunging into traffic. Then, sensing a threat from the state trooper, he showed no aggression, which is forbidden in a service dog and would have ended his career. Instead, he focused on my welfare, again trying to push me away from danger. He was never taught to do that. If anything, it ran counter to his training. He was smart enough, though, and concerned enough to understand what was needed in the moment. Jeanne calls that "intelligent disobedience," though maybe love is just as good an explanation.

Our relationship underwent a major change after the incident at Puget Sound Hospital. My respect and trust for this dog soared, and Bronson became even more loyal and vigilant about my safety. When the time came to seizure alert, he now did so with such intensity and determination that there was no mistaking his intention. With great urgency, he put his front legs onto my lap and licked my hands, face, and neck. Or he would bring me toy after toy. For my part, I finally took Jeanne's refrain to heart and began to obey my dog and get myself to safety.

That spring, Cindy Mack, who'd joined Jeanne for the initial home visit, called and invited Bronson and me to spend an afternoon with her at Tacoma's Freighthouse Square, a former railroad warehouse that had been converted into shops and restaurants.

Cindy and I had lunch, with Bronson properly tucked beneath our table, and explored a few of the stores, checking out T-shirts in one place and buying chocolate in another. We had a pleasant day, my first social outing with Cindy, who over the months would become a confidant and friend.

We were bound for home when Cindy turned to me and said matter of factly, "By the way, you and Bronson just passed your public access exam."

Seeing my confused expression, she explained that Jeanne figured I'd become too stressed if I knew we were undergoing a service dog certification test. So she instructed Cindy to say nothing but to closely observe Bronson and me going about our business.

The test, which Jeanne usually administered around ninety days after clients obtained their dogs, was to demonstrate that the team could operate in public without hazard to others. It was not required by law but helped the program monitor progress and determine where the teams needed work.

In all, the exam had fourteen categories including proper heeling, good behavior in a restaurant, ignoring noise and distractions, and how well the client and dog worked as a team. When my attention was elsewhere, Cindy even asked a fellow who ran one of the shops to approach me about petting the dog, to see how Bronson and I responded. Without even knowing it, we sailed through the exam almost flawlessly.

Not everything was going so well, however. The cough that began while shuffling along Interstate 5 only worsened. My suspicion is that when I was having seizures that day I aspirated some vomit. By the end of the month, I was again an in-patient at Madigan Army Medical Center, this time suffering from atypical pneumonia.

My only solace was that Bronson, on the mend himself, accompanied me in the hospital. (Harry took him out for potty runs until I felt up to it.) Half in jest and half to make sure the nurses understood Bronson was a welcomed visitor, my doctor scrawled special "dog orders," which he entered into my records. Included in his treatment regimen were "Milk Bone for good behavior" and "scratches behind ears."

GRACE McCARDLE

Bronson gave Leana a sense of having a friend, some self-confidence, and a feeling that she was special. Having Bronson gave her some extra attention. And probably some courage, too, when she needed it because he was always right there.

Bronson gave her a kind of strength, maybe an extra mission in life, and somebody that she knew would be her friend and a help to her.

She was very proud of Bronson, and rightfully so. He was very obedient, and such a friendly dog. She could relate to him and he wasn't going to talk back or disappoint her. And she had a certain amount of power over him.

Oh, that was a beautiful dog. Leana told me not to show any recognition of him or say anything to him while he was on duty. She would come in and sit down and the dog just lay on the floor right beside her. Very alert, though. It was always like he was at attention. Even when she would get excited or emotional he would just sit still, but he looked at her and watched her.

Our sessions were an hour and you could tell when the time was up—I almost didn't even have to see the clock—because he would start wiggling, getting a little bit restless. Then after the session I would pet him and talk to him. I loved that dog, too.

But there was this one session when all of a sudden he sat up and he went up to her and started pawing her, which he had never done before. I said, "Does that mean you're going to have a seizure?" And Leana said, "Yeah, he's alerting me."

I suggested she get down on the floor. She didn't have a real long grand mal seizure. She had a small seizure. Bronson took her by his mouth and just pulled her over onto her side, so that the fluids could come out of her mouth. Then he just watched her. I was so impressed with him. I didn't say a word. I wanted to praise him and say, "Good dog." But I knew that he was in control.

31

When it came down to it, all I wanted–and all Jeanne and everyone from the dog program wanted–were sincere apologies from Puget Sound Hospital and the Washington State Patrol as well as assurances, through education of their personnel, that other people with assistance dogs would be spared what I went through.

Besides her letter to the hospital's director, Jeanne continued to press my case. That's probably why on the day I returned from my hospitalization for pneumonia–more than two weeks after the incident–I received a gift basket of houseplants from Puget Sound with a card that read, "Please accept our apologies." More encouraging, the hospital agreed to allow Jeanne to hold a seminar on service dogs for the staff.

The state patrol, in the meantime, began to look into my complaint about trooper Veliz. Internal affairs called to say someone would be coming to interview me, a scary thought considering the resistance I'd already received. I expected belligerence from anyone they sent and that the true purpose would be to protect the offending officer.

The two-hour interview went smoothly enough. Besides giving my account of events, I taught the two investigators a bit about service dogs as well as epilepsy. Bronson, who adores practically everyone he meets, strolled over at one point and set a ball at one of the men's feet, hoping he'd found a willing playmate–and that I'd forgotten about the veterinarian's orders of bed rest. He settled for some friendly pats.

During this same period, we made headway with my access problems on Fort Lewis. A reporter from the base newspaper interviewed me about Bronson and took photographs, and shortly thereafter a good-sized feature article appeared, with the headline, "Woman's best friend."

But any hopes we had of an easy resolution of the Puget Sound-state trooper mess were soon dashed. Authorities at the hospital kept putting off Jeanne's seminar. Then, when Jeanne–joined by Rachelle and me and Bronson–was finally allowed to give her talk, the reception was decidedly chilly. Most of the handful of staff members that bothered to come refused to even take a seat, poking their heads in the door, glaring at us for a few minutes, then departing.

No doubt contributing to the atmosphere that day was a second newspaper piece about me and Bronson, this one in the Tacoma *News Tribune*.

A week or two earlier, one of the paper's columnists, C.R. Roberts, came to the base to interview me regarding the standoff at the hospital and to meet Bronson. When his column finally appeared, it was right on the money. Regrettably, it ran the very day of our visit to Puget Sound.

"Leana Beasley needed help," Roberts wrote. "She needed compassion, expert care, and a safe place to collect her mind. She doesn't think she was asking for too much.

"We're all in trouble if someone paid to enforce the law breaks the law. And one woman's pain is worth your attention when people whose job it is to relieve suffering do nothing but cause suffering all the more."

When we finished that morning, Jeanne left some pamphlets about service dogs on a table, though I doubt anyone so much as glanced at one. The wrongs of my previous experience were only compounded by the attitude we saw now.

RACHELLE LUNDE

When I first met Leana, she seemed very easily traumatized by everything. When she had to talk to the people coming out to interview her for the state patrol, when they did their internal investigation, she was sick before they even got there. I must have talked to her five times on the phone. About every other time my phone rang it was Leana. She kept saying, "They're going to make me so mad I know I'm going to say something I don't want to say." I just told her, "Whatever you do, don't lose your cool, because if you do, you're going to blow it for Bronson."

Leana will do anything for that dog. She can move mountains if she thinks it's going to help Bronson. And that's what kept her cool. She wanted to do this because in her opinion he had really been dishonored and treated very disrespectfully.

She might as well have not been there when we went to Puget Sound Hospital for the training session. It was supposed to be an opportunity to allow them to meet Bronson, if the doctors had any questions, or the people in the ER, if they had any questions about his role, what the law stated his public access rights were, anything like that. Leana was so intimidated that I don't think she could have said more than two words without completely falling apart. She was in tears the whole way there and the whole way back.

It was a very hostile environment. I don't think we got more than five words from any of them. They were very angry they had to be there. They felt they had more important things to do than deal with this woman and her dog. You would not have had any problem distinguishing the hostility in that room.

Through all of this, Leana had to be very courageous. At Fort Lewis, all the times she was denied access, that was a big fight, to try to work with all the different people to get that resolved. She got to the point where she was really tired of it and didn't think it was worth it. If you can't go anywhere without having to get into an argument for somebody to let you in, you start to feel, "The heck with it. It's just too hard."

But she got through that. And because of Leana I believe that public access is a little bit easier for other recipients who came down the road.

GRACE McCARDLE'S coming retirement from the VA that summer hit me hard. She was sixty-five and wanted to travel before she got much older. She had purchased an RV and with her boyfriend was planning to take in the sights and visit friends and family around the country. Although she'd spoken of retirement months earlier, I'd been unaware exactly when it would happen. When she finally told me, her last day was but a few weeks away.

To make matters worse, the woman chosen to replace her as my counselor, who joined our final few sessions, had a much different personality and temperament. Where Grace was accepting and open minded, Deb Steiner seemed judgmental and controlling, hardly someone I could easily entrust with the most intimate details of my life, particularly the rape.

I'd come so far with Grace. We had our differences, but I always saw her as an understanding friend. She played off of my strengths–my passion for animals, my determination, and my desire to heal–to help me find answers for myself, not just force-feed me her solutions. With her guidance, my self-esteem was on the rise and I was finally coming to accept myself.

No one with the type of problems I faced recovers overnight, but the dissociative episodes were down. There was the addition, of course, of Bronson, whom Grace helped me acquire. But I'd also learned so much about riding out difficulties and curbing my anxiety, which along with the medications prescribed by Dr. Cammermeyer, helped reduce my seizures, too.

Under the escalating stress that summer, I suffered seizures then a flashback and ended up once again in Madigan. Then, during my last counseling sessions with Grace, I fell into a dissociative episode–lapsing back into private Proctor–and shouted, nonsensically to Grace and Deb Steiner, who was also present, "That's not a legal order!" then charged from her office. Unaware Bronson even existed, I left the dog behind. While the VA police tracked me down, Grace contacted Harry.

HARRY BEASLEY

When Leana has a dissociative episode, I try to explain to her that it's no longer 1984 and that she's not in Virginia. But she doesn't believe me. "You're lying," she'll say, or "You're wrong." Then I say, "Look at the calendar, what does the calendar say?" Her answer to that is, "You faked this calendar, this is a fake calendar."

Usually, the first thing I do is try to get her to take a nap. A lot of time, if she lays down, takes a nap, she wakes up and remembers who she is again. Of course there are the times she doesn't want to take a nap. To her, this is 1984 and she's not tired. Usually, she's confused. She's lost. She doesn't understand where she is because she's supposed to be on Fort Lee, but obviously this is not Fort Lee. So she wants to get out. She wants to leave. She wants to walk away. She wants to catch a bus. She wants to do whatever she needs to get to base. But she doesn't have any clue where the base is.

I try to keep her in the house, but I can't. So my primary concern becomes trying to get her to a safe place until this wears off. And the only way I can do this is to notify the local cops to come out and make contact with her, so they can evaluate her, determine whether or not they need to take her into custody so somebody medical can evaluate her to determine if she needs to be put on a psych ward for a short period.

Dr. Cammermeyer had been successful in dealing with Leana's dissociative state by saying she was her commanding officer, and I did that once or twice, too. I got a call at work from the VA that said, "Your wife was here, she left, and the police are out looking for her." As I was driving onto the VA grounds, I saw Lee standing on the side of the woods with two VA cops. One of them was named Robin and she was a big, burly woman. I mean, she could body slam a man if she needed to. She didn't want to have to do that with Leana, so she was kind of keeping her distance. But she knew at the same time that the situation was extremely volatile and needed to end now, real quick.

I came walking up and Leana had a big old stick in her hand. She looked like she was going to whomp somebody if they got close to her. I was in uniform, and I told her to drop the stick. She wouldn't do it. And I said, "I am ordering you to drop that stick, soldier." She said, "Is that a lawful order?" And I said, "It is a directive."

Now, a directive is the same thing as an order. But I got the impression when she said, "Is that an order?" that she was going to say it's not a lawful order or find some way to circumvent it. So I kind of twisted the situation around. She couldn't say, "That's not a lawful directive." It doesn't sound right. It doesn't sing. So I said, "It is a directive." At that, she stopped, thought for a second, and dropped the stick. Then Robin came and slapped the cuffs on her.

By the time I was interviewed by a Pierce County mental health professional, late that night, I'd come around enough to agree to a voluntary admission to the psych ward, where I stayed for an uneventful four days.

After a call to the staff from Rachelle and assurances from Harry, Bronson was allowed onto the ward to stay with me, providing that I recognized him and could take him out and otherwise care for him on my own. And though one nurse scrawled a snide note in my records about "this pet" having the "run of the ward," another had far kinder words about Bronson and me. "She and dog are as one," she wrote.

Bronson's presence, I firmly believe, helped keep me grounded in the here and now, bringing about a faster recovery during my hospitalization and preventing a complete relapse that tough summer. Any dissociative episode is frightening and holds the potential for disaster, especially when I set off walking. But from the time Bronson came into my life, those episodes slowly diminished in duration as well as intensity. Even when I failed to recognize him or understand what he did for me, he seemed to stand as a beacon to reality. Not always, but oftentimes I knew through the fog of distant memory that this animal served some purpose in my life and that keeping him with me was paramount.

In August, the Prison Pet Partnership staged a graduation-reunion ceremony for all the recipients and service dogs that came through the program in the last year.

I dreaded returning to Purdy. Now, in addition to my old fears about prison, I'd convinced myself that the inmate trainers would be furious with me over the run-in with the state trooper and Bronson's injuries. I worried, too, if this wasn't a way for the program to reclaim the dog with the minimum of conflict. Of course, my fears were unfounded. Everyone seemed glad to see us and asked with heartfelt concern about the dog's condition.

Barbara Thompson, for her part, turned down Jeanne's invitation to attend, saying that seeing Bronson again would only be confusing for the dog and torturous for her.

In many ways, Barbara had an easier life now. The minimum security building where she was housed was less restrictive than medium security G-2. Most of the occupants were well behaved. She no longer had to face a boss she despised. And unlike her position as a dog trainer, when Barbara returned to her cell from her new job in the embroidery shop, where prison labor put the finishing touches on shirts and hats for the Hard Rock Cafe and other businesses, she could turn off and forget about her work until the next day.

Still, her longing for Bronson and the sting of her firing was like an open wound. For weeks after her departure from the dog program, Barbara held her emotions in check around the other inmates, typical for her. But under the rush of spray in the shower, unseen by the prison predators who regard vulnerability as weakness, she sobbed long and hard for missing Bronson.

> TO: Jeanne Hampl, PPPP
> FROM: Barbara Thompson
> DATE: August 9, 1995
>
> I received your memo on August 8 and was very pleased that I would be allowed to attend this reunion. However, I feel that I cannot attend because of feelings and emotions I am going through. I would be happy to write a little history down, but I don't think it would be fair to Bronson if I attended. I would like to be kept posted on how Bronson is doing whenever you and I see each other in the institution.
>
> I don't remember the exact date when Bronson came here, but I do remember how happy he made me. Bronson was always attentive and eager to learn, so he learned very easily. I remember how I used to have to be careful what I was saying because Bronson loved the word "outside" and would sit at attention, shaking his stub of a tail, and looking at me right in the eye until I would take him outside. There were other words, too, that I got into the habit of spelling around Bronson.
>
> Bronson brought me much happiness and joy and will always have a place in my heart. I wish Leana, her family, and Bronson all the best!

Despite my initial fears, we had a pleasant day. Family members were invited and Harry joined me. But because no children were allowed inside the prison, Michael had to stay home.

There were five other recipients and their dogs, three of which were golden retrievers, your more traditional-looking assistance dog. Spencer, Bronson's nemesis during his days in the program, was there with his owner, too. During our group picture, in fact, the onetime rivals sat but a few feet apart, both comporting themselves with dignity and drawing grins from those who recalled their former entanglements.

In the outdoor ceremony, Jeanne handed out diplomas and said a few words about each of the teams. She broke up the crowd when she introduced Bronson and me and alluded to the battles we'd endured so far. "These two," she joked, "have already been to the ends of the earth and back."

32

The confrontation at Puget Sound Hospital and Grace McCardle's retirement set me back emotionally. My physical health was worsening as well, with a rise in seizures and PTSD episodes, sometimes in concert and other times one or the other. Again I grew cautious about leaving home or doing much of anything without family or a trusted friend on hand.

I was also having trouble sleeping, a problem that had been going on for months. Numerous times each night, I'd open my eyes to find Bronson at my bedside in alerting mode, yet no convulsions would follow. In addition to her seizure work, Dr. Cammermeyer ran the VA's sleep apnea clinic, and that summer she diagnosed me with that ailment, most likely a result of complications from my tracheotomy. Tests showed that lack of oxygen was disrupting my sleep sixteen times an hour–causing me to gasp for air, cough, or choke–which explained Bronson's constant concern, not to mention my bone-wearying fatigue.

Now I had to sleep wearing a breathing mask attached to a CPAP (continuous positive airway pressure) machine. Although I was finally getting a steady flow of oxygen to my lungs, the mask itself took some getting used to. Many nights I'd awaken in a panic or full-blown flashback, believing that my assailant, Sgt. Stockton, was suffocating me.

When I returned to classes at Jeanne's, I was fragile, and always knew where my husband was standing in the yard. When Jeanne directed me to execute a command with Bronson, I'd glance at Harry, as if to make sure it was all right. Michael, meanwhile, tried to be helpful, too. Jeanne would tell the class to turn left with our dogs, for instance, and Michael would yell, "Mommy, she said left!"

After a few sessions like this, Jeanne had enough. One day, she gave my husband a friendly hello, thanked him for bringing me, then shooed him away. "All right," she said. "Bye." The message was clear: Take the kid out for a soda. Go shopping. Go look at the boats in the harbor. But leave. You can pick up Leana in an hour.

It wasn't that my family was disrupting the class per se, but they were diverting my attention from the work at hand. How was Bronson going to help me if I refused to stop using Harry as a crutch? How could the dog ever give any of us a normal life again if we failed to give him a chance?

My husband seemed stunned, and hesitant to leave me with an outsider. At the same time, he knew Jeanne was serious, that this was her turf, and that she wasn't someone to mess with.

So Harry and Michael reluctantly went and sat in the car. That lasted for a week or two–Harry scanning a newspaper and Michael playing an electronic game, both waiting to come running in an emergency. Before long, Jeanne delivered a few jibes about that too and Harry got her drift, finally driving off to window shop or to take our son to a toy store.

I did my best to conceal it, but I was near panic the first few times without them. My contact with Jeanne had been solely on a professional basis, and I had no idea she was also a registered nurse. The others in the class were complete strangers. And if something went wrong, the VA hospital and my doctors were a good distance away. As I managed to get through one session, then another, my fear faded. The more I got to know Jeanne, the more I trusted her, as well as Cindy Mack, who helped run some of the sessions.

Which is not to say the training itself went great at first or that Jeanne no longer intimidated me. My short-term memory remained a significant roadblock. I continued to confuse my left and my right, which foot to start on, and which to stop on. Jeanne would meticulously explain what she wanted the class to do and it would vanish from my mind just as quickly. How long, I worried, would Jeanne be patient?

At one point, she grabbed a leash and knotted it around my left ankle so I could distinguish it from my right. I was embarrassed at first, but found the physical reminder actually helped. Other times, I would be in tears, out of frustration with my own failings or from misinterpreting Jeanne's dry humor. She never intended to be hurtful, but if she came out with anything remotely critical, I took it to heart.

One day, while chatting with Rachelle, Jeanne commented on the difficulties I was having. She said she was stumped trying to figure out how to help me remember even basic steps. "Well, Jeanne," responded the volunteer, "if she's having memory problems, why not have her write it down?"

Jeanne looked at Rachelle as if she had solved a great riddle. "Of *course,*" she said.

The next class, when we began reviewing the footwork needed to walk with our dogs at a heel, Jeanne said, "Leana, write this down: Left. Right. Left. Together. Stop."

With that, I began to become unstuck. The very act of writing helped commit the steps to memory. And once I had them in hand, I could practice better at home. Pretty soon I was jotting down all of Jeanne's instructions.

Jeanne liked the concept so much that she began making up fliers and distributing them to the entire class, defining what "sit," "heel," or dozens of other commands meant, how they should be delivered to the dog, and how they should look when performed properly.

At home, I made flash cards. On one side, I'd scrawl the command in big letters, then the definition, often with a picture, on back, and reviewed them until I could no longer look at them anymore. As we progressed and the maneuvers grew more complicated and came to involve several steps, I'd make cards for each individual step, and tie them together with yarn, so I had a little book I could refer to.

I was constantly studying, thinking about the training, and practicing with Bronson in one way or another. We held sessions in the yard twice a day, but many lessons were just part of daily life around the house. To help me with right and left, I'd sometimes wear a shoe on one foot and a slipper on the other, or one blue sock and one white one. "Left, right, left, feet together, and stop," I'd say to myself, marching through our quarters.

Harry, seeing how impassioned I'd become, grew concerned. He thought I was pressing too hard, worrying too much, and that I was flirting with more seizures or a PTSD episode. I, on the other hand, was more afraid of the consequences should I let up. More than anything, I was propelled by fear, be it rational or not, that my keeping Bronson hinged on getting these steps perfect and that to stop or even to slow down might cause me to backslide and never catch up.

Performing the exercises over and over etched them into my long-term memory, where they were less likely to fade. At first, success was minuscule, but with each passing day I improved, and as I did I felt my self-confidence returning.

Bronson, for his part, loved training. I'd ask if he wanted to "go to work," and instantly he was up and about, retrieving his pouch, and dancing around me, his stubby tail spinning a hundred miles an hour. Just putting on my shoes was enough to have him doing a jig. Often, I'd have to tell him to hold on, that I wasn't ready for him yet.

The dog thrived on learning. Once he understood what was expected, he performed passionately and flawlessly. I gave him his much-deserved beef jerky treat as a reward and he'd anxiously await whatever was next. As Barbara Thompson discovered back in his days at the prison, Bronson was the quickest of studies. What's more, he retained his lessons well after we progressed to other exercises.

The more hours we spent working together, the greater our mutual trust. Just as I turned to my animals as a lonely girl on the farm, now too I found strength in Bronson. Steadily, he and I developed a feel for one another, to the point that we began to anticipate one another's movements–if not our very breaths–and response to circumstances.

My trust in Jeanne was growing as well. Between her, Rachelle, Cindy, and one or two other people who helped Jeanne, I sensed an understanding and acceptance that I rarely found since the seizures took command of my life. Having worked with people with disabilities, and counting them among friends and family, they understood this was a hurdle to overcome, not a reflection of me as a person or what I could accomplish. Jeanne respected the gravity of my condition, but never gave it undue weight. With her it was always, "This is what you need to do, do it, and get on with it."

One time, I had seizures during a class and fretted for days about Jeanne's reaction. Now that she had witnessed the brutality of my convulsions, with the spit and urine and a thousand frenzied contortions, I feared that she would lose clients or for reasons unspoken decide that it was best for me to stop attending the sessions.

When I showed up the following week, however, I got a much different response. Not only was Jeanne unfazed by the seizures, but she gently teased me about them, which no one had ever done before. "Now, if certain people will restrain themselves from giving unsolicited seizure demonstrations in the middle of my class," Jeanne said without batting an eye, "we'll begin."

ANNIE BRINGLOE, FRIEND

At this point, I lived in Gig Harbor. I was in my late forties, married, and my children were grown. I had a Scottish terrier named Riley that I thought could do well in AKC competition and I'd heard about Jeanne Hampl's classes and went over to start him in obedience.

I didn't know anything was wrong with Leana when I first met her, but soon learned Bronson had come from the prison program and that he was a seizure-alert dog. That's all I knew.

I think it was probably three or four classes after we started that it happened. Bronson was a very obedient dog, and he was going through all this obedience stuff, and having a good time, but suddenly stopped being an obedient dog. It was very clear that he went from being super-obedient to right in Leana's face. So she took him around to the other side of a row of rhododendron bushes.

I'm the kind of person that nothing bothers. If somebody needs a hand, I'll wade in. Jeanne knew that immediately about me and asked if I'd stay with Leana.

Eventually, she just sort of faded out. Then the seizure started. Her body was flying this way and that way. And Leana is so strong that if she hit anything she would hurt herself. When all those muscles are going and she has absolutely no control, it's pretty scary. I was really worried that she was going to choke on all this spit coming out of her mouth. It lasted, it seemed, like forever.

The thing I remember most was how powerful the seizures were, and how scary. I had never seen this before. I didn't know whether she was going to wake up, whether she was going to choke to death, or what was going to happen to her.

When the seizures died down, she was just laying there and I was wondering, "Is she going to wake up?" You know, what's going to happen now? The good part was that Jeanne had been a nurse for so many years. She said, "Oh, yeah, she'll wake up. Just don't let her swallow anything."

I wasn't very proud of this, but I thought, "What is she doing out here by herself?" I had some disbelief that she was out in the community walking around and having this happen to her. I didn't know much about epilepsy and thought she should be home or someplace.

I couldn't believe that she was out here in public doing everything perfectly normally and suddenly as if lightning came out of the sky there she was on the ground with these terrible seizures. To me, it looked like at any time she could just die.

JEANNE HAMPL

Leana was very high maintenance. When I think in terms of people that I placed dogs with over the years, with some of them you do your team training, touch base a couple of times, and they're off and running. Of course, these aren't people who have suffered brain injuries. These are people who have, say, multiple sclerosis, who have been in the business world all their lives. You pull them in, say this is the way it's going to be, and they say, "Okay, I can do that."

Leana's dedication to what we were doing balanced off the fact that it was harder with her. This was something that she really needed, she really wanted, and that made it worth all the effort.

The person I saw in Leana before Bronson was somebody who had a vision for what she wanted. But also, she didn't want to be a burden to her family. She realized that it wasn't right for her son to be an attendant to his mother, who would fall to the floor at any time and maybe die. Leana wanted to be a person again.

To this day, Leana still looks at me as the service dog police. She worried about the program taking Bronson back, but I never thought about that. I know the process peo-

ple have to go through to become competent service dog handlers and I don't care how long it takes us to get there. For me it was not an issue. For her, it definitely was. She was scared to death.

Leana has very violent grand mal seizures. They're frightening. She's a big girl, too, and moves around a lot. Every portion of her body is involved. We were at class one night and Bronson started to be bad. By that I mean, Leana would say something like, "I told you to fetch that," and he'd just look at her. People with seizures when their dogs alert don't always want to believe them. Not just Leana, but everybody.

I said, "Leana, listen to your dog." And she said, "No, I'm fine." I said, "Leana, listen to your dog."

Then, of course, he got really insistent. She was in her wheelchair at the time because she'd had a couple seizures previously. He put his paws up on her lap, licked her face, sniffed around her head.

I had this big hedge and she went off by the side and I went on teaching the class, figuring I'd give her time. Bronson gave like a thirty- to forty-minute warning. Well, I'm teaching and all of a sudden I heard Leana make a sound and one of the girls called me. I told the rest of the class to go home.

I went over and she had laid herself down and started this violent seizure. She went to the hospital that night because we couldn't get her to stop. I will let anybody seize three times, but when they hit number four, I call 911.

Afterward, Leana was so embarrassed because I had never seen her seize before. She was so upset and kept apologizing. I said, "It's okay, it's okay, it's no big deal."

"It's just nice that Bronson trusts me so much." I told her.

She goes, "Well, why?"

I said, "Because after I got over there and got you positioned and stuff, Bronson went off and took a little leak." He's trained to stay with her. But he had been alerting for like forty minutes at that point.

The look on his face was a riot. He looked up at me as if to say, "Oh, thank God you're here, Jeanne. I had to go to the bathroom so bad."

33

The better I came to know Bronson, the more baffling it seemed that anyone would willingly part with him. At the time, I had no idea why he was surrendered to the shelter. What I did know was that few dogs anywhere were as good-natured and soft-hearted. He was, in a word, a mush.

Many people are wary of Rottweilers, and to some extent I found comfort in that, especially in uncertain circumstances, around men I didn't know. Still, anyone who really knew dogs could take one look at Bronson's loving eyes and friendly face and know he was docile. That he was missing one of his lower front teeth, which never completely grew in and eventually dropped out while the dog was tugging at a soccer ball with my son, only made him that much more endearing.

In public, I saw to it that he practiced good etiquette, a must for properly trained service dogs. When we stopped to rest and Bronson laid down, his legs stayed tucked beneath his body, not sprawled out for someone to trip over. (In bathroom stalls, where Rachelle had problems with the dog and the floors were often unsanitary, I now kept him standing.) Yet when Bronson relaxed at home, he really relaxed. He had good flexibility in his hips and he liked to lay chest down, his hind legs splayed behind him like a frog's, and watch as I made dinner or we sat before the television.

Bronson held himself with confidence, especially when he was in working mode. He struck me as proud of what he'd learned and obviously loved to please. At the same time, his disposition was highly sensitive. Off duty, during quiet hours, he seemed almost needy. More than most dogs, Bronson craved being touched, stroked, and softly spoken to.

He gave of himself as only a dog could. I never had to prove myself to Bronson, or fulfill expectations, or feel embarrassed before him. Even Harry and the people who cared about me had limitations to their love. They were, after all, only human.

Counseling and medication obviously had their place in my slow return to health. But in my dark moments Bronson's sensitivity to my emotions was what kept me going. Other people might sympathize or claim they understood what I was going through, but only Bronson shared every moment with me. He seemed to understand not only when I was in despair but how to boost my spirits. If I was teary-eyed, he hurried to his milk-crate toy box and brought one plaything after another–tennis balls, stuffed animals, tug toys–until a dozen or more accumulated around me. A few minutes of that never failed to have me grinning.

As kind-hearted as Bronson was with me, he was also tender with other creatures. Despite his problems with chickens, which sealed his fate back on the farm, his prey-drive proved low. He had no real compulsion to chase squirrels, for instance, though he obviously enjoyed watching their antics. When cats would permit it, he liked nothing better than to preen them, licking their ears and faces. Over time, I saw him try to mother everything from baby rabbits to crickets.

Because of the parrots and parakeets that kept my home lively, Jeanne and Rachelle spent considerable time with the dog in pet stores before turning him over to me. They acclimated him to the squawks and sudden flapping of wings that might trigger primitive urges and made sure he understood that pursuing birds was forbidden.

During our time on Fort Lewis I had as many as six birds. Bronson put up with them without incident for the first few months. Sometimes he positioned himself before their cages and contemplated them. But he never barked or showed aggression, even when they were out, perched atop their cages or their tree-stand.

Then one day, while I was at my sewing machine and Bronson was dozing beneath the stand, something at the window startled Tangy, my yellow sun conure. She jumped from her perch, as if to take flight, but because her feathers had been trimmed–to prevent her from crashing about the house and hurting herself–she plummeted straight onto Bronson's back. Shocked from a sound sleep, the dog scrambled to his feet and started snapping, just a breath from Tangy's tail feathers as she bustled away. "Bronson, no!" I screamed. He pulled up short and dropped to the carpet, with as remorseful an expression as I'd ever seen on a dog.

With that incident I resolved to prevent future disaster. Bronson's prey-drive may have been low, but he was still a dog, with animal instincts and the potential for faulty judgment in what could be a mystifying human world.

Now, I would squat on the floor with a parrot in one hand and Bronson beside me. As the bird watched, I pet the dog, told him he was a good boy, then slowly set to stroking the parrot. I'd also have Bronson close at hand when I fed the birds, showing that the dog belonged to the flock and the parrots were part of the pack. Whenever Bronson received a treat, meanwhile, I'd give something to the parrots, too. Pretty soon, the dog would hardly raise an eyebrow as the birds confidently marched past him–and eventually over him–on their way across a room.

Occasionally, I'd run a towel through Bronson's backpack, deposit one of the parrots on it, and go for walks. We started by touring the living room but eventually voyaged all the way around the block. More than one passerby did a double-take at the sight of my dog strolling along with a parrot on his back, like some kind of canine pirate.

I also found it useful to run Bronson through the paces of basic obedience work with one of the birds on his back, ordering him to sit, heel, or come. It may not have been a conventional approach to training, but it strengthened his focus.

Bronson wasn't a guide dog in the sense of working for the blind, but through his loving heart, zeal to embrace new challenges, and ability to alert to my seizures, he became my guide on a deeper level, leading me away from chaos and despondency and back to the world of the living.

Progress came slowly, in situations that fully functioning individuals took for granted but that for me were major achievements. When my family and I went shopping, for instance, I always clung by my husband and son for fear of a seizure short-circuiting me, a dependency fed by my husband's overprotective nature. Like a lot of couples, though, Harry and I had our individual interests. At Wal-Mart, he liked to look at the tools, hunting and fishing equipment, or books. Although I enjoyed much of that, I tended to be drawn to the arts and crafts aisles, or kitchen wares, either of which had my husband fidgeting within minutes. He was so self-conscious, meanwhile, that he refused to go anywhere near the lingerie department.

On one expedition, while Harry was inspecting a rod and reel, I casually informed him that Bronson and I were off to browse on our own.

"Hold up," he said, "I'll be with you in second."

"*No*," I stamped. "I want to do this by myself."

And while my husband watched with apprehension, off I went, dog by my side. I ventured clear across the store, in fact, making sure Harry wasn't secretly following. Then, for the first time in years, I found myself shopping more or less solo. Never before or since has buying a spatula brought anyone such satisfaction.

Around that time, Cindy Mack invited Bronson and me to join her and her sheltie Gunny for a day trip to the oceanside community of Westport, Washington, a few hours west of Tacoma. I'd always loved the water, but since falling overboard in Panama was hesitant to go near it, especially alone. I envisioned having seizures on the beach, then being washed away by the tide. And though Cindy herself later admitted to being nervous that I might have an attack, the trip proved uneventful. Not only did my seizures stay dormant, but I experienced the roar of the ocean for the first time in ages, romping with the dogs on the beach. Even more significant, I'd left my usual source of security–my family–at home.

Grateful to the Prison Pet Partnership, which never requested a cent for Bronson or his prison training, I volunteered at a number of events at which the program had an information booth or was conducting service dog demonstrations. Sometimes I'd log two or three consecutive eight-to-ten-hour days, out distancing most volunteers and pushing the limits of my health.

One day that fall Jeanne asked if I'd be willing to work with Bronson at the Western Washington Fair in Puyallup, among the biggest fairs in the country, to demonstrate some of the tasks service dogs perform while Rachelle Lunde addressed the audience.

Less than a year earlier, I'd been afraid to tend to the crocuses in my garden for fear that neighbors would witness one of my attacks. Now, Bronson and I stood before a crowd of several hundred fair-goers and went through the basics of his training. What's more, our efforts helped the program take a blue ribbon for best educational exhibit. (A year later, Bronson and I would give three demos a day at the fair, with the dog doing everything from retrieving the telephone to bracing for me as I lifted myself from a would-be fall.)

Before long, Bronson and I were even performing service-dog demonstrations on our own, apart from the prison program, at Michael's school for instance. Sometimes I'd bring Tangy, a natural-born showoff, or one of the other parrots. They'd traverse the dog's backpack, hang upside down from his collar, and shimmy up and down the leash like circus performers, which of course electrified my son's classmates.

For all that Bronson did to bring me out of my shell, my fondest dream was more solitary in nature. Nothing, I thought, would be more wonderful than taking a bath again without worrying about drowning midst an onslaught of convulsions or harming myself on the porcelain or other hard surfaces of the bathroom. When I found faith enough in Bronson's ability to give me fair warning and courage enough in myself, I told Harry my intentions. Then I grabbed my favorite bath beads, slipped a Garth Brooks tape into my little boom box, and sank into a warm bath for the first time in four years.

Bronson, to whom this was all quite curious, sat by the tub, his ears high, eyes watching my every move. Basking in comfort, I eased back and slowly immersed myself beneath the bubbles, until in reverie I took a breath and submerged my head as well.

It was when I was coming up that I saw the flash of black and brown fur. Bronson, concerned that something was amiss, was leaping into the tub.

I bellowed, then let out an loud oomph as he landed squarely on my midsection. Harry heard the commotion and rushed to the bathroom door. "Are you okay?" he shouted, then pushed his way in to find the dog on top of me, both of us covered with suds. Despite this most inappropriate behavior for a service dog, I found myself laughing hard.

My husband, confused and embarrassed at what he'd come upon, shook his head in disbelief. "This is a little much, isn't it?" he said, then turned and walked out.

34

Over the previous couple years I had come to depend on, trust, and admire Grethe Cammermeyer. Harry and I followed the legal fight over her ban from the military for being a lesbian, which in June 1994 culminated in a federal court decision in her favor. Her dismissal was ruled unconstitutional and she returned to the National Guard, where she served as chief nurse for a Washington-based MASH. Harry even wrote a paper about her for a class he was taking, saying how his impressions changed and prejudices fell away as he got to know her and learned about her case.

By now, Grethe was something of a celebrity, speaking out on behalf of gays in the military and writing a well-received book, *Serving in Silence*, about her experience. When it hit bookstores, I immediately bought a copy. "To Leana, you are and probably always will be the most challenging and delightful client I know," she wrote when I requested an autograph. A subsequent made-for-TV movie—produced in part by Barbra Streisand and starring Glenn Close—won three Emmys and was nominated for three Golden Globe awards.

Reading about her life, I came to see that Grethe and I had more in common than I ever imagined. We both were interested in the outdoors, animals, and playing the guitar. As kids, each of us was a tomboy. We also were proud to serve our country but in our own ways were victims of the military.

Grethe served fourteen months in Vietnam. As chief nurse of the medical ward of a hectic evacuation hospital, and later, of its neurosurgical intensive-care unit, she saw a lot of tough sights. She understood the underpinnings of post-traumatic stress better than most doctors I'd come in contact with.

Grethe was the picture of a self-assured woman. To look at her, you would never suspect that she too had wrestled with tremendous despair. Years earlier, her marriage in turmoil, Cammermeyer nearly committed suicide. But she emerged from the fire stronger than ever, like steel from the forge. "My whole life is based on the belief that there's always a purpose, always a way of adapting, of taking what you have and making the most of it," she wrote in her book. "You can only find it by looking ahead."

Having the book as a window into her life provided me with ammunition for some friendly ribbing. When Grethe rode me for continuing to smoke despite my lung problems, I teasingly volleyed back that at least I never taught my younger brother to smoke and drink beer as she wrote about having done as a youngster. Grethe laughed out loud to find her words coming back to haunt her.

I think Grethe appreciated that I felt comfortable with her. Her honesty and openness broke down some of the barriers I often found with medical professionals, which in the end promoted trust and healing. Grethe offered more than good medical advice. She gave of herself. She listened. And she showed respect for my opinions and experiences. Many veterans felt the same about her, but with Grethe Cammermeyer I was never just another patient.

I believe that's what ultimately saved me that tough summer of 1995. Grace McCardle was gone from the VA, and though I tried, I never did adjust to her replacement, Deb Steiner. As a result, I came to lean more and more on Grethe for advice about all kinds of matters.

It was the end of August when the many stressors in my life finally reached the breaking point. For weeks, I'd been harassed by intermittent flashbacks, dissociative episodes, seizures, and breathing problems, and even landed in the hospital once or twice. With Bronson accompanying me, however, I pushed through, staying on top of Michael's activities, attending Jeanne's classes as faithfully as possible, and regularly taking the shuttle bus to the VA for my appointments.

Then, the Washington State Patrol issued the findings of its supposed investigation into the Puget Sound Hospital incident. "Trooper Veliz exercised his training, good judgment, and extreme patience at all times while dealing with an extremely difficult situation," the report concluded. I was angry over such a whitewash, but more than that, I began to doubt whether I'd ever win vindication for Bronson—or myself.

All that month I'd been on edge and jittery. With the additional diagnosis of sleep apnea—and subsequent flashbacks brought on by wearing the CPAP breathing mask—I was also growing despondent about my health.

I was at the VA all day that Tuesday, for a variety of appointments, when the wheels finally came off the cart. In the morning, I saw Grethe about my difficulties with the oxygen mask and a bout I was having with bronchitis.

Then, at the canteen, while waiting for an afternoon session with Deb, I was stunned to see Jill Porter, an MP friend from my Army days, the first person on Fort Lee I'd gone to after the rape. In retrospect, I'm sure it wasn't really Jill. Whether I was experiencing a flashback or if it was just someone who looked like her, I can't say. It was certainly an indication of the direction my thoughts were taking, a foreshadowing of trouble.

I went to my counseling session and for the most part was fine. But with five minutes left, I inexplicably marched straight out of the room, paying no mind to Bronson or my stunned counselor. "I called her name, but she would not respond," Deb wrote in my records. "I followed her out of the building as she put her imaginary hat on her head.... She stopped in front of the building, scanned left to right, and proceeded over to find the locked gates. She jumped the gate and walked down the dirt road."

That fence, I should point out, was taller than me. Deb told me I planted my foot on a bar that ran across its center, grabbed near the top of the fence, and sailed over as smoothly as if mounting a horse.

Deb shouted for me to stop. But I was in another world and determinedly headed down the road that ran through the woods behind the VA. Unable to give chase, Deb hurried to her office, called Harry at work, then summoned the VA police. Leaving Bronson locked in her office, she rushed back out to join the search.

When the VA police officer and Deb found me, I was down the road, holding a three-foot-long stick, and smoking. "She verbally responded to the officer that she was setting up some MP check point and wanted M60 (machine gun) from arms room," Deb wrote in my records.

It took about forty-five minutes, but the officer and paramedics who arrived shortly afterward managed to handcuff me and drove me over to Building 61, the VA's psychiatric facility.

But the excitement was only starting. Once there, I commenced battling in an attempt to escape. The police and paramedics overpowered me and wrestled me to the floor, but then I erupted into a series of seizures and had to be rushed across the grounds to the ER.

That's where I was when I came to, on a gurney with an IV in my arm. I looked and there was a smear of blood on my forearm, apparently from the insertion of the needle. Suddenly, I was again flashing back to my rape. Sitting bolt upright, I ripped out the IV and sent blood spurting. Shocked staffers—most of them men—grabbed at me, trying to bring me under control. In my mind, I was being attacked all over again.

I went crashing from the main section of the ER into an adjacent treatment room. Unable to escape, I curled up quaking in a corner like a wounded creature. An alert female nurse ordered all the men away and shouted for someone to get Cammermeyer. My blood, both real and imagined, soaked the floor and I was tearfully smearing my hands in it, trying to clean it up but only making a bigger mess. I was reliving the aftermath of my rape now, cleaning my room and trying to wipe the blood off my flesh.

Cammermeyer arrived and quickly took control. She got down on the floor with me and by speaking softly and reassuringly, managed to calm me down. I was still murmuring about my rape when she got me back up on the gurney and went through the motions of helping me wash away non-existent blood from my arms.

Deb Steiner arrived a few minutes later to find I had regressed to early childhood. As Grethe tended to me, Deb later wrote, I was curled in the fetal position and sucking my thumb.

Soon after, Harry showed up, still dressed in his camouflage BDUs (battle dress uniform.) On training status, he had been able to break away from the base almost as soon as he got Deb's call. Once he got to the ER, no one thought it a problem for him to go right in and see me.

"Lee, are you okay?" he said, coming over and rubbing my arm.

I looked up. Rather than my husband, I saw my attacker. Furiously, I rained punches on him, striking him hard in the chest and arms. Harry went to restrain me, but Grethe grabbed me instead.

"It's the uniform!" she yelled. "Harry, get out of here!"

He backed out, stunned, but now I was again terrorized, trying desperately to climb atop some steel wall lockers. I finally settled down, but again it was back to the fetal position and sucking my thumb.

I spent several turbulent days in the hospital, first on the medical ward, then the psych unit, to which I was transferred in five-point restraints. For much of that time I was like a child. When I slept, I sucked my thumb. When interacting with the staff, I asked for "my mommy" and otherwise spoke like a five-year-old. At other points, I was private Proctor, once even punching my way out of my room in a panic when a tech tried to draw blood. Periodically, I was myself again, too, and was shocked and saddened when Harry visited and showed me the big bruise my blows had produced on his chest.

When the worst was past, I foolishly checked out of the hospital against medical advice. I didn't realize that Grethe had helped me through one of the worst PTSD episodes I'd ever experienced. Instead, I was determined to leave the hospital before she learned I was there. Although it wasn't really in Grethe's nature, my fear was that she would think less of me.

Hollywood depictions to the contrary, the turmoil I'd produced during my stay was far from an everyday occurrence at the VA or any hospital. Nor was checking out AMA something that the staff looked kindly upon, especially if you've done it before. So when the head of psychiatry announced a meeting of all my caregivers to review my treatment plan, I feared the worst.

With Grace retired, no one at American Lake except Grethe knew me very well. During that tumultuous admission, the staff on several occasions resorted to restraints to control me, failing to understand that strapping me down only prolonged and intensified my trauma. What's more, it was a dangerous practice, especially given my breathing problems and heart condition. (One subsequent study, in fact, showed that as many as one-hundred-and-fifty people die each year as a result of restraints, be it from inadequate training or outright neglect.)

Now, I worried that straps across my wrists and ankles and a seclusion room were about to become standard operating procedure whenever I was in the hospital for my PTSD. I was also concerned that administrators might decide the VA was ill-equipped to handle me and in the future would direct me to Western State Hospital. That I was being excluded from attending the review upset me all the more.

In anticipation of the meeting, I wrote two letters, one of which outlined for the staff how I felt it best to deal with my PTSD. I asked for patience, to start with, and a gentle hand. It only agitated the situation, I explained, if doctors and nurses insisted that the year was 1995 when I had it in my head it was 1984. And rather than put me in restraints, I'd always done better if I was eased back to reality in a safe, quiet room, preferably with an empathetic woman on hand to assure me everything was all right. Cammermeyer's ability to play into my perception of reality, I wrote, also seemed to keep me calm and shortened the episodes.

The other letter went to Cammermeyer, whom I desperately wanted to understand what I was going through. In it, I recounted the story of my rape and its aftermath, right down to my commanding officer's accusations that I was lying and that he would have me thrown in prison if I ever mentioned the word "rape," and how my MPI school was canceled and my dream of ever becoming an MP was over.

But most of all, I told her how sorry I was about being out of control at the hospital and how I didn't even understand all that was happening. I also explained how fearful I was about what action the doctors at American Lake would now take against me:

> Deb told me about the staff meeting that will take place on Tuesday. I feel like I will be tried and judged without a chance to explain to anyone what I live with everyday. These people don't know the real me. They only know what they see when I'm "sick" or out of it. I'm not mad at anyone. I know that they

are only doing their jobs and what they think is best. My only concern is whether they have all the evidence or facts.

Sometimes when I'm not "all together," I see things that are not real. I love my husband dearly and would never hurt him on purpose. And yet you saw me hit him. But I did not "see" my husband. I saw SSG Stockton over me. More than likely the BDUs set me off. Sometimes people change into people I knew from the past. When Deb ordered me not to fight the handcuffs or police out in the woods, she says that I called her Lieutenant Ferguson (one of my superiors during my Army days.) But Deb is not a tall, thin black woman. This is why I'm concerned about what the outcome of the staff meeting will be. If people don't know what is in my head or what I went through, how can they make just judgments about me?

I know that none of this helps the person on the receiving end of my fist. And I know that I scare people. And this puts a heavy ache in my heart. I don't want people to dislike me or to be afraid of me. But no one could be more afraid or dislike me more than I do.

35

Grethe Cammermeyer had never heard the complete story of my rape and how it affected me. Reading my letter moved her. Having served in the military, Grethe knew the dangers that many female soldiers faced from their male counterparts. She knew sexual assault occurred more than those in power admitted. She had friends, in fact, who were raped in Vietnam but who never spoke of it, out of shame and fear, until years later.

The only other individual at the VA with whom I shared my story was Grace McCardle, and that, too, was mainly through a hard-wrought written account.

Now, when my caregivers met to go over my treatment plan, Grethe immediately sensed the sentiment against me. Spearheaded by psychiatry, the conference consisted of nearly a dozen individuals from various disciplines and sections of the hospital.

Among the participants were those who wrote me off as a problem patient and treated me as such. Others wondered if I wasn't faking my seizures or my dissociative episodes. The head of psychiatry, meanwhile, opposed Bronson's presence when I was hospitalized on the psych ward.

For her part, Grethe saw the individual behind the illness and knew that compassion went a lot further in helping a person than controlling behavior. She requested a brief delay to call me and ask if she could read my letter aloud at the meeting.

"Do what you think is best," I told her. "I trust you, Grethe."

And so she read my letter. Hearing what I wrote changed almost everyone's attitude, Cammermeyer later said. For the first time, many of the staff put themselves in my shoes. Also hitting home was the deep complexity of my case and the daily tightrope walk that living with my conditions involved.

Grethe was much respected throughout American Lake VA, by patients and staff alike. With her on my side, efforts to take a hard line fell away, at least temporarily. For now, the staff agreed to work closer with me and my family to understand how best to help me emerge from my dissociative episodes. With Grethe's help, my feelings about my own care carried weight.

But Cammermeyer was more than my advocate; she was my inspiration. Second only to Bronson, she stirred in me a growing will to stand up for myself. I wasn't going to be testifying before Congress like her, but I realized that I too could take a stand on matters that affected my life. In the process, I thought, perhaps I could benefit those with similar problems who came later.

That fall, Jeanne Hampl referred me to Tacoma attorney Richard Levandowski, who was on the board of the Prison Pet Partnership Program. Repeated efforts by myself, Jeanne, and others to convince Puget Sound Hospital and the Washington State Patrol to own up to their mistreatment of me and Bronson and to educate their personnel about service dogs had gotten nowhere. Now, after numerous conversations with Jeanne, I decided to move forward with a lawsuit over my denial of access and let a court decide who was right and who was wrong.

As the end of my first year with Bronson neared, change was coming in other ways as well. After fifteen years, Harry would soon be leaving the Army. In preparation for civilian life, we moved off Fort Lewis to an apartment in Puyallup, fifteen miles away. And though I was apprehensive at first, having spent so many years on military bases, I felt a burden slowly lifting.

We chose Puyallup, a solidly middle-class community, because it was one of the more service-dog friendly places in the state. Pam Reader, whom I met through Jeanne, was the wife of the city's police chief. She suffered from multiple sclerosis and had obtained a service dog through the prison program. As a result, Pam and her husband Lockheed became active in the organization and even served on its board of trustees.

Seeing firsthand the ignorance and discrimination that many with assistance dogs faced, chief Reader saw to it that his officers knew the applicable laws. Regularly seeing Pam and her dog visit the police station and attend community meetings no doubt got the message across as well.

Not once during our time in Puyallup were we denied access. The manager at our apartment complex, we were happy to discover, knew all about service dogs, having a nephew who also received one through the prison program. But all around town, in stores and restaurants, we came and went without challenge or confrontation.

Getting away from the military base made a big difference. Gone were the constant reminders of my rape, from the khaki uniforms to the regimented atmosphere. And with Harry leaving the Army, it would be that much harder for my attacker, should he try to trace my whereabouts, to find me.

Early in 1996, in the meantime, at the insistence of Deb Steiner, I began group therapy at the VA with eight or nine other women who suffered from post-traumatic stress. The roots of their traumas varied, ranging from domestic abuse to a military equipment accident, but like me these women were working to rebuild their lives.

Joyce Moody, who oversaw the sessions, had few hard and fast rules, the main one being that we reserve conversation about our individual traumas for private counseling. These gatherings were to focus on mutual support and the day-to-day problems of living.

At first I hesitated to say much. In many ways, I was still wary to come out of my shell. To open myself to strangers, to endure their judgment and the possibility of rejection, remained daunting. Bronson, as always, smoothed the way. He made the rounds before or after every session, collecting pats and scratches behind the ears. He was the cheerful face and steady presence I showed the group, indeed the world, before I dared show myself.

MARGARETHE CAMMERMEYER

I could have just dealt with Leana's epilepsy, but that assumes that it exists in isolation. If you're working with a client you try to figure out those stressors that make the seizures worse. And Leana's psychological distress made her seizures worse.

What really gets me angry is when people make assumptions that the patient is somehow at fault if she has flashbacks, for example, or if she is not responding the way she should according to the textbook.

There was this undercurrent in our VA hospital as well as in other hospitals that were seeing her of "Let's blame the victim." Things like, "Her seizures aren't real," or "She's malingering." All of this is something that I have always been infuriated by.

Leana never exhibited anything to me other than that her problems were real and that she wasn't being validated. As a woman that's something that I could relate to. So I became her advocate with some of the other staff members, because they just didn't get it. And I, of course, in my arrogance presumed that I did.

I used to give Leana a lot of advice, and I would try to find ways of simplifying things. Much of it was probably along the lines of the Serenity Prayer: Those things you can do something about, do something about. The rest of it let go because you don't have any control over a lot that happens.

It seems to me that she became empowered during the time we worked together, and a lot of that was because she was the expert about her own life. She found that if she doesn't speak up for herself, who else is going to?

Part of coming to healing and to achieving self-esteem is recognizing that bad things happen to you. For her, coming to acknowledge her experience and being able to put it into the present, so that she didn't have to have a flashback was really an important part of all this. She began to take control of her life as she began facing it.

Once you begin to deal with the past you can then begin to take charge of it in the present. That's where Bronson came in. We said, "Okay, if we can't make the seizures go away, then what can we do to minimize the risks?"

To begin to move forward you have to also say, "I'm an okay person and I deserve to have a life and not to be dependent on my husband or my neighbor or my son." For her this was a tremendous growing time.

I remember when she told me she was going to pursue the lawsuit. I said, "Well, what do you hope to accomplish by it?" And she looked at me with this look that sort of said, "You're asking me this?"

She said, "I don't want any money. I want them to change how we're treated and to recognize service dogs." It was the principle. She felt she was in a position of being able to make a change. And I certainly wasn't one to argue with that. It was just very interesting because she was still very vulnerable herself.

36

Healing, growth, and change came at a steep price. Even with Bronson leading the way, new risks meant new challenges, confrontations, and problems, some of which I was ill-prepared to handle. And as much as I tried to move my life forward, the past remained no more than a thought, a smell, or a haunting phrase behind.

As winter edged toward spring, I again descended into depression. This was the season of dark anniversaries: my hysterectomy, the coma, and the rape. An added blow was that Grethe, giving fair warning, said she planned to retire later that year. Old issues of abandonment and loss again rose from the depths.

Life at home, for its part, was tense. Harry was soon to be unemployed. Because he was seeking a job with the Washington State Patrol, among other law enforcement agencies, he argued against my pursuing the lawsuit. I refused to back down, but I was frustrated by his opposition.

I'd only been in group therapy about two months, meanwhile, when one of the women brought in a videotape of her family, complete with background music. Among the songs was "Seasons in the Sun," the Terry Jacks hit of the 1970s, which is told from the perspective of a dying man. Drippingly sentimental, it includes the line, "Goodbye papa, please pray for me, I was the black sheep of the family."

That song, popular near the peak of my family's upheaval, and the term "black sheep," which my father had used to describe me, gave way to a flood of memories and emotions. I grabbed Bronson's leash and charged out, leaving everyone bewildered and concerned.

Harry, as luck would have it, was arriving to pick me up around this same time. As he wheeled into the entrance of the American Lake VA campus, he spied Bronson and me sitting on the curb. I'd completely blanked out and had no memory of anything after leaving the session. It was the dog urgently licking my face and whining that returned me to sensibility.

My will to live receded. I was unable to sleep. The flashbacks–of my attacker, my wrists being bound, and blood on the carpet–struck with growing frequency. As I had after the rape, I was again scrubbing myself raw in the shower.

Soon, Bronson went on red alert and the epilepsy kicked in. On one ambulance trip to Good Samaritan Hospital in Puyallup, I experienced seven seizures en route and another three in the emergency room.

Hope again seemed lost. But rather than impulsively try to kill myself as I'd done before, I hatched a plan which were it not so sad might be funny.

The newspapers and television news had reported numerous incidents in recent months of gang-related shootings in Washington state and around the country. My idea was to pay someone to kill me–at a prearranged place and time–and make it look like a drive-by shooting gone awry. Bronson would stay behind, leaving everyone to conclude that I simply walked off during a PTSD or postical event and blindly wandered into the crossfire. Skewed as it was, my rationale was that I'd be free of my pain and Michael would be spared the psychic scars of knowing his mother committed suicide.

With Bronson beside me and five hundred dollars of Social Security money in my pocket, I found my way into a tough Tacoma neighborhood and approached several individuals who appeared to be selling drugs. Hearing my proposition, the first few ignored me or moved away.

Finally, I found one dangerous-looking character and a buddy, who after probing me about being a cop, heard me out. At first, the pair demanded more money than I had with me, saying such a job didn't come cheap. Finally, they said they would do it, at an agreed-upon intersection, just a few days later. All I had to do, they promised, was show up and they'd take care of the rest.

I believed wholeheartedly they would do it, though in all likelihood, they just planned to take the money and run. As my suicide date neared, I found myself both repulsed and tempted to follow through. Finally, I tried to be admitted into American Lake–and thereby skirt my appointment in Tacoma–but was informed that Bronson wouldn't be allowed in the psychiatric unit.

The problem had been brewing for months, and it had more to do with controlling behavior than what was best for the patient. Although Bronson was welcomed on the medical wards, intensive care, and even the emergency room, the head of psychiatry opposed his presence on the psych ward.

It started with her saying that the dog served no purpose if I was suffering flashbacks or dissociative episodes. If I didn't recognize the dog, she said, how could I know he was alerting? How could I care for him?

Bronson's behavior, however, warned not just me but the staff of my oncoming seizures. By now doctors and nurses in the ER, among others at the hospital, had seen him in action several times.

I also emerged from the dissociative states much quicker when he was there, whether I outwardly recognized him or not. Something about the dog was grounding for me. He was a shard of my life to focus on, that unlike Harry or Michael could stay with me day and night.

I often knew Bronson, in fact, before even my own son, who took it hard when I treated him like a stranger. I have no definite explanation. Maybe my awareness of Bronson had something to do with the dog being nonjudgmental or nonthreatening, or the solace I found in animals since childhood, or the drum beat of Jeanne Hampl emphasizing my responsibility for this dog. Whatever the case, Bronson was my best anchor to reality.

Care of the dog while I was on the psych ward was hardly an issue. When I was hospitalized for other reasons and was unable to take Bronson out, Harry or Rachelle Lunde pitched in. Even in the mindset of private Proctor, I knew enough to tend to a dog while sitting around my room. On a couple occasions, when I'd slipped into a dissociative state at home and failed to recognize Bronson, Harry simply told me I'd been ordered to watch him. I gladly did so.

In despair over the VA's refusal, I called Rachelle in tears. She, in turn, contacted Jeanne, who made a phone call to someone she knew. That night, I had a bed on the psychiatric ward at St. Joseph Medical Center in Tacoma—with Bronson right next to me.

I stayed at St. Joe's four days, long enough to stabilize and remain safe. Privately operated, the hospital was expensive for us, especially given the uncertainty of Harry's job prospects. Still, it was well run, complete with milieu therapy that kept patients productively occupied and a staff that was well-educated about service dogs.

My stay was uneventful but for a single incident: One evening as I stepped out to potty Bronson and smoke a cigarette, a man concerned about the dog being in the hospital and on the grounds came from behind me and placed his hand on my shoulder to get my attention. Startled, I dissociated and wound up walking the streets of Tacoma, again believing I was in the Army in Virginia.

Much of that excursion is a blur. I know I briefly stopped at a McDonald's. Not only was I thirsty but I wanted some water for this strange dog who was following me. While I went in and ordered he sat patiently outside peering in.

Soldiering on, I saw what I perceived as a radio tower and a military structure and forged toward them. A mile from the hospital, this in actuality was the County-City Building, which among other government offices housed the Tacoma Police Department. A little earlier, St. Joe's had called to report my disappearance.

The cops approached us as we crossed the parking lot. In my mind, these were fellow MPs. When I asked to see a woman lieutenant, again from my time in the Army, the officers were more than obliging.

"She's in another building," one of them said. "Why don't we give you a lift over?"

So into the squad car Bronson and I went, back to St. Joe's, no worse for wear.

RACHELLE LUNDE

There were times when mentally Leana was just not stable and she would feel like she was losing control. She knew that Harry could take care of Michael. She didn't really have to be stable for him. But because of Bronson, she didn't get off the hook that easily.

I would tell her, "If this is something that you're not going to be able to take care of Bronson, I will come get him." But she didn't really want me to come get him. Maybe she interpreted that as I was going to get him and keep him. I never meant it that way.

There were a couple times that Harry called to let me know what was going on, that she was in the psychiatric unit, and he didn't know how long she was going to be there. He didn't know how long it was going to take for her to come out of this, but said she kept asking for Bronson.

He would go and talk to her and she could have a conversation with him, but in her mind it was as if they were still dating; it was like she was stuck in the past. They hadn't gotten married yet. She hadn't had a child yet. She knew him but she couldn't quite place where he fit into her life. But, she wanted Bronson.

I believe that Leana felt, "I have to take care of him at all costs." It was almost like everything was going black around her, but there was this tiny light in the distance, and that was Bronson. She had to take care of him. She had to continue moving toward him.

That spring another incident occurred that revealed how prominent a place Bronson held in my thoughts when I was compromised. At around six-thirty one Saturday morning state troopers found me walking at the side of State Route 512, a normally busy highway that connects Puyallup to Interstate 5. I was a couple miles from home. The dog was nowhere in sight.

I'm uncertain what set off this event, which seemed to have elements of both epilepsy and PTSD. I suspect I suffered a seizure at home and in my postical state trudged out the door. My anticonvulsive medication had been nauseating me in recent days and I stopped taking it.

When the troopers approached me I was confused and struggling to speak, signs that usually indicate that I've had convulsions. But I had no cuts or bruises, nor had I been incontinent. What's more, my thoughts were for the most part back in my military days. That's usually a function of my PTSD.

The state patrol contacted the Puyallup police–who categorized me on their report as a "mental case"–and I was brought to the station. Since I was unable to speak, one of the cops tried putting his questions for me on paper:

What is your name? Where do you live? What city? Phone number?

My responses show just how out of touch I was. In addition to my rudimentary drawing of a house, I scrawled a single-striped private's patch, my rank; a map to the quartermaster company on Fort Lee; the word "Petersburg," where Fort Lee is located; and "95B," military code for an MP. I did identify myself as Leana, but also wrote "Dr. Grethe," and most prominently, dead center on the page, "Dog my need."

I didn't know where Bronson was or what happened to him, but I was concerned and desperately wanted him there.

After conferring with a mental health official, the cops transported me to Puget Sound Hospital, which given my lawsuit and all that occurred the previous May was the last place I'd want to be.

As an officer waited with me at the desk, a male nurse who'd been involved in the confrontation last time saw me and did a double take.

"I remember that bitch," I heard him say. "She's the one with the service dog."

As I slowly came around and it struck me where I was, I panicked. With my lawsuit, I said, I couldn't be treated there. I had to leave.

Someone reached Harry in the meantime and we spoke before he came to get me. To my lasting relief, he told me to relax about Bronson. Apparently I left him behind when I headed out. The dog, he assured me, was safe and sound.

OF ALL BRONSON'S contributions, none was greater than his constancy in alerting to my seizures, the very reason Jeanne Hampl brought us together in the first place.

When I initially took him to the VA, few there were familiar with service dogs, let alone one with such a special talent. It was telling that posted around the hospital were outdated rules and regulations prohibiting all animals except seeing eye dogs. Seemingly, American Lake was locked in a time before the Americans with Disabilities Act and widespread acceptance of the benefits that thousands of dogs–and other animals–provided their human companions.

Medical professionals in general have been slow to accept a dog's ability to detect seizures or other conditions. To many, it smacks of card tricks, voices from the beyond, and the telepathic bending of spoons. Doctors, in particular, if they never learned about such dogs in school or in their text books, could be dismissive. That is, until they saw Bronson in action.

On several occasions, the dog alerted right in the VA hospital–in the waiting area, in the ER, and on the medical wards–with seizures rocking me soon thereafter. He not only allowed me time to prepare but gave the medical staff precious extra minutes as well.

For those who knew Bronson's purpose, the signs were unmistakable. Usually mellow, the dog would shift into urgent mode, licking my face, stepping into my lap, sometimes barking. With such warning, the staff could hurry me to the ER or a quiet room, before the convulsions even came.

References to Bronson also began appearing in the hurried reports of paramedics arriving at one scene or another to pick me up, with information provided by neighbors, family, and friends that the dog alerted or that he rolled me over before rescue workers got there. Some paramedics were excited, because they'd seen something about such dogs on television or in an article they'd read. Others were skeptical.

The fact remained, however, that my trips to the emergency room dropped dramatically as did my secondary injuries, the head wounds and broken bones. The only seizures that Bronson failed to alert to were those that arrived without buildup, if I tripped and struck my head for instance.

During one stay at St. Joseph Medical Center, now a regular alternative to the VA, Bronson alerted with a higher level of intensity than usual, leaping like a jackrabbit onto my bed when I followed his advice and lay down.

I informed the staff that he was giving warning and a nurse was dispatched to my room to sit with me. As the aura came on, more help was called and sure enough, a grand mal seizure rocked me, followed a few minutes later by another.

The staff was in the midst of transferring me from my bed to a gurney when Bronson began making his excited "woo-woo-woo" sounds, or what I describe as "talking."

I was halfway off the bed when they heeded him and set me back down. Seconds later, a third seizure hit. So violent were the convulsions, I was told, that if they had continued to move me, I stood a good chance of being dropped or otherwise hurt.

At Good Samaritan Hospital, where I usually was brought when an ambulance was called to my home, one of the nurses was so impressed by the dog that she took a Polaroid of me with Bronson while I was convalescing. Three years later, that picture still hung on a bulletin board near the ER.

At the VA, Cammermeyer remained Bronson's champion. Dr. Koerker, my neurologist, who worked with her and whom she consulted with, never said much to me about the seizure alerting, though he was supportive and seemed intrigued by the possibilities.

Over time, both he and Grethe grew curious about what exactly was stirring Bronson to alert. In the spring of 1996, during a scheduled EEG, they decided to monitor the dog's reactions. Though informal–and far from a scientific study–it was the only such test of a seizure dog I'd ever heard about, and Bronson came through magnificently.

MARGARETHE CAMMERMEYER

We had by this time seen Bronson alert in the emergency room a couple times. We never followed through with long, complicated testing. But we did have an occasion where we were doing an EEG and Bronson was on the floor beside Leana. He was laying there very calmly and when we began doing the photic stimulation he immediately changed his demeanor and jumped on the bed and started licking her. When the neurologist read the EEG at the time when Bronson was alerting Leana also had some changes in her background EEG activity. So we felt that there really was something substantive that Bronson was alerting to.

But it's very stressful for patients to go through this. It's not something you say, "Well, let's do this again." Just because of the nature and complexity of her medical disorder we decided not to pursue it any further. But certainly we felt that he was responding to some physiological change that was taking place in her. We were looking for corroboration of his behavior and felt we had gotten that. It was at least a first-step corroboration.

37

Only once did seizures fail to follow one of Bronson's alerts. That was a May evening in 1996. Harry and I were relaxing in the living room around nine o'clock, watching television. The dog, who was dozing on the floor, awoke with a start. He hurried over to me on the couch, sniffed, and stared as if puzzling over something. Then he scanned the room and hastened to deliver one toy after another.

Harry and I figured seizures were on their way. I'd had some recent episodes and like bad luck they tended to come in streaks.

My husband smoothed a blanket on the carpet.

"Come on, Lee," he said. "Lie down."

"Hang on," I said. "Something's different about this. It's not building like it usually does."

Obviously, the dog was concerned. But when he warned of seizures it was always with an escalating urgency, as if the electrical storm in my brain, or the odor, or whatever it was that set him off, was bearing down like a locomotive. As uneasy as the dog seemed, this behavior was steady paced. Even his facial expression was more quizzical than demanding.

No sooner than I spoke, Bronson became all but frantic. He sprang into my lap, then burrowed his head into my side, as if to plead, "Save me, Mom!"

At that, the earth rumbled ominously, the dishes rattled in the cabinet, and the pendulum on our grandfather clock swayed not side to side but front to back.

We looked around in astonishment. The shaking seemed to go on forever, though in reality only about thirty seconds lapsed before it stopped. When it did, Bronson stepped off my lap and with the excitement over lay down as if nothing happened.

My husband and I were still catching our breath when it came on the television that the region had just experienced its mightiest earthquake in thirty-one years, a 5.3 on the Richter scale. No one was hurt and damage was minimal, but it was enough for umpires at the Kingdome to suspend the Seattle Mariners's baseball game, then in the seventh inning.

I never regarded Bronson as having magical powers. He was an intuitive, intelligent creature. Indeed, much of the joy he brought to my life—and my family's life–stemmed from his simply being a dog. Bronson had a spirit, a friendliness, and a pure enjoyment of life found only in innocent beings like dogs and children.

Once we were fishing for trout off a dock in Spanaway, near Tacoma. Bronson, who was outfitted in just his collar and harness, was beside me, fascinated by these glimmering creatures we kept pulling from the lake.

"Look at the fishy," I'd say when someone caught one. I'd let him sniff, then set it aside with the rest of our catch.

Everything was fine until I reeled in one that was too small. I removed the hook and tossed it back, with hardly a second thought. But as often happens the trout was stunned and took a moment on the water's surface.

From the corner of my eye, I saw Bronson uncoil from his down position. And though I screamed his name, I was too late. Off the pier he leaped, splashed down, and retrieved that fish like he would a favorite stick. To my surprise, the trout was unharmed and I was able to release it again.

Harry growled at me to correct Bronson immediately. But if anyone was at fault, it was me, for failing to command the dog to stay before any of this happened.

I felt sheepish the rest of the afternoon. What's more, no one around us caught another fish for almost an hour. And though there was plenty of grumbling, at least one of our neighbors found humor in it.

"Hey," I heard a guy shout as Bronson paddled toward me with the catch of the day, "that dog's going fishing!"

Then there was the time we introduced Bronson to snow. We were on our way to my mother's place in eastern Washington, when we stopped at Snoqualmie Pass, a ski area in the Cascade mountains.

When we got out of the car Bronson was more excited than he could bear. He bounded through the white stuff, sank, dug his way out, and jumped again, looking like a cartoon rabbit. Then he burrowed through, plow-like, gobbling as he went. We tossed him snowballs and threw up handfuls of the powder, which he futilely tried to catch. He rolled around in it, emerging with his muzzle and head covered in white and an expression of such joy that we had to laugh.

RACHELLE LUNDE

When I've seen Bronson and Leana working together, the thing that's different is that Bronson is always in contact with her. He likes to have his body touching her. It's not obnoxious. But instead of doing the correct heel, where he's walking in place alongside her, he'll tend to rub up against her a little bit and she will unconsciously reach down and pat him on the head. There's a lot of physical connection between the two of them.

It's almost as if their souls have somehow merged. That sounds corny, but there's a connection there. I have some friends that are blind that have guide dogs. They love their dogs. They depend on their dogs. But there's still that line of division. The dog is basically a worker for them. I believe Leana sees Bronson as important to her as her arm. And I do believe that Bronson senses that in some way. I'm not ready to give him human emotions, but in some way he has decided that he has to take care of her. And he does.

Bronson gave me reassurance and strength. Despite the setbacks, and there were many, I was engaged in life again, growing braver, and attempting new activities. One success fueled another.

When we were still living on Fort Lewis, I would occasionally join my friend Theresa and one or two other women at an NCO club that had a karaoke night. On the evening that I finally gave into Theresa's needling to go up and sing, I was in my wheelchair because of the Todd's paralysis. Two muscle-bound Marines hoisted me onto the stage. Overcome with stage fright, I stroked Bronson's fur and kept my gaze on him as I offered a heartfelt rendition of Lee Greenwood's "God Bless the USA," a favorite with military crowds and a song I knew by heart. By the time I was done, everyone in the place was up and cheering like crazy.

Bronson was the steadying force that allowed me to do what others did, even those activities that most people would rather avoid. When I received my notice for jury duty, everyone said I had the perfect out, that my disability was enough for me to be waived. Yet the dog's purpose was to get me back into society. To make excuses would be to say Bronson wasn't much help after all.

We spent a week at the county court. The long hours, however, took their toll. I had seizures at home after my second day and the Todd's paralysis returned. Still, I showed up at the courthouse in my wheelchair.

I was considered for three trials. That my husband was in law enforcement and I had a police background dampened my prospects. But then there was also an exchange I had with a prosecutor who questioned me for a narcotics trial.

"I see you have a helper dog," he said. "What if we were to bring a police dog into court to demonstrate how the drugs were found? What is your dog going to do?"

His patronizing tone and his insinuation galled me. He was ignorant, for starters, and disrespectful of Bronson's extensive training.

"My dog is going to do what he's doing right now," I replied, nodding at Bronson laying contentedly at my feet. "But I can't guarantee what your dog is going to do."

The judge covered his face to hide his smile and the DA quickly wrapped up. I was disappointed when we were dismissed; I would have liked the chance to prove Bronson's mettle.

Typically, he found his own way to impress. As the weeks passed, I became more involved in volunteering for Jeanne and the Prison Pet Partnership. I was so appreciative of Bronson that I offered my services whenever an activity was planned away from Purdy. I liked getting out, but it was also an opportunity to spread the word about service dogs.

ANNIE BRINGLOE

Leana and I were at the Puyallup dog show, where over a weekend two or three clubs put on a big show. We agreed to man the Prison Pet Partnership table, which was set up right across from the superintendent's desk. We had brochures and were trying to educate people about service dogs and the program and maybe get some donations.

Leana left to potty Bronson. And on her way back from the grassy area there was some sort of scuffle. At dog shows there's always a lot of people going back and forth and they're not always paying attention to whether their dogs are misbehaving, be it growling or snapping at other dogs. I think that's what happened. Some incident occurred and it scared her. When she came back, Bronson was alerting.

Here we are, it's on an asphalt surface. It's not clean. This was not a good place. But I had my Scottie Riley's really thick dog bed with me. I put it on the floor for Leana's head and got her down quickly. Within just two minutes she started seizing. I asked someone to call 911 because the last time I saw this I was really concerned. And these seizures were more violent than the ones she had in Jeanne's yard. And this time, Bronson was even better. He was right there with her, licking her face.

Riley had been through this before, too. So he just sat down beside her. Here's Bronson and Riley, the most unlikely dog companions, comforting Leana, while I'm trying to keep her from hurting herself, and she's having all these seizures. Meanwhile, people started coming around and they were very alarmed.

Sometime after the third seizure, the emergency vehicle drove right into the dog show area. Leana was quiet for a few moments, and I told them that this was her service dog and that he was to go with her to the hospital. They had no problem with that. So they loaded Leana in the back of the ambulance and they loaded Bronson right up in the front seat.

I still have this picture of him in my mind, riding with men he didn't know in the front of the emergency vehicle as it took Leana away. He was sitting up in that front seat just as proud as could be.

38

It would be wrong to say that Bronson ended my problems. Some ugly, wrenching days remained, and probably never would be completely behind me. They were becoming fewer and further between, though, and that was a blessing. There were also more happy days, accomplishments, and improvement in my health and memory. Yet as I got out and became involved with more people, it only followed that others would witness my seizures or dissociative episodes, increasing my humiliation and shame. That, too, would have to be faced and overcome.

Some of the roughest times came that spring, when Cammermeyer reported that her last day at the VA would be in June. I'd known it was coming, but now that a date was set the news was devastating. On the Monday Grethe told me, in fact, I suffered seizures on the hospital grounds, was hospitalized, and trudged out of my room in a dissociated state. I was found walking on a nearby street and brought back by Harry, the VA police, and a sheriff's deputy who happened upon them trying to restrain me.

Over the next several days, I would be in and out of the psych ward because of dissociative episodes and my husband's fears that I was suicidal.

When I was home, I wept for hours on end. Nausea overcame me and I'd vomit. Typical of depression, little in my life seemed to matter to me. One night I downed several wine coolers, which given the various medications I was on was hardly a good idea. But as I told one of the VA doctors, I wasn't necessarily trying to hurt myself; I was "just trying to get numb."

In some ways, Grethe's impending departure seemed like death was in the offing. She was perfectly healthy, of course. She had no concrete plans for retirement other than to landscape her new home on Whidbey Island in Puget Sound. Though physically not very far away, Cammermeyer was beginning a new phase of her life, away from the VA and her former patients. It went without saying that once she left the hospital our contact would be minimal. Perhaps we'd exchange Christmas cards or a note now and then, but that was it.

Grethe's leaving opened old wounds: the rejection by my father, losing Les Weaver, even Grace's retirement one year earlier. The individuals I held in highest regard, whose approval I most hungered for, I was unable to keep in my life. It seemed like I wasn't meant to have such people, that they'd always leave.

Yet it wasn't just the emotional support I would miss. Cammermeyer had pinpointed the proper medications and dosages that, combined with Bronson and an improvement in my psychological outlook, made the seizures–and my PTSD–bearable. After all I'd been through–the many doctors I'd seen, the doubts that my seizures were epileptic, and countless adjustments to get the doses just right–Cammermeyer had me on a combination of the drugs Valproate, Gabapentin, and Lamotrigine that beat back my seizures and the subsequent Todd's paralysis to the point that I sometimes went months without incident. No one could help me before Grethe came along. Why should I believe that someone could help me after her?

I wasn't alone in my gloom either. Many of Cammermeyer's patients, some of them war-hardened veterans, were teary-eyed that spring, because they knew what I knew: They were never going to find another healthcare professional like her.

By mid-June, I began to come to terms with the inevitable. To show my gratitude for all Grethe had done for me, I brought her some farewell gifts: a dozen red roses mixed with white carnations and baby's breath; a lovely music box; and a figurine of a little girl bandaging a teddy bear, with the inscription, "When I grow up I want to be a nurse."

Grethe seemed pleased to receive them, then drew serious.

"You know," she said, "we're not supposed to accept gifts from our patients."

I expected her to say that therefore she had to refuse them. I was stricken and my face must have showed it.

"But in this case," Grethe said reassuringly, "we'll make an exception."

AT HOME, worries about money plagued us. Harry's separation pay from the Army was dwindling and would soon be gone, as would his unemployment benefits, leaving only my Social Security check to pay the rent.

My husband's refusal to consider any job outside of law enforcement became a point of contention between us. And though he applied at nearly a dozen police departments and agencies around Puget Sound–the state patrol, Pierce County Sheriff's Office, Seattle PD, to name a few–none panned out.

Finally, he accepted a part-time position as a security guard for our apartment complex. In the meantime, we waited to hear about a possible position with the U.S. Immigration and Naturalization Service–in Phoenix, Arizona.

On another front, my lawsuit was gathering steam. Early efforts to settle collapsed and lawyers on all sides got ready for the possibility of a trial. Records were subpoenaed and depositions were scheduled.

In plotting his courtroom strategy, Richard Levandowski even considered calling Bronson to the witness stand, to show how intelligent and well behaved a creature he was. Such a move would undoubtedly have gotten the jury's attention. Whether any judge this side of a television courtroom would have ever allowed such a stunt was another question.

Among the treasure-trove of documents Levandowski and his staff obtained through discovery was Trooper Veliz's personnel file, which bolstered my claims about his controlling, combustible temper. Included in his complaint file were letters from motorists outraged by his behavior during traffic stops.

One driver, cited for speeding, wrote that Veliz had a "miserable attitude." He charged that at one point the trooper unnecessarily threatened to "haul him off to the nearest jail," which sounded a lot like his promise to toss Bronson in the pound.

Another citizen said that when Veliz pulled him over for following another vehicle too closely, the trooper was "extremely confrontive (sic) and loud." He described his voice as "aggressive" and his body language as "antagonistic."

"A traffic violation does not warrant this type of conduct," the man continued. "A badge and a gun do not give him the right to treat minor traffic violators as if they are the scum of the earth."

And though the state patrol predictably ruled that these claims lacked merit, it didn't take much to see a disturbing pattern that culminated in the run-in with Bronson and me.

As the litigation proceeded, state troopers were deposed, as were hospital nurses, administrators, security guards on duty that day, and others. Before it was over, Harry, Jeanne Hampl, and Cammermeyer would also be called.

The pressure was high when opposing counsel finally had the opportunity to question me. But by staying focused on Bronson–and of all things, my cup of coffee–I managed to calmly ride the waves over the course of an intense, all-day deposition of one insinuating question after another.

My lawyer was appalled that they would put someone with my health problems through the wringer. But nothing would have pleased the defendants more than if I became so upset that I had convulsions or, worse, a dissociative episode right then and there. They had to figure I'd back down once I realized how rigorous a trial would be. And if I did go forward despite my vulnerabilities, they were undoubtedly counting on a jury finding me too frightening–or too crazy–to take seriously.

JEANNE HAMPL

Being a nurse it really made me mad when I learned what happened to Leana at Puget Sound Hospital. My feeling is as a nurse you are there to help a patient; you're there to do what's best for them.

Hospitals have a responsibility to treat people. Even if they thought her problem was totally psychological that didn't give them any right to treat her that way. Are you any less a citizen of the world?

When I was doing my deposition the one thing that the attorney kept saying to me is, "Why would you give a dog to somebody who has a psychiatric disease?" Basically, she meant, why would you give a dog to somebody who was crazy? And I said, Leana came to me because she has seizures. She also had a brain injury, from the coma. There is no reason she could not be a competent dog handler. But if she has a psychiatric disease, it's like she has leprosy or something.

We stigmatize mental illness in society today and when we'll get over it I don't know. The whole fact that this lawsuit ever happened tells you where society is today on mental illness. If it had been you or I with no history of mental illness, with just a seizure disorder, that lawsuit would never have happened.

It's just amazing that we still will not accept psychiatric disease like we accept diabetes, heart disease, aneurysms. They thought they were going to win because they were going to prove that Leana was crazy, therefore you don't have to listen to anything she said.

That's why they went after her like they did. And it was so obvious during my deposition what they were trying to do. It was so painfully obvious. They didn't even hide it. And I'm sitting there going, "Get a clue."

WITH CAMMERMEYER gone, it didn't take long for the head of American Lake's psychiatry department to implement over my objections a formal treatment plan that kept Bronson off the psych ward, even if I wasn't dissociating. "If seizures become a risk," the document stated, "she will have to accept restriction to the unit and staff will be responsible for her safety. The service dog, Bronson, will *not* therefore, be on the unit."

It was a power play, pure and simple, designed to keep me lined up with all the other psych patients and under house control. Banning Bronson put me at risk. It threatened to mar his training. Despite my admonishments, my treatment team, including counselor Deb Steiner and women's group facilitator Joyce Moody, signed off on it in a unified front.

In the months that followed, I railed against this policy, appealing to the VA's Seattle division, which had jurisdiction over American Lake, and enlisting Wilson Hulley of the President's Committee on Employment of People with Disabilities, a highly respected advocate for individuals with assistance dogs. Jeanne Hampl even buttonholed H. Norman Schwarzkopf on my behalf when the retired general, working for *NBC Nightly News*, came out to Washington for a segment about the prison program. All of it was for naught.

I dropped Deb Steiner as my counselor and quit group therapy. As a last resort, I filed an administrative tort claim for more than two million dollars with the Department of Veterans Affairs regional office in Seattle. That, too, would ultimately be denied.

In the fall of 1997, Harry was offered the job with the INS in Arizona. When we discussed the position months earlier, I was reluctant to trade beautiful Washington and my healthcare providers at American Lake for the searing heat and smog of Phoenix. Now, I saw no reason to stay.

39

As anyone who's lived there knows, autumn and winter are most pleasant in the Valley of the Sun. Residents take great satisfaction in watching news reports of snowstorms back East or in the Rockies, or of record-breaking rains in the Pacific Northwest.

Although I missed Washington and my friends from the prison program, even I couldn't resist sending a rain-dampened Jeanne Hampl a wish-you-were-here E-mail from Arizona: "Yesterday was sunny and seventy degrees. Today is sunny and seventy-two degrees. The weatherman says sunny and seventy-five for tomorrow. Ha ha."

Being busy kept me happy. Michael was enrolled in a new school. Harry soon left for six months at the INS police academy in Georgia. And not long after I got settled with a counselor and neurologist at the Carl T. Hayden VA Medical Center, I was invited to use Bronson as a therapy dog.

The hospital had just established its dog visitation program, looking to tap into the well-established health benefits that animals provide people who are fond of them. My hope was that Bronson could bring to long-term and elderly patients some degree of what he brought to me. The volunteer department even issued him a special photo ID

Once a month we made the rounds at the VA's nursing home care unit and on Fridays we visited the Arizona State Veterans Home, located behind the hospital. Affectionate and sensitive, Bronson comforted patients. Many lit up, some smiling for the first time in weeks, when he padded into the room.

Seeing those former soldiers laid so low was hard for me, especially at first. I'd go home and cry at the utter sadness of their stories. But as the weeks passed, I found myself looking forward to the visits and the smiles we brought to the men's faces.

Bronson seemed attracted to the patients most in need of companionship, those with neither friends nor family. As he showed with me, the dog had a talent for drawing people out of themselves. After a nurse assured me that it was all right, he even climbed on the bed with patients and nuzzled them

One of his favorites was an older man who'd lost both his legs to a land mine and because of a stroke had little movement in his arms. When Bronson inched his way up the bed and rested his head on the man's chest, the gentleman hugged him and broke down sobbing.

Another veteran lost a leg to bone cancer and was suffering from severe depression. The dog licked his hand while the man and I talked about whatever came to mind. His wife had recently died, and a nurse told me that the first time he allowed himself to cry was with Bronson there.

We even amazed the staff by convincing one blind patient who for months refused to leave his room to play fetch with Bronson out in the courtyard. The fellow would toss the tennis ball and I'd describe the dog's efforts to retrieve it, snatching it in mid-air or racing after a grounder. Then Bronson deposited it in his lap and we'd do it again.

When we lived in Washington, I made a couple friends in Arizona through an on-line service-dog bulletin board. Now that I was there, Bronson and I tagged along with one of them, Liz Carabine, to a training program run by a fledgling organization called Happy Tails Service Dog. There were half a dozen clients, with disabilities that ranged from Multiple Sclerosis to the after-effects of stroke. The program provided no dogs to clients, but helped people prepare their own animals for certification.

In large part, the sessions, which were free, consisted of building a sound obedience foundation. I volunteered to help the trainer and pretty soon I was teaching some of the service-dog skills I'd learned, such as having the dog retrieve items that fell beneath one's wheelchair, opening doors, bracing to help a person lift themselves from the floor, and others.

I did so well that when the instructor left, I was asked to take over the classes, which I did for several months, often using Bronson to demonstrate proper technique. In that time, my assistants and I won an award from J.C. Penney for volunteer community work, including a thousand-dollar donation to Happy Tails. A year later, the state veterinary association honored one of my students' dogs, a golden retriever named Sheba, for her service-dog work with induction into the Arizona Animal Hall of Fame.

In December 1998, my lawyer advanced me funds and Bronson and I flew to Seattle for mediation of my lawsuit. The trip alone was an accomplishment. It had been years since I traveled on my own. Moreover, getting on a plane and flying somewhere–anywhere–was something I never imagined I'd be able to do again.

Bronson behaved like a seasoned traveler, settling in on his blanket before me at the very front of the coach section, and, for most of the trip, sleeping with his stuffed lion.

When I had to use the plane's cramped lavatory, I left the dog in the aisle, ran his leash under the door, and commanded him, "Get close." When I heard him press tight against the door and lay down, I gathered up the slack on his leash, to allow passersby as much room as possible.

In Washington, we spent a grueling day in mediation with lawyers from the state and Puget Sound Hospital, going back and forth with proposals and counterproposals. As evening neared, the defendants offered to pay a total of thirty-three thousand dollars. And though that seemed inadequate to me, they also came around on some conditions that would rectify much of what went wrong at the hospital that day.

Both defendants agreed to work with the Prison Pet Partnership to implement educational programs about service dogs for their personnel. Each new class at the state police academy was to receive a half-hour course on the subject. At the hospital, a half-hour in-service training session was established. The organizations were also to include service-dog information in their literature, such as policy manuals and pamphlets.

And so we came to terms and my lawsuit was settled. C.R. Roberts, the Tacoma *News Tribune* columnist who rose to our defense when the incident occurred, now reported the outcome to his readers:

> It's not just the money. It was never about money. It's about defending what she knew was the truth. And now, if promises are kept, no one in Washington will ever need experience the fear and humiliation Leana Beasley suffered four years ago....
>
> A State Patrol trooper delivered Beasley and Bronson to Puget Sound Hospital, but hospital employees would not allow the dog inside. They were unaware of laws that require access. Also unaware, the trooper took the side of the hospital.
>
> In the angry confrontation that followed, Beasley says she and Bronson were threatened by the trooper. As I read them, later court records seem to confirm her version. She says her rights were violated. She says she knew—as she regained her wits—that she was correct to stand against the misuse of authority. That's what she told me a month after the incident, and that's what I said in a column four years ago. Now comes the end.
>
> She won.

Technically, neither side wins when a lawsuit is settled, but Bronson and I were vindicated. And though bigger financial problems ultimately drove Puget Sound Hospital out of business and the Washington State Patrol was slow to fulfill its end of the agreement, Bronson and I had made a contribution, pushing forward the protection of service dogs and their human companions.

On that trip, we also visited old friends. When Bronson saw Rachelle Lunde again, he was bursting with glee, refusing to even wait until I gave the command that released him to say hello. He danced around her, shaking his hindquarters and whining happily. It was more unrestrained love and kisses when he laid eyes on Jeanne Hampl.

I had some training questions–Bronson was having trouble holding objects for any length of time–and we returned to the prison for a visit and a quick lesson. One of the inmate handlers, Sue Ortega, took the dog through his paces. She and everyone who knew him complimented me on how he looked and how well I'd done not only in maintaining his training but furthering it.

Back home, more good news was coming. My neurologist, Dr. Richard L. Matthews, added a newly developed seizure drug, Topiramate, to my regimen, with great results. In Washington, I was never able to go the full six months without a seizure that the law required to regain my driver's license. Now, I went eight straight months without one.

When I filled out the forms and asked Dr. Matthews for the required physician's letter for the Arizona Department of Motor Vehicles, he gave me a quizzical look and asked why I waited so long: State law there required that I go seizure-free only three months.

I brought my documents to the Arizona DMV, where to my surprise I was handed the written part of the driver's test and directed to a desk to take it. Without so much as an opportunity to read the study guide, I passed. Soon after, behind the wheel of our new Honda CRV–paid for in part with the settlement money–I also cinched the road test,

When we were done and I pulled into the DMV parking lot, Bronson's head popped up in back.

"Bronson, down," I said.

"Who are you talking to?" asked the man who administered my test.

"Oh, my medical assistance dog is in the very back."

"Man, that's one quiet dog," he said. "I didn't know a dog was in here."

"Bronson!" I called, to show him, and up came his head again.

"And it's a Rottweiler!" the guy said, only partly feigning shock.

A few minutes later I said cheese; they snapped my picture; and I bounced happily out the door, kissing my new driver's license.

The next month, Bronson and I got in the truck and followed Liz Carabine and her husband from Phoenix to Anaheim, California for the joint conference of the

International Association of Assistance Dog Partners and Assistance Dogs International.

Jeanne Hampl, who'd recently left the prison program to spend more time with her newly retired husband, was going to be there, along with other friends I'd made through the program as well as the Internet service-dog community. There would be lectures, exhibitions, and accessories and books for sale. Now that I could travel, I wanted to be there, too.

I'd registered at the last minute, unfortunately, and was unable to attend the banquet. But in the lobby of the hotel I met two women attending the conference who were heading to Disneyland. Feeling out of place and unsure what to do with myself, I asked if Bronson and I could tag along. They said sure.

They turned out to be trainers from the largest assistance dog training program in the country, the Michigan-based Paws With a Cause. I was in my wheelchair because I'd twisted my knee, but I didn't want to be a drag on their fun. So while they went off on the rides, Bronson and I toured the amusement park, shopping for Harry and Michael and taking in the sights.

In the time we spent together, the trainers seemed taken by how well Bronson and I worked as a team, the eye contact we made, and how he provided for my needs. When we stopped for a bite to eat, for instance, I dropped my napkin and the dog picked it up for me. But rather than take it whole in his mouth, Bronson knew to grasp it by the edge, with just his front teeth.

The conference went well. I learned, for example, a good method of lifting myself from the wheelchair when crippled with Todd's paralysis. And when the opportunity came for audience members to give short talks on new techniques or equipment they invented or came across, I spoke about a cloth patch I'd recently started using on Bronson's backpack—the blue star of life with a snake coiled around a staff, used by paramedics—so strangers would understand that the animal had a medical purpose.

Jeanne, in the meantime, was hearing from a number of colleagues, including the trainers I'd met from Paws With A Cause, about how impressed they were by Bronson and me and what a great job she and the Prison Pet Partnership had done in preparing us. As in many fields, those who train assistance dogs tend to be territorial. When someone does break down and compliment the competition, it's a good bet that it's heartfelt.

During an intermission, people were milling around outside the hotel, getting some air and chatting. I was there with Bronson when Jeanne approached me, grinning. I looked back at her, bewildered by her expression.

"I am so proud of you," was all she said before she spun around and hurried off.

SELECTED BIBLIOGRAPHY

BOOKS

Cammermeyer, Margarethe, with Fisher, Chris. *Serving in Silence*. New York: Penguin Books, Viking Penguin, 1994; Penguin Books, 1995.

Covan, Frederick L., with Kahn, Carol. *Crazy All the Time: On the Psych Ward of Bellevue Hospital*. New York: Simon & Schuster, 1994; Random House, Ballentine Books, 1995.

Gaddis, Thomas E. *Birdman of Alcatraz: The Story of Robert Stroud*. New York: Random House, 1955; New American Library of World Literature, Signet Books, 1958.

Gordon, Barbara. *I'm Dancing as Fast as I Can*. New York: Harper & Row, 1979; Bantam Books, 1987.

Hales, Dianne and Hales, Robert E. *Caring for the Mind: The Comprehensive Guide to Mental Health*. New York: Bantam Books, 1995; Bantam Books, 1996.

Herman, Judith Lewis. *Trauma and Recovery*. New York: Basic Books, 1992; reprint ed., Basic Books, 1997.

Jamison, Kay Redfield. *An Unquiet Mind: A Memoir of Moods and Madness*. New York: Alfred A. Knopf, 1995; Random House, Vintage Books, 1996.

————. *Night Falls Fast: Understanding Suicide*. New York: Alfred A. Knopf, 1999; Random House, Vintage Books, 2000.

Kaysen, Susanna. *Girl, Interrupted*. New York: Random House, 1993; Random House, Vintage Books, 1994.

Keve, Paul W. *The McNeil Century: The Life and Times of an Island Prison.* Chicago: Nelson-Hall, 1984.

Masson, Jeffrey Moussaieff. *Dogs Never Lie About Love.* New York: Crown Publishers, 1997; Crown Publishers, Three Rivers Press, 1998 .

Moskovitz, Richard. *Lost in the Mirror: An Inside Look at Borderline Personality Disorder*, 2nd ed. Dallas, Tex.: Taylor Publishing Co., 2001.

Rothschild, Babette. *The Body Remembers: The Psychophysiology of Trauma and Trauma Treatment.* New York: W.W. Norton & Company, 2000.

Sheldrake, Rupert. *Dogs That Know When Their Owners Are Coming Home.* New York: Crown Publishers, 1999.

Van der Kolk, Bessel A.; McFarlene, Alexander C.; Weisaeth, Lars; editors. *Traumatic Stress: The Effects of Overwhelming Experience on Mind, Body, and Science.* New York: Guilford Press, 1996.

ARTICLES

Arnold, J. Cleveland. "Therapy Dogs and the Dissociative Patient: Preliminary Observations." *Dissociation* 8 (December 1995): 247-252.

Associated Press, "Study tests if dogs can predict seizures." *Lewiston* (Wash.) *Tribune*, Jan. 29, 1992.

Barker, Sandra B. and Dawson, Kathryn S. "The Effects of Animal-Assisted Therapy on Anxiety Ratings of Hospitalized Psychiatric Patients." *Psychiatric Services.* 49 (June 1998): 797-801.

Candy, Dana. "Seizure-Alert Dogs May Get Seeing-Eye Status in Florida." *The New York Times*, March 29, 2002, p. A22.

Carmichael, Mary; with Reno, Jamie; Shenfeld, Hilary. "Animal Emotions." *Newsweek,* July 21, 2003, pp.44-47.

Carroll, Linda. "Mounting Data on Epilepsy Point to Dangers of Repeated Seizures." *The New York Times*, February 18, 2003, pp.F5-F6.

Chandrasekaran, Rajiv. "More than a best friend; epileptics credit their dogs with life saving warnings." *Washington Post*, June 20, 1995, p. B3.

Chiacchia, Kenneth. "VNO: the 6th Sense." *Bark*, spring 2002, pp.43-45.

Dale, Steve. "The Sick Sense." *USA Weekend*, Dec.28-30-2001, pp.14-15.

Devi, Swaha. "Beyond Words: Animals as Healers." *Alternative Medicine*, November, 2000, pp.31-34, 36-37.

Glazer, Fern. "A New Leash on Life." *Bark*, summer 2003, pp.50-55.

Green, Ranny. "When businesses turn away service-dog owner they should consider repercussions." *Seattle Times*, April 4, 1999.

Holcomb, Ralph and Meachem, Mary. "Effectiveness of an Animal-Assisted Therapy Program in an Inpatient Psychiatric Unit." *Anthrozoos*. 2, No. 4: 259-264. 1989.

Miller, Peggy Sue. "Pet therapy advances: seizure-alert dogs." *Dog World*, April 1992, pp.52-53.

Pflaumer, Sharon. "Seizure alert dogs." *Dog World*, January 1992, pp. 42-44.

Sawicki, Stephen. "Seizure Alert." *Animals*, January/February 1999, pp.9-13.

Shulins, Nancy, Associated Press. "Researchers probe cases of seizure-sensing canines." *Yakima* (Wash.) *Herald-Republic*, August 7, 1994, pp. 5E-6E.

Teagarden, Rebecca. "Canines who Care." *Seattle Post-Intelligencer*, February 1, 1990.

Waldsmith, Lynn. "What Explains Their Sixth Sense?" *Reader's Digest*, October 2000, pp.106-111.

Wren, Christopher S., "Harnessing the Powerful Secrets of a Dog's Nose." *The New York Times,* August 17, 1999, p.F5.

————. "Seizure-Alert Dogs: Are They Fact or Fiction?" *Dog World,* March 1998, p.10.

ABOUT THE AUTHORS

LEANA BEASLEY currently lives in Washington state, where she has been an advocate for people with assistance dogs. In addition to conducting well-received service-dog demonstrations for schools and businesses, she has also worked with organizations, including fire departments and hospitals, to adopt service-dog policies to help their employees better understand state and federal laws regarding service dogs. In 2004, she and Bronson were honored by the Delta Society, a national organization that promotes the human-animal bond, for Bronson's service-dog work. With Bronson in retirement, Leana has since obtained a second service dog, a Rottweiler named Faith.

STEPHEN SAWICKI is the author of *Teach Me to Kill* (1991), a true-crime book about Pamela Smart, a New Hampshire school worker who enlisted her teenage lover and his friends to murder her husband. He also wrote *Animal Hospital* (1996), an account of his year inside Angell Memorial Animal Hospital in Boston, a renowned medical center for pets.

Stephen's journalism has appeared in *People*, *Time*, *U.S. News & World Report*, *The New York Times*, and other national and regional publications.

He holds degrees from Ohio Wesleyan University and Stanford University.

978-0-595-47488-2
0-595-47488-8